ECOLOGY AND KOREAN CONFUCIANISM

Korean Studies series 34

KEIMYUNG UNIVERSITY PRESS

ECOLOGY AND KOREAN CONFUCIANISM

Korean Studies series 34

초판 1쇄 인쇄 2013년 4월 25일
초판 1쇄 발행 2013년 5월 10일

지 은 이 계명대학교 한국학연구원 편
펴 낸 이 신일희

펴 낸 곳 계명대학교출판부
출판등록 제347-1998-1호(1970. 9. 1)
주 소 대구광역시 달서구 달구벌대로 1095
대표전화 053-580-6233
팩 스 053-580-6235
홈페이지 www.kmupress.com

ISBN 978-89-7585-630-3 93150 정가 30,000원

이 도서의 국립중앙도서관 출판시도서목록(CIP)은 서지정보유통지원시스템 홈페이지(http://seoji.nl.go.kr)와 국가자료공동목록시스템(http://www.nl.go.kr/kolisnet)에서 이용하실 수 있습니다.
(CIP제어번호: CIP2013004355)

Preface

This book is a collection of papers that were presented at the Fifth Keimyung International Conference on Korean Studies (KICKS 2011) on the theme, "Korean Confucianism and Ecology." Professors Tu Wei-ming and Hong Won-sik gave the keynote speeches, which were followed by presentations by Professors Michael C. Kalton, Philippe Thiébault, Kwon Chee-yun, Edward Y. J. Chung, Ro Young-chan, Donald Baker, Yu Kwon-jong, Kim Se-jeong, and Kim Jong-won. Having already appeared in Acta Koreana (indexed in A&HCI and Scopus) and Hangukhak nonjip (registered with the Korea Research Foundation), both published by Academia Koreana of Keimyung University, these papers have now been compiled for publication in this book.

Many years ago Rachel Carson in her book *Silent Spring* and John Cobb in his book *Is it too late*? expressed their grave concerns about the global environmental crisis facing humanity today. In the meantime many efforts have been made to solve this crisis on various levels by means of environmental engineering in the scientific arena, and environmental policy in the political arena. Such efforts have been made not only in developed nations but in all the nations of the world, and not only by individuals and governments, but also by dedicated international environmental movements. Nevertheless, the situation has grown gradually worse. Of course, existing efforts need to be continued, but we are now being challenged to reflect deeply on our ways of thinking and attitudes to life. This problem is related to our worldview as well as our awareness and ethical outlook. It is now high time for philosophers to step forward and make their voices heard.

At present various western scholars, who are frequently referred to as "deep-structure ecologists," are rushing forward to provide answers. With one accord they criticize contemporary western philosophy's anthropocentricism and instrumental reasoning, and some of them trace the problem further back to ancient times and the Hellenistic idealist philosophical tradition on the one hand and Hebraic humanistic religious philosophy on the other. Also, some of them have focused their attention on traditional East Asian thought, namely, Confucianism, Buddhism, and Daoism. *Confucianism and Ecology*, published by Harvard University Press in 1998, is representative of such studies, and this book, *Korean Confucianism and Ecology*, can be seen as its successor. In Korea there have been many outstanding Neo-Confucian scholars such as Toegye Yi Hwang, Yulgok Yi Yi and Dasan Jeong Yagyong, and Neo-Confucianism has exerted a greater influence on Korea than on any other country. It is to be hoped that the thought and exemplary lives of these philosophers of the past can help us even in a small way to overcome the global ecological crisis that is facing all humanity today.

February 7, 2013

Hong Won-sik on behalf of the authors

(Translated by Michael Finch)

Content

● Content

By Tu Wei-ming

(Professor Emeritus, Harvard University, USA, Lifetime Professor, Peking University, China)

I congratulate the organizers at Academia Koreana for this conference on ecology and Korean Confucianism as the Fifth Keimyung International Conference on Korean Studies. I am very privileged to have this chance to share some of my ideas on ecology and Confucianism. I cherish the opportunity to be part of this international adventure. My ideas are still evolving. They are tentative but I have addressed this question on several occasions. I and a number of scholars try to relate ecology to Confucian humanism in different ways. For example there is a serious attempt to identify the spiritual and cultural resources of the Confucian tradition for formulating a new vision of ecology in the 21st century. What I would like to propose for this particular presentation is to first look at some of the core values of the Confucian tradition. On the surface they are intrinsic to the Confucian concern and yet this very focused investigation of the Confucian project should show rather explicitly that Confucian humanism at the core of its overall concern is ecological. You can even say that Confucian humanism is based upon an ecological vision. We all know that the core value of the Confucian tradition is to learn to be human. Learning to be human is the core Confucian concern.

Of course the idea of the human is variously understood. Sometimes it is defined as a rational animal. Sometimes it is understood as a tool user or as an animal that is gifted with linguistic ability. But from the Confucian point of view a human is multi-dimensional. We cannot understand the full meaning of being human in a reductionist model. We do not define being human in terms of one particular quality. There are many important qualities that have to be recognized in order to understand the meaning of being human. Human beings are necessarily emotional beings. Human beings are social beings. Human beings are political, are historical are aesthetic and of course human beings in the search for the meaning of life are philosophical and metaphysical. This multi-dimensional nature of being human underlies the Confucian idea of learning to be human as an infinite process of self-realization or self-perfection. This process of self-realization takes self-knowledge as its point of departure. Self-knowledge of course is not simply to know something it is also to know in order to do, in order to transform. So it is a transformative knowledge. The more we know ourselves the more we will be shaped by our knowledge and transform ourselves accordingly. This dynamic process of learning is predicated on a belief that the self, a person, a human self is always a center of relationships, never an isolated individual. Of course, the idea of the self as an intrinsic value has its own what may be called subjectivity, and this subjectivity is not reducible to the environment, to the world beyond. This idea of the self is the core of human realization, personal realization, and that is the reason why the idea of self-cultivation features most prominently in the Confucian tradition as a whole. The idea of self-cultivation is predicated on the improvability, the perfectibility, certainly the moral ability of human nature. And since human nature is shared not only among all human beings but by all modalities of being. This is predicated on the belief that everything in the universe consists of a vital energy, not a static structure but a dynamic process, and this vital energy is shared by all modalities of being in the universe. Rocks, trees, animals, humans, even spiritual beings are an integral part of this ever expanding network of relationship. This idea of the vital energy that permeates every aspect of the universe is an important background understanding of human self-realization as a process of not only personal flourishing but in communication with society, with nation and the world beyond.

Let's stay focused on the question of learning to be human as the basis for our ecological thinking. The human being is social therefore the human being needs to be communicated with an ever enlarging network of relationships. Human beings are historical so human beings are not only concerned about the situation at present. Human beings have a deep memory, and memory is the basis for human beings to look forward in a long-term perspective. Human beings are also metaphysical beings who search for meaning because human beings are not simply confined to the world here and now. Paradoxically the Confucian tradition compared to many other spiritual traditions in the world seems to put more emphasis on the world here and now. The idea of the transcendent world is certainly very significant, but the primary concern is the world here and now. Even though that is the case human beings are not simply secular beings. Human beings are sacred because human beings are not simply this-worldly. The transcendent world, heaven for example is intrinsically valuable for human self-understanding and self-appreciation. This interaction between the humans committed to the world here and now and the human aspiration for extending its relationships beyond the self, community, nation and world to the cosmos as a whole makes the Confucian humanistic tradition a very comprehensive humanistic tradition. It is not secular humanism. It is to regard the secular world here and now as sacred. In fact it moves beyond this separation between secularity and sacredness. The distinction itself actually is being overcome in the Confucian humanistic world. By being rooted in the world here and now the human being is not simply confined to the world, to this particular world. It is one of the reasons why the Confucian idea of being human is both immanent and transcendent. Immanent in the sense that within the spiritual resources of being human we have not only necessary but also sufficient conditions for full self-realization. And this intrinsic meaningfulness of being human is an attempt to overcome the limited and limiting understanding of the person simply as part of the lived world here and now. Human beings must move beyond the lived concreteness in order to extend to a much larger universe to find the intrinsic meaning of being human. And yet the strong belief that the ultimate meaning of life is not only realizable being our ordinary human existence but ought to be realized in our human existence here and now. This interplay between a sense of rootedness in the world here and now and the necessity of going beyond the various limited and limiting structures of relationships makes the Confucian project of self-cultivation a complex, fruitful and nuanced approach to the process of learning to be human.

Maybe it is important for us to recognize in this connection that a human being in terms of a multidimensional perspective should first be recognized as an observer. Human beings like animals are major observers and yet the ability of the human being to observe is more penetrating, more systematic, more comprehensive than any other members of the animal kingdom with the aid of the various kinds of scientific, technological advances. As an observer human beings have a very comprehensive view of not only themselves, their society, but the environment as a whole. And it is important to note that for the first time in human history since the 1960s, the late 1960s, we human beings with the naked eye with the help of astronauts are able to observe the earth in its holistic structure. Every aspect of the earth, minerals, earth, soil, plants, water, air, every aspect of the earth can be perceived or observed by human beings in a holistic sense. This is unprecedented in human history and of course it is a very important event in understanding the true nature of being human as an observer. Human beings are not only observers of nature. Human beings are also appreciators of nature. It is very difficult for us to know whether other animals have this aesthetic sense of appreciation but it is very important to note that human beings have this totally—not just disinterested—totally free and non-utilitarian vision of the word, of our own environment, trees, rocks, water, of mountains, and human beings appreciate the environment in order not just for self-gratification but also for self spiritual transformation. Human beings as appreciators, of course, are extensions of observations, but there is a difference between human beings as observers, often in the scientific sense of the term, and human beings as appreciators. Using Martin Buber's notion that human beings can establish an I-Thou relationship with the world beyond, with nature rather than regarding nature as something out there, as an object, but to regard nature as an integral part of one's own self-understanding. In other words that which is being observed is an extension of one's own inner self rather than simply an object out there. I very much enjoy Thomas Perry's notion that nature is not a collection of objects. Nature should be considered a union of subjects. In the Confucian tradition human beings as appreciators through art, through music, through literature in a way try to embody nature in one's own self-consciousness and self-knowledge. More actively there is also a notion in Confucianism that human beings are participants in nature, participants in the sense that human beings are not simply creatures of the evolutionary process or of the creative process or the transformative process. Human beings are also active participants. As active participants human beings take part in this transformative process as an active agent. Human beings are not simply the outcome of the evolutionary process. As an agent human beings try to realize themselves by incorporating the various resources, vital energy, spiritual resources from the world beyond. There is a very beautiful statement in the Doctrine of the Mean which says that if we really understand our own nature, we will be able to understand the nature of human beings. If we can understand the nature of human beings, the fully realized nature of human beings, we can help to fully realize the nature of things. If we can fully realize the nature of things, we can take part in the transformative and nourishing processes of heaven and earth. If we can transform and if we can take part in the transforming and nourishing processes of heaven and earth, then we can form a trinity with heaven and earth so the human in this sense is on the one hand rooted on earth but at the same time extends to heaven. The trinity heaven, human and earth formed an integrated wholeness. This is of course a very basic Confucian cosmological vision. If we can extend this one step further human beings are not only observers, appreciators and co-participants in the process of nature, human beings can then be considered co-creators of the cosmic process. As co-creators, human beings add something new to the process of the cosmic transformation and this newness that human beings are able to contribute is often understood in the Confucian tradition as culture. Cultural creation is what human beings are capable of contributing to the cosmic process. So culture is not simply a limited artificial construction but culture could be considered as an extension of the creativity of heaven and earth. Of course the negative consequence, an unintended negative consequence of this vision is that because human beings are also co-creators, human beings can become major destroyers. The destructive force embodied in the human capacity is so extensive and is not simply restricted to the human community. So human beings are positively co-creators of the cosmic process, but at the same time human beings are dangerous animals for human beings can also become one of the most powerful destructive forces in the world. Even before Confucius there was a very deep understanding of this rather complex relationship between creativity and destructiveness of being human. There is a notion that human beings will always survive all kinds of natural disasters. Human beings have this capacity to survive disasters. On the other hand human beings will never be able to survive man-made disasters. So human beings will be destroyed not by nature but by human beings themselves. This vision is very deeply rooted in the Confucian tradition. So every human being in the process of learning to be human through self-cultivation is no longer simply a narrowly defined humanistic project. It is a much broader not just humanistic but naturalistic and a spiritual project. In this sense it is important to note that Confucian humanism is not a form of secular humanism it is a humanism that relates to nature on the one hand and the spiritual world on the other as an integral part of learning to be human. Human beings in this sense ought to be understood in terms of four inseparable relationships. The important relationship between human beings as individuals and society, the relationship between self and community, the relationship between the human species and nature. The third one the relationship between the human heart and mind and heaven and then human self-understanding, the integration of the person, the relationship between the human heart and mind and the human body and how to embody heart and mind, soul and spirit in one's own existence, in one's own being is an extremely important aspect. This idea of integration of the self, interaction between self and community, sustainable relationship between human beings and nature and the mutual responsiveness, the mutuality between the human heart and mind and heaven. These four dimensions are fully integrated as defining characteristics of Confucian humanism as comprehensive, spiritual humanism. We need to explain of course in this connection the idea of heaven, which often is understood as the function or equivalent of God, Allah, Logos or Brahman. But heaven in the Confucian tradition as compared to Christianity for example is omniscient, omnipresent but most likely not omnipotent. Heaven knows everything, heaven can sense and feel everything, but heaven is not all powerful. Part of the reason is because of the human. Human beings can be understood as co-creators and also human beings can be understood as partners as not only partners but also as transformative agents in themselves. Of course as I pointed out there is the other aspect, the tragic aspect, that human beings are major destroyers. In this sense the ethic of responsibility is absolutely critical for human self-understanding. The responsibility is not only to oneself to one's community but also to nature and to heaven. So what we do in the privacy of our home is not only important for ourselves for our family members but it is also important in a sociological, naturalistic and even a spiritual sense. So the idea that humans can make the Way great, the Way or the Heavenly Way cannot make humans great is not a sense of humans self ... a kind of exaggerated human power, rather it is the notion that human beings with incredible power of changing themselves and the environment around them should have responsibility for the cosmos, the cosmic order as a whole and human beings are not simply anthropological.

To go beyond anthropocentrism is this process of learning to be human. Specifically self-cultivation begins with one's ability to go beyond privatized egoism. So one's own subjectivity is being realized because of one's ability to go beyond egoism, and we cherish the warmth of the family, but we have to go beyond nepotism. Nepotism is a distorted version of family closeness, and we need to go beyond parochialism in order to fully integrate ourselves in our own community. We need to go beyond chauvinistic nationalism and even anthropocentrism. If we do not go beyond anthropocentrism, we will not be able to fully realize ourselves as human beings. That is the reason why the anthropocentric idea is not humanistic enough. Human beings are not simply anthropological beings.

Now these very basic Confucian ideas, I would argue, are absolutely critical for the development of an ecological consciousness in the 21st century. An ecological consciousness is of course very much linked to our knowledge, our knowledge about our environment and our knowledge about ourselves, our body, about the food chain, about water, about air, about the interactions of various kinds of important elements that constitute the human environment. And much of this important scientific knowledge is totally absent from many spiritual traditions. It is only in the modern times with the advent of science and technology that we are able to understand how complex each ecological interactions are in shaping the environment in which we not only survive but flourish. And yet one of the deepest concerns of the ecological movement is not simply the behavior based upon well-established factual knowledge but our attitude towards nature, our belief, our cosmological thinking, our way of life, our own sense if what it means to be human in reference to nature and how will we be able to establish a long, sustainable, harmonious relationship with nature, The question of attitude and the question of belief are predicated on something much deeper than the knowledge on how to deal with the world here and now. The ecological crisis can certainly be met, confronted, with scientific advances, with new technology, with new ways of dealing with energy, recycling various kinds of wastes, and all these scientific enterprises are absolutely critical for our better understanding of the ecological system, but much more significant in my view is the absolute necessity of achieving a change of the mindset, a change of the attitude, a change of our belief and change of our human self-understanding with nature. Now whether human beings are a viable species or not is highly problematical, and a different vision of being human is necessary. The Confucian tradition seems to offer one of these possibilities for understanding ourselves and our relationship to nature.

I would like to summarize by citing a number of key texts in the Confucian tradition that can help us understand how this new ecological vision based on comprehensive Confucian spiritual humanism takes shape. Now if human beings are centers of relationships from the self all the way to the cosmos, the relationship between the human being and nature ought to be intrinsically valuable in a sense that human beings should learn from now on never to regard nature as something out there to be exploited not just to understand to be appreciated but to be exploited, to be used for human consumption. This idea is very elegantly presented in the Western Inscription of Tsangzai, a great Neo-Confucian thinker. In the opening statement of the Western Inscription he states that heaven is my father and earth is my mother. Even such a small creature as I finds intimacy in their midst. That which fills the universe is my body. That which directs or gives direction to the universe is my nature because my nature is ordained by heaven. All people are my brothers and sisters and all things are my companions. And this sense that everything is an integral part of a communion rather than something simply out there to be exploited is based upon a comprehensive vision, which is not a romantic assertion about human consciousness. It is an experiential understanding of the human capacity, the human capacity of forming one body with heaven, earth and with the myriad things. This idea of forming one body is to consider everything in the universe as connected with me organically as an integral part of myself even in the very physical sense of my body. This is a kind of embodied knowing, embodied understanding of nature. This does not necessarily mean that we form a body with heaven and earth and myriad things in a totally undifferentiated way. The idea of differentiation, the idea of division is absolutely critical. From the Confucian point of view the analogy is the human community first of all. In the human community we should regard every person as either a brother or sister, but at the same time we need to know that our relationships to the ever extending network of relationships ought to be differentiated. Our relationship to the closest kin is different from our relationship to a stranger. Our relationship to human beings should be differentiated from our relationship to animals, to plants, to rocks, to trees. So these differentiations will have to be made in order to make the human world a realistic lived reality rather than simply an abstract understanding of a romantic assertion about togetherness. But these differentiations do not at all undermine the sense of being connected in a meaningful, long lasting organic way with all modalities of being in the world. And the distinction between differentiation and union is to be decided and to be negotiated, discussed every moment and in all kinds of situations. Therefore the human is the center of communality and communication. The human is related to everything, and the human self-understanding is to say everything matters and in a concrete way throughout Chinese history, throughout East Asian history, this sense of respect, respect not only for ourselves, respect for other human beings, respect for nature, respect for heaven. The sense of respect is based upon a sense of gratitude. The sense of reverence is because we are offered incredibly rich resources for our survival and for our flourishment. We are grateful for nature which is the source, which is the proper home for us. We are grateful for the cosmic order. We are not only grateful. We consider ourselves active participants, agents, in shaping our environment together with nature that will allow human beings not only to survive but also to flourish. And self-cultivation in the deepest sense is to move beyond a limited privatized person to an ever extending network of relationships, and this particular movement is deeply rooted in the ecological thinking of why human beings are not only observers, appreciators but participants and co-creators.

My understanding of Korean Confucianism is very limited but I have a very deep impression that ecological thinking, especially the relationship between human beings and nature featured most prominently in Korean Confucianism. In China in the Neo-Confucian period the major debate was between the School of Heart and Mind on the one hand and the School of Principle. Shin and li, but in Korea the major debate is between li on the one hand and ki. Now li and ki are both integral parts of nature so the human heart and mind in a way does not feature that prominently in Korean Neo-Confucianism and I think part of the reason is because the debate between principle on the one hand and vital energy and material force on the other integrate the person into a whole natural and cosmological process. And the cultivation of heart and mind of course is critical but it is the principle which underlies not only human beings but the world at large that becomes most attractive as a major concern for T'oegye for example. And Yulgok was also deeply concerned about how the vital energy is in the lived concreteness of the human and is able to unfold rather than being simply abstract universalism. And this debate, the more you look at it, the more I am convinced that nature has always been an integral part of it. And so there is no subjectivism that is considered as prominent. There is a very strong emphasis on objectivity and subjectivity. And subjectivity and objectivity are interconnected, interrelated, and the human and nature are considered as a continuum, an integral part. The other thing in Korean Confucianism is that there is a great deal of emphasis on holism. All kinds of diagrams, most of these diagrams are diagrams about human flourishing, how human self-cultivation, not only with society but with community and with heaven and earth are to be visualized, and this holism on the one hand and this understanding of nature as an integral part of human self-reflection make Korean Confucianism not only ecologically sound, ecologically significant, but also in itself a kind of deep ecological vision. The vision is often related to another very important feature of Korean Confucianism, that is this emphasis on feeling, on emotion, on the human responses to not only other human beings but to the world beyond. And this notion, for example the Four-Seven Debate is not only a debate between the Four Beginnings and the Seven Emotions, it's a debate about how human beings as rational emotive, emotional beings have to understand themselves in reference to the world at large—the relationship between the body and the heart and mind, the relationship between individual and community, the relationship between human species and nature, and of course the relationship between the human heart and mind. What are complex relationships are very much captured by nuanced and subtle discussions on the nature of being human and the nature of being human is by definition an integral part of nature. This continuous interaction of being human on one hand and being human in nature, therefore, being an extension of nature. Human beings can be understood not only as an integral part of nature but also as the reason that nature becomes meaningful and of course the meaningfulness of nature is the reason why human beings ought to learn from the harmonization of the four seasons, the cosmic transformation of nature. And this close interaction between the human on the one hand and nature on the other helps us to understand the holistic interactive mode of Korean humanistic thinking. A distinctive feature of Korean Confucianism is its emphasis on human sensitivity and of course human sensitivity is often understood in terms of human interactions or social communication, or communicative rationality, but I think in the Korean sense that sensitivity is not only sociologically significant but also aesthetically significant. How nature, how mountains, rivers, trees and the whole naturalistic world can be meaningfully related to one's self-cultivation and self-understanding.

Human survival is based upon our friendly, sustainable, harmonious relationship to nature, but human flourishing is based upon our ability to interact with nature, not in a utilitarian mode but in an aesthetic and mutually self-reflexive way. In Confucianism there is a very fruitful understanding of the dialogical relationship between humans and nature. In other words nature is never an aesthetic structure out there as the dynamic transformation of the vital energy. Nature speaks to us to inspire us. Nature provokes us, nature evokes some very deep sentiments in us so this interactive dialogical mode is a mode of not just tolerance but recognition. We recognize nature as an integral part of human self-understanding and we imagine that our participation in nature enhances the aesthetic quality of nature with this recognition this real respect—you can even say reverence—for nature. Nature is awe-inspiring, especially beautiful scenery, even a tree is a source of inspiration not only for poets, for painters, but also for philosophers, for thinkers. And this sense of mutuality with nature—not only do you learn from nature, you use nature as a reference for ordering society. You never think about the human as totally independent of the natural world.

I would like to offer a concluding remark that since human beings are a viable species the question has loomed very large in our minds, we need to think about the human in a totally new perspective. The old way of understanding nature has to be fundamentally changed. The modernizing process that has created all kinds of creative energy and new possibilities is also a devastating process of disrupting the relationship between humans and nature, and the ecological thinking from a Confucian point of view ought to serve as a critique of modernization as understood in terms of economism, materialism, consumerism with insatiable demand for goods and services. We have to rethink what is necessary for human beings to survive and what is the minimum condition for human beings to lead meaningful lives in a world where the environment has been polluted and resources have been totally depleted.

● KEYNOTE SPEECH

CONFUCIANISM, KOREAN CONFUCIANISM AND ECOLOGICAL DISCOURSE

By Hong Won-sik

(Professor, Keimyung University, Korea)

1. INTRODUCTION—THE DREAM AND LIMITATIONS OF THE NOTIONS OF 'ENVIRONMENTAL SOUNDNESS AND SUSTAINABLE DEVELOPMENT'

Yangip wich'ul (量入爲出, To spend according to one's income). I just wrote this down out of the blue because it suddenly came to mind as I started to contemplate this study. This expression is not directly related to the theme of this study. However, it was one that was always affixed to the door of my grandparents' house in Hahoe Village, Andong. Every year, the piece of paper on which this was written was replaced by a new one that bore the same characters. Of course, I had no idea what it meant, and I did not even pay attention to it during my childhood. However, once I gained some knowledge of Chinese characters (*hancha*), I began to wonder about the meaning of this expression that was different from the signs reading *ipch'un taegil* (立春大吉, Great luck on the onset of spring) that were attached to the gate of all the other houses. It was only as a high school student that I finally learned the meaning of the expression, 'to spend according to one's income' from my uncle. Whenever I visit my grandparents' house, I still find myself looking for this expression. My uncle passed away a few years ago after ninety-three years on this earth. My mother's family hailed from the P'ungsan Ryu clan, which continued the traditions of the Yi Hwang (1501–1570) School of Learning for some 400 years. My uncle was the director of the Tosan Confucian Academy (陶山書院, Tosan Sŏwŏn) during his latter days.

Almost half a century has elapsed since Rachel Carson first warned in her book Silent Spring that life forms were being rendered extinct by man. A long time has also passed since John Cobb asked, "Is it too late?" Nevertheless, it feels like discussions on the actual state of the destruction of ecosystems and the environmental crisis have just begun. The deepwater horizon oil spill (or BP oil spill) that occurred in the Gulf of Mexico in 2010 because of an explosion on a drilling rig brought mass death to the ocean. Another catastrophic disaster occurred after a nuclear power plant exploded in Fukushima, Japan this last spring. Sadly, it is too early to identify this as the biggest disaster of the twenty-first century because there are almost ninety years left before this century will come to a close. Such incidents have also happened in other countries. Currently, the Naktong River Project, which is the biggest civil engineering undertaking since the prehistoric era on the Korean peninsula, is being implemented in the name of 'environmental-friendliness' and 'Naktong River Restoration,' not even 1 km away from where I sit as I write this article.

Faced with food shortages, resources depletion, and environmental pollution, the denizens of the world finally got together in Rome in 1972 to discuss the "Limits to Growth"; meanwhile, "Environmentally Sound and Sustainable Development (ESSD)" began to be emphasized following the *United Nations* Conference on the Human Environment held in Stockholm. This can be regarded as he point in time where a developmental model which addressed environmental problems was adopted. This is a reality and dream which we naturally should seek to bring about.

It is clear that this 'Environmentally Sound and Sustainable Development (ESSD)' was a step forward from the reckless developmentfirst principle. However, this line of reasoning was endowed with a certain overconfidence in the capability of environmental engineering. As is commonly said, one may only begin to think about cleaning up after having made a mess. The current mess created by mankind is clearly one that environmental engineering cannot cope with. This cannot be perceived as a wise approach. A wiser approach would have been to make less of a mess in the first place. Thus, the sustainable development theory is one that is rooted in an optimistic technological theory that revolves around engineering methods, and should be perceived as nothing more than symptomatic therapy. The production of an effective and fundamental cure that represents more than symptomatic therapy is predicated on a solution to environmental and ecological problems that is developed in conjunction with the humanities. Let me point out the two limitations of the sustainable development theory prior to moving on to the next topic for discussion.

First, although the sustainable development theory has brought environmental and ecological problems into the debate, its focus remains on development. This so-called 'environment-friendly' development theory regards development as the top priority, and the ecological and environmental problem as being secondary. Such a theory runs the risk of being employed as logic to justify development. One salient example of this phenomenon is the 'Four Major Rivers Restoration Project.' The government has argued that the development of the four major rivers is the only way to restore the natural ecosystem and to develop the economy for local residents. I have emphasized that the four major rivers, especially the Naktong River, should be developed in a manner that takes into consideration not only the natural ecosystem, but also humanistic ecology.[1] The Naktong River area can be regarded as the last place on earth where the spirit and soul of Confucianism, which constitutes one of the four civilizations in the world, survives and is cherished. I emphasize once again, "Rivers should flow and the Naktong River should flow like the Naktong River."

Second, the sustainable development theory remains based on the anthropocentric viewpoint in that it is centered on the prioritization of man's exclusive interests at the expense of the environmental ecosystem. Ecological theory is rooted in the perception of man and nature as equal beings. Viewed from this standpoint, any sustainable development theory that seeks to develop and preserve nature based on man's necessity cannot be regarded as ecological or as having ecological ethics.

---

1 Hong Won-sik (Hong Wŏnsik) and Lee Sangho (Yi Sangho), "Kyŏngbu taeunha p'ŭrojekt'ŭ wa Naktonggang kaebal e taehan 'inmun saengt'aejŏgin' chŏpkŭn [A humanistic ecological approach to the Pan-Korea Grand Waterway Project and Naktong River Development]," *Han'gukhak nonjip* (Academia Koreana) 36 (2008).

2. THE ECOLOGICAL DISCOURSES OF ECOLOGY, DEEP ECOLOGY AND CONFUCIANISM

A group of scholars has identified anthropocentrism as the main culprit behind the destruction of the environment and the ecosystem. These individuals have commonly been referred to as ecologists. They have asserted that all life forms on earth are equal from the standpoint that they all share 'life.' While Peter Singer and Tom Regan called for animal liberation, Paul Taylor broke down biocentrism as follows: First, man is a member of a global community to the same extent as all other life forms. Second, all species, including man, are part of an interdependent system. Third, all life forms pursue goodness in their own manner. Fourth, man is not internally inherently superior to other life forms.[2]

Deep ecology criticizes the above assertions as examples of individualism, and focuses on the necessity for an ecological philosophy that includes all life forms as well as non-living beings. Arne Naess can be regarded as an ardent proponent of such opinions. Naess identified existing environmental ethics, for example, Gifford Pinchot's resources conservation and development theory, Garrett Hardin's lifeboat ethics, as well as Peter Singer and Tom Regan's animal liberation, as 'superficial ecological theories,' and referred to his own ecological theory as 'deep ecology'. Arne Naess' deep ecology advocated 'self-realization' and 'biocentric equality' as the ultimate norms. Here, self-realization refers to

---

[2] Joseph R. Desjardins, trans. Kim Myŏngsik, *Hwan'gyŏngyulli* [Environmental ethics: an introduction to environmental philosophy] (Chajak namu, 1999), 237.

the process of gaining awareness of the self through mutual relations with nature; meanwhile, biocentric equality indicates the acceptance of the fact that all life forms are equal members of an interrelated whole, and as such have an equal fundamental value.[3]

As such, while tracing the primal causes of the ecological crisis and searching for detailed solutions that reflect such causes, the center of ecological theories has moved from life to ecosystems, and various ecological thoughts, philosophies and ethics have been added to the spectrum. It was during this process that social ecology, eco-Marxism, ecofeminism and ecoanarchism emerged.[4] While various ecological discourses were produced, various critical discussions of these ecological discourses were also introduced. For example, the theory of an 'environmental doomsday' was criticized as an extreme exaggeration of the impending ecological crisis. 'Ecofascism' was criticized for having not only placed man in a position of absolute equality with other life forms, but for in many instances having subjugated man to other life forms. Meanwhile, ecologism was panned for having become politicized and transformed into an ideology, and was regarded as little more than a self-protection discourse introduced by the economically advanced countries. Viewed from the standpoint of the greater framework, such criticisms of ecological theories can also be regarded as part of the ecological discourse.

The focus of ecological philosophy and ethics has long been

---

3 Ibid, 353.

4 For more on the classification of ecological groups, please refer to Mun Sunhong, *Saengt'ae wigi wa noksaek ŭi taean* [The ecological crisis and green alternatives] (Nara sarang, 1992) and Han Myŏnhŭi, *Hwan'gyŏng yulli* [Environmental ethics] (Ch'ŏrhak kwa hyŏnsilsa, 1997).

concentrated on anthropocentrism. This is inherently connected to the modern view of the world which has separated man and nature, and also to the mechanical and instrumental view of nature. Consequently, the fundamental and primary cause of the ecological crisis in the contemporary era has been the dichotomous perception of man and nature, namely the anthropocentric, mechanical and instrumental views of nature. As such, the starting point for the resolution of the ecological crisis of today, as well as the fundamental solution to such problems, should be based on the removal of the dichotomous perception of man and nature and the actualization of the oneness between man and nature. Although various kinds of ecological philosophies and ethics have been suggested, the majority have been unable to move beyond this line of reasoning. Let us look at Pak Imun's assertions.

Under the anthropocentric view of the world, man as a species is first separated from all the other objects as well as all animals in a metaphysical manner. Second, man is superior to all other beings. Third, man is the most precious being. Four, man has the right to rule, possess, operate, and use all other beings as tools or materials with which to actualize his satisfaction. In other words, man's rule over nature is metaphysically justified.[5]

Tu Weiming[6] has focused on the modern anthropocentrism brought about by enlightenment, and concludes that the enlightenment mentality,

---

5 Pak Imun, "Noksaek ŭi yulli [Green ethics]," *Noksaek p'yŏngnon* 15 (1994), 47.

6 Tu Weiming, "Kyemongjuŭi chŏngsin ŭl nŏmŏsŏ [Beyond the enlightenment mentality]," *Yuhak sasang kwa saengt'aehak* [Confucianism and Ecology: The Interrelation of Heaven, Earth, and Humans]. ed. Mary Evelyn Tucker and John Berthrong (Harvard University Press, 1998), trans. O Chŏngsŏn (Yemoon sowon [Yemun sŏwŏn], 2010): 59–63.

which he identifies as the most dynamic, reformative, and potent ruling ideology in the history of mankind, had become the basis for the modern Western world.

> Because we have become so immersed in this enlightenment mentality, we assume that the general ideologies of enlightenment are rational. This reality is further evidenced by the fact that both capitalism and socialism are in keeping with excessive anthropocentrism, which has become the basis of the modern thinking structure. Man is not only the standard for all beings in the universe, but also the source and only power that can bring about economic prosperity, political stabilization, and social development. Although some of the modern scholars in the West have challenged this enlightenment mentality rooted in progress, reason, and individualism, the enlightenment continues to inspire intellectual leaders the world over.[7]

Tu Weiming asserted that any attempt to establish an ethical or value system which is fundamentally different from or has no relation with the enlightenment mentality rooted in anthropocentrism, progress, reason, and individualism would inevitably draw harsh criticisms and sardonic laughter. Tu emphasized,

---

[7] Tu Weiming, "Kyemongjuŭi chŏngsin ŭl nŏmŏsŏ [Beyond the enlightenment mentality]," *Yuhak sasang kwa saengt'aehak* [Confucianism and Ecology: The Interrelation of Heaven, Earth, and Humans], ed. Mary Evelyn Tucker and John Berthrong (Harvard University Press, 1998), trans. O Chŏngsŏn (Yemoon sowon [Yemun sŏwŏn], 2010): 60.

> We should now widen the sphere of enlightenment in a manner that makes possible the strengthening of moral sensibility, and explore spiritual materials which can bring about creative changes in the inherent limitations of enlightenment so that enlightenment truly becomes a world view for man.

To this end, after having pointed out that the origin of this enlightenment mentality was the ethical and religious traditions of the modern Western world symbolized by Greek Philosophy, Judaism, and Christianity, Tu presented a detailed analysis of what we should do.

> The time has come to transcend the exclusive and dichotomous thinking exemplified by the division between material-spirit, body-soul, holiness-vulgarity, man-nature, and creator-creature, which has ruled the spiritual world of the West. We must, at the level of contemporary philosophy, religion and theology, highlight the characteristics of ultimate values which emphasize the sacredness of the earth, the continuity of being, the reciprocal relationship between human communities and nature, and the interrelationship between heaven and man.[8]

We can thus see that Tu Weiming has advocated the need to conduct

---

[8] Tu Weiming, "Kyemongjuŭi chŏngsin ŭl nŏmŏsŏ [Beyond the enlightenment mentality]," *Yuhak sasangkwa saengt'aehak* [Confucianism and Ecology: The Interrelation of Heaven, Earth, and Humans], ed. Mary Evelyn Tucker and John Berthrong (Harvard University Press, 1998), trans. O Chŏngsŏn (Yemoon sowon, 2010), 63.

a comprehensive review of not only modern Western thought, but also of traditional schools of thought which have become the roots of modern Western thought such as the Hellenism of ancient Greece, Judaism, and Hebraism of Christianity.[9] Under these circumstances, many ecologists have searched for alternative views of the world that could be used to overcome the dichotomous and dualistic worldview of the West. In this regard, some of them have focused on Asian philosophies, which contain an abundance of unitary, organic and relational contents. Encouraged by the fact that Western ecologists were paying attention to Asian philosophies, East Asian scholars also joined in the 'East Asian discourse' that emerged at the end of the twentieth century.

The translation by scholars who majored in ethics of Western ecology books that began in Korea[10] in the 1980s spurred the implementation

---

9 In her work, *The Historical Roots of Our Ecologic Crisis*, Lynn White argues that Judaism and Christianity's emphasis on the transcendence of God over nature and on man's rule over nature has had the effect of devaluating the value of nature, which in turn has allowed nature to become a resource that can be used for utilitarian purposes.
Tu Weiming, "Kyemongjuŭi chŏngsin ŭl nŏmŏsŏ [Beyond the enlightenment mentality]," *Yuhak sasang kwa saengt'aehak* [Confucianism and Ecology: The Interrelation of Heaven, Earth, and Humans], ed. Mary Evelyn Tucker and John Berthrong (Harvard University Press, 1998), trans. O Chŏngsŏn (Yemoon sowon, 2010), 26.

10 Examples include: Murray Bookchin, trans. Mun Sunhong, *Saeho saengt'aeron ŭi ch'ŏrhak* [Toward an ecological society]; Reiner Grundmann, trans. Pak Manjun and Pak Chun'gŏn, Marŭk'ŭsŭjuŭi wa saengt'aehak [Marxism and ecology]; Peter Singer, trans. Kim Sŏnghwan, *Tongmul haebang* [Animal liberation]; Hans Jonas, trans. Han Chŏnsŏn, Saengmyŏng ŭi wŏlli [The phenomenon of Life: toward a philosophical biology]; Joseph R. Desjardins, trans. Kim Myŏngsik, *Hwan'gyŏng yulli* [Environmental ethics: an introduction to environmental philosophy].

of ecological studies in a full scale manner, which in turn led to the publication of study results.[11] In this regard, the most outstanding work can be identified as natural scientist Chang Hoeik's philosophy of 'global life'.[12] Chang's global life theory identified all individual life forms on earth as 'co life' and the entire life phenomenon as global life. Moreover, Chang asserted that all life forms on earth were organically related to each other as part of a huge life mass governed by infinite relations. Han Myŏnhŭi not only expanded on Chang's theory of global life, but also introduced the *ki*-ecological theory.[13]

Here, two important joint studies can be identified. One is the compilation of ten sessions of lectures carried out from May to June 1993

---

11 Examples include: Pak Imun, *Munmyŏng ŭi wigi wa munhwa ŭi chŏnhwan* [The crisis of civilization and cultural transition], *Munmyŏng ŭi mirae wa saengt'aehakchŏk segyegwan* [The future of civilization and the ecological view of the world], *Hwan'gyŏng ch'ŏrhak* [Environmental philosophy]; Mun Sunhong, *Saengt'ae wigi wa noksaek ŭi taean* [The ecological crisis and green alternatives]; Han Myŏnhŭi, *Hwan'gyŏng yulli* [Environmental ethics]; Chang Hoeik, *Sam kwa onsaengmyŏng* [Living and global life]; Chin Kyohun, *Hwan'gyŏng yulli* [Environmental ethics]; Lee Chinu (Yi Chinu), *Noksaek sayuwa ek'otop'ia* [Green thought and ecotopia]; Ku Sŭnghoe, *Saengt'ae ch'ŏrhak kwa hwan'gyŏng yulli* [Ecological philosophy and environmental ethics], *Ecophilosophy*; Ch'oe Chongdŏk, *Hamkke hanŭn hwan'gyŏng ch'ŏrhak* [Environmental philosophy for all]; Kim Myŏngsik, *Hwan'gyŏng, saengmyŏng, simŭi minjujuŭi* [Environment, life, and deliberative democracy]; Kim Seajeong (Kim Sejŏng), *Wang Yangmyŏng ŭi saengmyŏng ch'ŏrhak* [Wang Yangming's philosophy of life].

12 Chang Hoeik, *Sam kwa onsaengmyŏng* [Living and global life] (Sol, 1998).

13 Han Myŏnhŭi, *Hwan'gyŏng yulli* [Environmental ethics] (Ch'ŏrhak kwa hyŏnsilsa, 1997).

by the Buddhist Academy for Ecological Awakening.[14] The preface to this book states,

> The segmented and reductionist thinking structure of the West has resulted in the separation of man and nature, and in man being pointed out as the primary cause of the environmental problems we now face. For this reason, those who have been concerned about environmental problems have focused on the holistic and organic thought of Asia, as well as on its 'life sustaining' standpoint. Internally, they hoped that great alternatives would emerge from these Asian themes.

As such, we can deduce the goals of the book. This particular work includes ten sections dealing with topics such as Confucianism, Buddhism and Daoism, the Hinduism of India, as well as Tonghak (Eastern Learning) and other traditional philosophies of Korea.

The other is the publication from 1996 to 1998 by the Center for the Study of World Religions at Harvard University of collections of works based on the theme 'world religions and the ecosystem.' One of these collections was a work entitled Confucianism and Ecology: *The Interrelation of Heaven, Earth, and Humans.*[15] In the book's preface, the

---

14 Buddhist Academy for Ecological Awakening, Tongyang sasang kwa hwan'gyŏng munje [Asian Thought and Environmental Issues] (Mosaek, 1996).

15 *Confucianism and Ecology: The Interrelation of Heaven, Earth, and Humans* ed. Mary Evelyn Tucker and John Berthrong (Harvard University Press, 1998).

editors Mary Evelyn Tucker and John Berthrong referred to Confucian ecology as being characterized by

> a dynamic and organic view of the world, dynamic perceptions of *qi*, respect for the infinite continuity of life, caring mind for those who suffer, efforts to establish the basis for the construction of a society in which justice and the environment are continuously preserved, emphasis on holistic theory, emphasis on moral education, and a cognition and appreciation of life which is deeply embedded in the interrelated groups.

This book is composed of sixteen papers written by seventeen scholars, including Tu Weiming, William Theodore de Bary, Rodney L. Taylor, Michael C. Kalton, Joseph A. Adler, Young-chan Ro and Cheng Chung-ying. The work includes discussions on Pre-Confucianism and Neo-Confucianism, as well as on theoretical and practical themes. For instance, Young-chan Ro's paper, "Yulgok ujuron ŭi saengt'aeronjŏk amsi tŭl (The Korean Neo-Confucianism of Yi Yulgok)," a work related to Korean Confucianism, is included in the book.

At the "Korean Confucianism and Ecology" conference held at Keimyung University from June 2 to June 4, 2011, the relationship between Korean Confucianism and ecology was discussed. All in all, nine papers were presented as well as two keynote speeches. This was the first conference concentrating on ecological discourse from the standpoint of Korean Confucianism.

3. WHAT DO CONFUCIANISM AND KOREAN CONFUCIANISM HAVE TO TELL WITH REGARDS TO THE ECOLOGICAL DISCOURSE?

Several ecological discussions centering on Confucianism have been organized. However, few ecological discussions revolving around Korean Confucianism have to date been carried out. In his paper presented during the Fifth Kei-myung International Conference on Korean Studies held in June 2011, Kim Sea-jeong (Kim Sejŏng) revealed that the ecological discourses related to Korean Confucianism started during the late 1990s, and that approximately twenty papers on the topic were produced during this period. Kim pointed out that most of these studies were focused on the Neo-Confucian scholars Yi Hwang and Yi Yi as well as the Sirhak (Practical Learning) scholars Hong Tayong and Ch'oe Han'gi. This focus on such a limited number of Confucian scholars has rendered the tasks of attempting to identify the characteristics of Korean Confucianism pertaining to ecological discussions very complicated. In this regard, it is particularly difficult to separate the Neo-Confucianism of Yi Hwang and Yi Yi from Chinese Neo-Confucianism. The development of an ecological discourse that is limited to Korean Confucianism can also be perceived as being complex when we consider that Sirhak scholars also fall within the sphere of Confucian thought. Let us first discuss about Confucianism in general, therefore.

In the past, Western ecologists' examination of Asian thought mostly revolved around the Hinduism and Buddhism of India and the Daoism of China. However, Confucian researchers and scholars have now followed in their footsteps in search of the ecological thought embedded in

Confucianism. The main Confucian texts which they have paid attention to include the *Book of Changes* (周易), the *Doctrine of the Mean* (中庸) and the Mencius (孟子). Ecophilosophical interpretations have been focused on Zhang Zai's Qi philosophy, Cheng Hao and Wang Shouren's theory of *wanwu yiti/manmul ilch'e* (萬物一體, all things are of one body). At some point, the Li-Qi theory (理氣論, theory of principle and force/energy) in Neo-Confucianism was interpreted in an ecological philosophical manner.

However, one important obstacle to the perception of Confucian thought in an ecological manner was the concept of the moral man embedded in Confucianism. Leaving aside Xun Zi's view of the division between heaven and man (天人分二), we find that while Mencius argued that what separated man from other beings such as animals was morality, Zhou Dunyi of the Northern Song dynasty regarded man as the most intelligent of all beings. Meanwhile, in accordance with the inherent inclination, completeness, substance, and remnants of *qi*, Neo-Confucianism also granted the discriminative status to man. In fact, these can be regarded as the fundamental characteristics and viviparous limitations of the moral philosophy known as Confucianism.

However, the problem is that ecology, and in particular deep ecology has taken issue with anthropocentrism. This has forced individuals who intended to depict Confucian thought in an ecological manner to struggle to explain the anthropocentric characteristics of Confucianism. While some developed their own logic with regards to the issue of anthropocentrism, others attempted to provide an indirect explanation by instead evoking the other philosophical characteristics of Confucianism. Examples include those who attempted to interpret Confucianism from the standpoint of the organicism theory (有機體論), relational theory, life theory, and the theory of *wanwu yiti/manmul ilch'e*. Let us take a closer look at these assertions.

First of all, the majority of scholars and researchers have accepted that Confucianism possessed anthropocentric tendencies. Nevertheless, they have stressed the fact that the anthropocentrism found in Confucianism was different from that embedded in Western modernity. To this end, Kim Pyŏnghwan stated the following.

> The anthropocentrism found in Confucianism should be interpreted differently from the Western anthropocentrism that has been the root cause of the destruction of nature. This is because Confucianism describes oneness with heaven and nature as the ultimate goal of man and suggested an image of man as the core participant in the achievement of harmony between heaven and earth.[16]

Kim Pyŏnghwan asserted that not all anthropocentric philosophies caused ecological crises, and that the anthropocentric tendencies in Confucianism differed from the anthropocentrism embedded in Western modernity, the latter of which was regarded as having caused the ecological crisis. In other words, by establishing a confrontational relationship between man and nature, the anthropocentrism embedded in Western modernity made possible the establishment of a perception whereby

---

16 Kim Pyŏnghwan, "21 segi yuhak ŭi kwaje wa chŏnmang—yuhak sasang kwa saengt'ae munje rŭl chungsim ŭro [The tasks of Confucianism in the twenty-first century and the outlook thereof—with a special focus on Confucian thought and ecological problems]," *Chungguk hakpo* 42: 391.

nature was viewed in an instrumental manner. Meanwhile, although also based on anthropocentric thought, Confucianism pursued a unitary relationship between man and nature as its ultimate ideal. Kim pointed out that as Confucianism did not view nature in an instrumental manner, it did not entail the inevitable destruction of the ecosystem. Some of the examples of Confucian anthropocentrism identified in this particular work were the notions of 'great man and virtuous man (大人君子)' and 'thought of three essences (三才思想: heaven, earth, and humans)' taken from the *Book of Changes*, the concept of the fulfillment of one's nature (盡性) found in the *Doctrine of the Mean*, and the notion of love for all creatures (愛物) found in *Mencius*.

Tu Weiming also regarded Confucian humanism (人本主義) as being in essence anthropocosmic rather than anthropocentric. Tu claimed that the self-transcendental anthropocosmic spirit of Confucianism was connected to the unity of heaven and man (天人合一論), and that communications between communities were carried out based on the discovery of the correlations between man and nature and between heaven and man. Tu's detailed outlook was based on Wang Shouren's theory of *wanwu yiti/manmul ilch'e*.[17] The assertion that Confucian anthropocentrism differed from the Western variant in that it did not regard man and nature as contradictory entities was one that was also

---

17 Tu Weiming, "Kyemongjuŭi chŏngsin ŭl nŏmŏsŏ [Beyond the enlightenment mentality]," *Yuhak sasang kwa saengt'aehak* [Confucianism and Ecology: The Interrelation of Heaven, Earth, and Humans] ed. Mary Evelyn Tucker and John Berthrong (Harvard University Press, 1998), trans. O Chŏngsŏn (Yemoon sowon, 2010), 78–79.

shared by modern scholars such as Hwang Kapyŏn,[18] Chŏn Pyŏngsul[19] and Yi Tonghŭi. Despite being laden with anthropocentrism, Yi Tonghŭi nevertheless labeled Confucian thought and its inherent respect for nature as humanistic ecologism, and pointed out the eco-philosophical elements of Confucianism, particularly Neo-Confucianism.[20]

Some of the scholars that had reservations about the anthropocentric characteristics of Confucianism instead emphasized the organic characteristics of Confucian thought. The emphasis on the organic characteristics of Confucianism was suggested as a view of nature or the world that could stand up as an alternative to the mechanical view of nature embedded in Western modernity, a view which as mentioned above has been pointed out as the cause of the ecological crisis. In the same context, the relational view of the world was suggested as the alternative to the ontological view of the world and the life-ism view of the world as an alternative to the material view of the world. They believed that the organic, relational, life-ism-based view of the world found in Confucian thought was in keeping with the ecological view of the world. The spread

18 Hwang Kapyŏn, "21 segi yuga ch'ŏrhak ŭi paljŏn panghyang—hwan'gyŏng yulli rŭl chungsim ŭro [The developmental direction of Confucian philosophy in the twenty-first century—with a special focus on environmental ethics]," *Tongyang ch'ŏrhak* (The Society for Asian Philosophy in Korea) 12 (2000).

19 Chŏn Pyŏngsul, "Tongyang ch'ŏrhak ŭi in'gan chungsimjŏk hwan'gyŏng yulli [The anthropocentric environmental ethics of Asian philosophy]," *Chungguk hakpo* (The Korean Association of Chinese Studies) 47 (2003).

20 Lee Dong-hee (Yi Tonghŭi), "Han'guk Sŏngnihak ŭi hwan'gyŏng ch'ŏrhakchŏk sisa [Environmental philosophical implications of Korean Neo-Confucianism]," *Tongyang ch'ŏrhak* [The Society for Asian Philosophy in Korea] 13 (2000).

of such views of the world would inevitably reduce man's exclusive and discriminative status.

As part of his analysis of the discussion of the relationship between man and nature found in the *Book of Changes*, Ch'oe Yŏngjin focused on the oppositeness of *yin* and *yang* (陰陽對待) rooted in the view of others (他者觀). Ch'oe identified the oppositeness of yin and yang as both a relational theory and as an essential preposition designed to ensure the existence of the self vis-à-vis others.[21] Therefore man and nature were formed in accordance with an oppositional rather than confrontational relationship. Ch'oe further claimed that the relationship between man and nature was not the only oppositional one, but rather all beings in the universe existed in oppositional relationships with one another. Moreover, he went on to add that all beings within the universe are embedded in each being. As support for his argument, he introduced the example of the kwe (卦, hexagram) found in the *Book of Changes*.

> One *kwe* contains the whole. In other words, all 64 *kwe* include one another. Therefore, one represents the whole and the whole is one. This shows that the world is composed of an organic net of objects (物).[22]

---

21 Ch'oe Yŏngjin, "*Chuyŏk* esŏ ponŭn in'gan kwa chayŏn ŭi kwan'gye—tajagwan ŭl chungsim ŭro [The relationship between man and nature as viewed through the *Book of Changes*]," *Tongyang ch'ŏrhak* (The Society for Asian Philosophy in Korea) 13 (2000): 15.

22 Ch'oe Yŏngjin, "*Chuyŏk* esŏ ponŭn in'gan kwa chayŏn ŭi kwan'gye—tajagwan ŭl chungsim ŭro [The relationship between man and nature as viewed through the *Book of Changes*]," *Tongyang ch'ŏrhak* (The Society for Asian Philosophy in Korea) 13 (2000): 16.

This can be regarded as a typical organic and relational theory-based interpretation of the *Book of Changes*. However, Ch'oe stressed the fact that this organic and relational philosophy was not only exhibited in the *Book of Changes*, but also—as evidenced by the notions of loyalty and forgiveness (忠恕), the principle of measuring square (絜矩之道), and interconnected realizations of self and of all others (成己成物)—included in the general characteristics of Confucian thought. Kwak Sinhwan also interpreted the *Book of Changes* from the standpoint of organic theory, and concluded that this work greatly influenced future generations.

> The fundamental classic of philosophy from the Han dynasty was the *Book of Changes*. Many scholars from China and Korea who were engaged in the study of Li (principle) believed that the *Book of Changes*, which included the Appended Statements or *Great* (繫辭傳, Xicizhuan), was the origin of the study of Li (principle). The cosmic extension of the notions of benevolence (仁) and honesty (誠) evident in Zhou Lianxi's *Tung Shu* (通書, All-knowing Book), *Zhang* Zai's *Ximing* (西銘, Western inscription), Cheng Hao's *Shi ren pian* (識仁篇, On understanding benevolence), and Zhu Xi's *Renshuo* (仁说, On benevolence) took the form of the Confucian theory of an organic cosmos.[23]

Kwak Sinhwan also interpreted the *Book of Changes* from the

---

23 Kwak Sinhwan, "Yuhak ŭi yugich'ejŏk ujuron [The Confucian theory of the organic cosmos]," "*Kisul chŏngbohwa sidae ŭi in'gan munje* [Mankind in the age of technology and information]," (Hyeonamsa, 1994).

standpoint of life-ism theory.[24] In fact, such an interpretation of the *Book of Changes* had already been made by previous generations of scholars such as Thome H. Fang (Fang Dongmei). Fang claimed that concepts found in the Book of Changes such as endless vitalization (生生不已) pointed at no death or extinction in the universe, but rather endless generation and change. As such, the *Book of Changes* regards nature and all the beings in the universe as living things, which become a huge living organism in and of themselves. While nature moves around alongside the self and the two are interconnected to one another, each possesses its own intrinsic value. Fang asserted that the life-ism-based view of nature found in the Book of Changes was further expanded upon during the Song Dynasty.

The Song dynasty established the structure of moral metaphysics by adding the Qi-philosophy, Daoist and Buddhist thought, as well as the Book of Changes, in particular the cosmic theory found in the Yi Chuan/ Yi Zhuan (易傳, The Annotation) section, to Confucius and Mencius' theory of the moral man. The establishment of such *moral* metaphysics was begun in earnest by *Zhou* Dunyi, who sought to interpret all beings as part of one overarching system. Many philosophers attempted to interpret the infinite, discriminative world or universe as a complete and holistic structure. For example, while Shao Yong interpreted the universe based on numbers (數), Zhang Zai did so based on *qi* (氣). Meanwhile, Cheng Hao interpreted the universe based on benevolence (仁), and Cheng Yi from the standpoint of *li* (理). Finally, Zhu Xi of the Southern Song dynasty established moral metaphysics that were based on the Li-

---

24 Kwak Sinhwan, "*Chuyŏk* esŏ ŭi chayŏn'gwan [The view of nature contained in the *Book of Changes*]," *Tongyang sasang kwa hwan'gyŏng munje* [Asian thought and environmental problems] (Mosaek, 1996).

Qi theory by combining Zhang Zai's Qi-philosophy with Cheng Yi's Li-philosophy.

These philosophers' metaphysics share the commonality that all beings are unable to escape from the net of existence, and this regardless of whether this net is structured based on numbers, *qi*, benevolence, *li*, or *li-qi*. Viewed from this standpoint, it is clear that the organic and relational view of the world found in Confucianism was completed during the Song dynasty. Meanwhile, the life-ism based view of the world can be perceived as having already been embedded in Confucian thought. For example, it is difficult to regard *qi* in Zhang Zai's Qi philosophy as nothing more than a physical or material being. This is also evident in Zhang Zai's notion of *wuwo tongbaolun/mul-a tongp'oron* (物我同胞論, the self and objects share the same origin). Here, we can see that rather than limiting himself to interpreting the universe as a simple organic and relational theory based on *qi* Zhang Zai interpreted the world from the standpoint of life-ism. Such an approach can also be found in Cheng Hao's notion of benevolence. For Cheng, benevolence was akin to a vitality or will to live which all beings possessed. Moreover, benevolence could be expanded to become a theory of the cosmos. As such, Confucianism established a more complete organic and relational view of the universe and nature during the Song dynasty. In particular, it encompassed the contents of life-ism theory that revolved around the notions of *qi* and benevolence. The *Yangming* Learning (陽明學) that held sway during the Ming dynasty helped to further strengthen the Neo-Confucian characteristics that prevailed during the Song dynasty, which eventually resulted in the advent of the theory of *wanwu yiti/manmul ilch'e*.

Wang Shouren said, "All the beings in the universe are made up of the same body (一體) as man, ... wind and rain, dew and lightening, the sun, moon and stars, animals and trees, mountains and rivers, earth and stone are all originally of the same body as man."[25] In addition, Wang pointed out, "A great man (大人) refers to a person who regards all the beings in the universe as one body, ... The reason why a great man can regard all the beings as one body is not because he forces himself to regard things in such a manner. Rather, it is the original benevolence in his mind that becomes one body with all beings."[26] Wang went on to add, "The petty man (小人) separates the self from others based solely on outer appearances."[27] Wang's theory of *wanwu yiti/manmul ilch'e* is supported by the theory of circulation of one *qi* (一氣流通). As such, this indicates that there is responsiveness (感應) between man and all beings.

Thus, Wang Shouren's theory of *wanwu yiti/manmul ilch'e* can be seen as having borrowed from the theory of the unity of heaven and man (天人合一) found in Pre-Confucianism, and from the organic and relational view of the universe and nature that prevailed during the Song dynasty, in particular Zhang Zai's *qi*-based *wuwo tongbaolun/mula tongp'oron* and Cheng Hao's life-ism based view of the universe. Kim Sea-jeong summarized Wang Shouren's *wuwo yiti/mul-a ilch'e* (物我一體, oneness of objects and man) as follows.

> Based on the perception of all beings (in the universe) as an organism, Wang's theory of *wuwo yiti/mul-a ilch'e* granted

---

25 Wang Shouren, *Chuanxilu* [傳習錄, Instructions for practical living], 黃省曾錄, 274.

26 Wang Shouren, *Collection of Wang Yangming's Studies* [王陽明全集], vol. 26, 大學問, 968.

27 Ibid.

> a value to the life of all beings, and expanded the subjects of *ch'inmin* (親民, approach the people with dignity) to the members of natural ecosystems. As such, it created the opportunity to abandon the anthropocentric instrumental view of nature, which is rooted in a dichotomous view of the world that has led to the destruction of natural ecosystems, under which the relationship between man and nature is viewed as being contradictory and conflictive in nature, in favor of a life-centered 'ecological view of the world' in which the relationship between man and nature and is perceived as mutually complementary and harmonious.[28]

Kim Sea-jeong asserted that as all beings in the universe possessed life and constituted a huge organism, man should, in accordance with the principle of *qinmin/ch'inmin* found in Yangming Learning, extend the scope of affection to include all beings. Yangming Learning, which advocated that all beings originated from one body, can be regarded as a life-oriented ecological view of the world. Such interpretations of Wang Shouren's theory of *wanwu yiti/manmul ilch'e* from the standpoint of ecological philosophy can be found in the work of Tu Weiming, Ch'oe

---

28 Kim Sea-jeong, "Wang Yangmyŏng ŭi ch'inminsŏl e taehan saengt'aeronjŏk chŏpkŭn [The ecological approach contained in Wang Yangming's theory of *ch'inmin*]," *Tongyang ch'ŏrhak* (The Society for Asian Philosophy in Korea) 11 (1999): 272.

Chaemok[29], Kim Kyobin,[30] and Han Yewŏn[31].

Let us now take a look at the ecological discourse from the standpoint of Korean Confucianism. As previously mentioned, few studies have to date been conducted in this field. As many of these studies have been focused on only a few figures, the number of studies which approach Korean Confucianism from the standpoint of ecological philosophy, is actually even smaller. This, on the other hand, will make today's presentations and discussions even more significant. We will herein separate Korean Confucianism into the Neo-Confucian group centering on Yi Hwang and Yi Yi, and the Sirhak (practical Learning) group centering on Hong Taeyong and Ch'oe Han'gi. As Kim Sea-jeong examined this very theme during the Keimyung conference on Korean Confucianism and Ecology, special attention will be paid herein to his detailed analysis of this theme.

First, Han Myŏnhŭi analyzed Korean Neo-Confucianism from the ecological standpoint. Han divided the main ecological issues into 1) the connectivity of nature, 2) the non-instrumental value of nature, 3) ecological limitedness of society, and 4) the ideological concretization program. As it incorporated issues 1) and 2), Han classified Korean Neo-

---

29 Ch'oe Chaemok, "Yangmyŏnghak kwa hwan'gyŏng yulli [Yangming learning and environmental ethics]," *Tongasia munhwa wa sasang* (East Asian Culture and Philosophy) vol. 1 (East Asian Forum on Cultural Diversity, 1998).

30 Kim Kyobin, "Yangmyŏnghak kwa saengmyŏng sasang [Yangming learning and life-ism]," *Tongyang ch'ŏrhak* 13 (The Society for Asian Philosophy in Korea, 2000).

31 Han Yewŏn, "Yangmyŏnghak ŭi manmul ilch'egwan esŏ pon saengmyŏng yulli [Life ethics as viewed through the perception of *manmul ilch'e* found in Yangming Learning]," *Yangming Study* 6 (Korean Association of Yangming Study, 2001).

Confucianism as falling under the category of 'passive ecologism.'[32] For his part, Lee Dong-hee (Yi Tonghŭi) asserted that while Yi Hwang's theory of principle (主理論, churiron) could be regarded as having anthropocentric tendencies, Yi Yi's theory of vital energy (主氣論, chugiron) could be viewed as having physiocentric or nature-centered tendencies. Nevertheless, unlike the anthropocentrism of the West and the physiocentrism of ecologists, these were based on 'humanistic' and 'organic' ecologism.[33] Chang Sŭnggu[34] and Yi Chongho[35] also analyzed Yi Hwang's study from the standpoint of ecological philosophy. These scholars maintained that Yi Hwang's theory of the unity of *heaven and* man included both aspects of anthropocentrism and physiocentrism, and sought to identify the ecological potential of an organic view of the

---

32 Han Myŏnhŭi, *Tongasia munmyŏnggwa Han'guk ŭi saengt'aejuŭi* [East Asian Civilization and Korean Ecologism] (Philosophy and Reality Publishing, 2009), 49–52.

33 Lee Dong-hee, "Han'guk Sŏngnihak ŭi hwan'gyŏng ch'ŏrhakchŏk sisa [Environmental philosophical implications of Korean Neo-Confucianism)," *Tongyang ch'ŏrhak* (The Society for Asian Philosophy in Korea) 13 (2000).

34 Chang Sŭnggu, "T'oegye sasang ŭi saengt'ae ch'ŏrhakchŏk chomyŏng [Highlighting Yi Hwang's ecological philosophy]," *T'oegye hakpo* (The T'oegye Studies Institute) (2001).

35 Yi Chongho, "T'oegye Yi Hwang ŭi yugich'e ujuron kwa saengt'ae sasang [Yi Hwang's theory of the organic universe and ecological thought]," *Han'guk hanmunhak yŏn'gu* [Journal of Korean Literature in Hanmun] (Society of Korean Literature in Hanmun) (2004).

universe based on the notion of manmul ilch'e. Yi Kiyong,[36] Yu Sŏngsŏn[37] and Young-chan Ro[38] conducted eco-philosophical analyses of Yi Yi's study. While Young-chan Ro identified Yi Yi's theory of the universe as a 'value-neutral theory of the cosmos,' he maintained that Yi Hwang's theory of the universe was in fact an 'anthropocentric-based theory of the cosmos.' Ro pointed out that because Yi Yi regarded the relationship between man and universe as one between subject and subject rather than that between subject and object, Yi Yi's thought had the potential to develop into universal ecology. As such, these researchers, based on the fact that it contained fewer anthropocentric tendencies than Yi Hwang's school of thought, sought to identify the eco-philosophical potential in Yi Yi's school of thought.

In terms of the ecological leanings of Hong Taeyong, special attention should be paid to the study conducted by Pak Hŭibyŏng.[39] Pak identified Hong Taeyong's thought as being ecological in that his notion of equality between man and objects (人物均) was one that viewed man and nature

---

36 Yi Kiyong, "Yulgok ŭi chayŏn ihae wa ch'ŏnin kyoyŏ [Yi Yi's perception of nature and the relationship between heaven and man]," *Tongyang ch'ŏrhak* (The Society for Asian Philosophy in Korea) 13 (2000).

37 Yu Sŏngsŏn, "Yulgok simnon e kŭn'gŏhan hwan'gyŏng yulli ŭi mosaek [Searching for environmental ethics bases on Yi Yi's theory of the mind]," *Yulgok sasang yŏn'gu* (Association of Yulgok Study) 4 (2001).

38 Young-chan Ro (Ro Yŏngch'an), "Yulgok ujuronŭi saengt'aeronjŏk amsi tŭl [The Korean Neo-Confucianism of Yi Yulgok], *Yuhak sasang kwa saengt'aehak* [Confucianism and Ecology: The Interrelation of Heaven, Earth, and Humans], trans. O Chŏngsŏn (Yemoonsŏwŏn, 2010).

39 Pak Hŭibyŏng, "Hong taeyong sasang e isŏsŏ mu-la ŭi sangdaesŏng kwa tongilsŏng [The relativity and similarity between nature and the self found in Hong Taeyong's thought]," *Han'guk ŭi saengt'ae sasang* [Ecological Philosophy of Korea] (Tolbegae, 1999).

as being equal. On the other hand, few studies have been conducted on the main symbol of the Sirhak (Practical Learning) School, Chŏng Yagyong.[40] Kim T'aeo's study can be regarded as a leading example of an eco-philosophical study conducted on Ch'oe Han'gi's thought.[41] Kim focused on the eco-philosophical implications of Ch'oe Han'gi's thought from the standpoint of the theory of *ki*-circulation (運化), which he linked to his viewpoint on educational philosophy. Thus, we can see that there have only been a few studies on the ecological discourses within Korean Confucianism, and that these have in essence failed to move beyond the scope of Chinese Confucianism.

---

40 While Ch'a Sŏnghwan wrote one paper on this subject, it is difficult to regard his paper as constituting a full-fledged ecological discussion. Ch'a Sŏnghwan, "Chŏng Yagyong kyŏnghak sasang i saengt'ae hwan'gyŏng wigi ŭi sidae e chunŭn sisajŏm [The implications of Chŏng Yakyong's thought regarding the Confucian Classics in terms of the ecological crisis]," *Tamnon* 201 (The Korean Association of Socio-Historical Studies) (2010).

41 Kim T'aeo, "Hyegang sasang ŭi saengt'aejuŭijŏk kyoyuk wŏlli [The ecological education principle contained in Hyegang's thought]," *Philosophy Education* (The Philosophy Education Society of Korea) 35 (2008); "Hyegang ŭi taedongnon kwa sot'ongnon kŭrigo kyoyuk saengt'aehak [Hyegang's theories of great harmony and communication and educational ecology]," *Philosophy Education* (The Philosophy Education Society of Korea) 41 (2010).

4. CONFUCIANISM IN THE ECOLOGICAL DISCOURSES

We have regarded the anthropocentric characteristics of Confucianism as the biggest obstacle to the interpretation of Confucian thought in an ecological manner. In this regard, the interpretation of Confucian thought in an eco-philosophical manner is predicated on the explanation of the anthropocentric characteristics of Confucianism. With an eye towards explaining such characteristics, we reviewed the existing ecological discourse within Confucianism. Only a quick look or common sense is required to conclude that Confucianism is clearly anthropocentric. At the center of this anthropocentrism is the perception of moral man that is embedded in everything from Pre-Confucianism to Yangming Learning. The deep ecologists in the West, ecologists in Asia, and further those who developed the ecological discourse based on Confucian thought, have all identified the anthropocentrism of the modern West as the primal cause of the current ecological crisis. That being the case, the following question inevitably comes to mind: If Confucianism also falls under the category of anthropocentric philosophy, then how can one interpret Confucianism in an ecological manner?

A group of scholars and researchers have attempted to answer this question. The following can be regarded as a summary of the answers that have been provided to date: the anthropocentrism embedded in Confucian thought differs from that of the modern West. Moreover, while the anthropocentrism in Confucian thought perceives man and nature as existing in an oppositional relationship, that of the modern West, which is based on a dichotomous view, regards man and nature as being governed by a contradictory relationship.

Meanwhile, other scholars failed to directly deal with the anthropocentric characteristics of Confucianism, preferring instead to focus on its organic, relational, and life-ism-based characteristics. The focus on these characteristics can be explained by their belief that the primal cause of the current ecological crisis has been the mechanical, practical, and physical view of nature that has prevailed in the modern West. These various inherent philosophical characteristics of Confucianism have been identified as philosophical alternatives with which to overcome the ecological crisis. From the same context, researchers involved in the field of Yangming Learning have stressed the fact that this school of thought rooted in the theory of *wanwu yiti/manmul ilch'e* constitutes an ecological philosophy.

Let us now review the ecological interpretation of Confucian thought. The first question is that of identifying the problems as pertains to the interpretation of the ecological characteristics of Confucianism. As seen in our review of the work conducted by the relevant scholars and researchers above, Confucian thought clearly includes eco-philosophical contents that have no relation to anthropocentrism. These include the organic, relational and life-ism based view of the world and the theory of *wanwu yiti/manmul ilch'e*. However, even though Confucianism does contain such philosophical contents and characteristics, this does not mean that it can be interpreted as ecological thought. Confucianism is clearly not a philosophy that was established based on an ecological foundation. In this regard, Pre-Confucianism's philosophical interest was man and its range of philosophical inquiry was limited to man alone. Thus, the hasty inclusion of Confucian thought in ecologism runs the risk of falling into the trap of Apologetics and Orientalism.

The biggest obstacle to perceiving Confucianism as ecologism is not anthropocentrism, but rather moralism and the concept of moral man. As those in Asia who have participated in the ecological discourse have asserted, the organic, relational view of nature and the world is a concept that is embedded in Confucianism. Such views of nature and the world were further expanded upon by later generations. For instance, Yangming Learning suggested that the self and all other beings essentially became one body. In this regard, the conclusion can also be reached that moralism and the view of moral man were further expanded upon through such organic and relational views of nature and the world, as well as the theory of *wanwu yiti/manmul ilch'e*. Efforts to increasingly incorporate eco-philosophical contents in Confucian thought will inevitably lead to more space being occupied by the notion of the moral man, which in turn will result in nature and all beings in the universe having to abandon their status to ethics and man. Once this comes to pass, nature will become nothing more than a personified nature. The development of ecological discourses based on a personified nature which does not possess any intrinsic value is like building a house on sand.

Another problem which has emerged has been the analysis of the causes of the current ecological crisis and the methodology to overcome it that has been suggested by those in Asia who have participated in the ecological discourses. These individuals have sought to locate the cause of the ecological crisis in the dichotomous separation of man and nature in the West, as well as in the anthropocentrism, instrumental view of nature, and mechanical view of world that stem from this dichotomous separation. To this end, the answers to this problem can be found in the very causes thereof. The ecological crisis can be resolved by altering or outright abandoning these problematic viewpoints. In addition, these scholars have indicated that infallible remedies are already embedded in

Asian thought. Of course, such assertions have been the prerogative of those who have sought to excessively oversimplify the prevailing problems and who have been deeply swayed by the tenets of deep ecology.

Yi Hyogŏl raised the following question with regards to the development of a deep ecology-centered ecological discourse, "If the ultimate cause of the environmental destruction is the dichotomous view of the world and the anthropocentric view of nature under which nature is perceived as a subjected being, then can, even if a long period of time is required, environmental destruction be done away with by establishing a pluralism-based view of the world and a physiocentric view of nature?"[42] Kim Pyŏnghwa shared Yi's opinion.

> One cannot help but wonder whether the conclusion that the environmental crisis caused by anthropocentrism and individual metaphysics can be overcome by Asian thought, for example, the nature-friendly thought of the Confucian School and the naturalism contained in Laozhuang Thought (老莊思想), is not in reality an oversimplification of things. Furthermore, Asian thought has also been hailed by some as an alternative with which to bring about a new civilization. Western scholars have increasingly paid attention to Asian thought as a means of solving the ecological crisis. However, the convenient interpretation of this denouement by those

---

42 Yi Hyogŏl, "Hwan'gyŏng saengt'ae munje e taehan tongyang ch'ŏrhak ŭi taean [Asian philosophy as an alternative with which to resolve environmental and ecological problems]," *Chunggukhak nonch'ong* (Chinese Studies Institute) 9–1 (1996): 163.

> who specialize in Asian philosophies in a manner that makes it look as if Western civilization will be replaced by Asian civilization in the twenty-first century or that all the problems caused by Western civilization, including the ecological crisis, can be solved based on Asian wisdom, should be regarded as little more than an exercise in vanity on the part of such individuals.[43]

Yi Hyogŏl and Kim Pyŏnghwan's criticism can be regarded as a clear sign of the limitations of the ecological discourses based on Asian thought, and of the need to overcome these limitations. In this regard, Kim Sea-jeong stressed that scholars and researchers in the field of Asian philosophy,

> ...cannot solve the environmental crisis merely by asserting that Asian philosophy possesses an abundance of organic and ecological characteristics. It is necessary to analyze the various and complex causes of the environmental crisis in a continuous, exact and structural manner. It is also necessary, in order to solve the environmental crisis, to conduct comparative studies and interdisciplinary cooperation that includes the field of environmental philosophy, and, based on this process, to reestablish Asian philosophy as

---

[43] Kim Pyŏnghwan, "21 segi yuhak ŭi kwajewa chŏnmang—yuhak sasang kwa saengt'ae munje rŭl chungsim ŭro [The tasks of Confucianism in the twenty-first century and the outlook thereof—with a special focus on Confucian thought and ecological problems]," *Chungguk hakpo* 42: 381.

environmental ethics or an environmental philosophy.[44]

As such, some of the scholars and researchers in the field of Asian ecology have pointed out that there have been problems with regards to the diagnostic of the ecological crisis and the establishment of countermeasures. Be that as it may, these individuals have also sought in their own studies to bring about an alternative Asian ecological thought. Then, has it become impossible for these Asian ecological discourses to move forward? Should we not move beyond the scope of philosophical discourses? I do not think that is the case. By changing our way of thinking a little bit we can see that the ecological crisis was not only the result of the prevailing world view, but also of a capitalist economic system that values the pursuit of infinite profits and of the capitalist humans who pursue infinite desires under this capitalist economic structure. As such, those engaged in the study of the relationship between the ecological discourse and Asian thought should actively concentrate not only on the development of new and alternative ecological thought, but also on the establishment of ecological politics and economy as well as means to abstain from desire. The ecological discourse has already been pushed to new lengths and depths in the West, and various hands-on activities have been implemented. We should not allow our thinking and activities to be limited by a strict adherence to the tenets of deep ecology.

Efforts have been made to implement the notions and ideologies that

---

44 Kim Sea-jeong, "Hwangyŏng yulli e taehan tongyang ch'ŏrhakchŏk chŏpkŭn: yuga ch'ŏrhak ŭl chungsim ŭro [The Asian philosophical approach to environmental ethics: with a special focus on Confucian philosophy]," *Pŏmhan ch'ŏrhak* 29 (2003).

make up Confucian thought in the real world for over 2,000 years. To this end, if ecological ideology does in fact represent the most important value to mankind at the present point in time, then one can in fact use Confucian thought, which has gone through a similar experience, as a means to uncover how such an ecological ideology can be actualized in the reality of East Asia. Furthermore, attention should also be drawn to the ecological views of politics and economics contained in the Confucianism-based ruling structure established in the past. Confucian thought can in particular provide many answers with regards to the issue of how one can live as the owner rather the slave to desire under the current capitalist economic structure in which one desire leads to the advent of another. Of course, this issue should also be addressed with perceptions and means of persuasion that are rooted in an understanding of a contemporary society that is based on a complex mesh of desire rather than rigid moral reprimands.

Hong Won-sik (wsh683@kmu.ac.kr) *is a professor in the Department of Philosophy at Keimyung University, Korea.*

Translated by Michael Bujold and Young-ki You

THE CONTEMPORARY CONFUCIAN HERITAGE AND THE ENVIRONMENT OF WORLDLY CONFUCIANS AND TOHAK CONFUCIANS

By Michael C. Kalton

INTRODUCTION

In the January 15, 2011 issue of the New York Times, columnist Nicholas D. Kristof writes as follows:

> An international study published last month looked at how students in 65 countries performed in math, science and reading. The winner was: Confucianism!
> At the very top of the charts, in all three fields and by a wide margin, was Shanghai. Three of the next top four performers were also societies with a Confucian legacy of reverence for education: Hong Kong, Singapore and South Korea. The only non-Confucian country in the mix was Finland.
> The larger issue is that the greatest strength of the Chinese system is the Confucian reverence for education that is steeped into the culture. In Chinese schools, teachers are much respected, and the most admired kid is often the brain

rather than the jock or class clown.[1]

Among those who observe global economic trends, the various East Asian "tigers" have long attracted exactly this kind of attention. There is widespread agreement that this aspect of their Confucian heritage has played a critical role in the unmatched economic surge of East Asia. First the tigers, and now China, dwarfing in population, production, and consumption any consumer surge in world history.

Reverence for education is only half the story, however. In order to achieve such success children must study more diligently, parents must be able to demand more from them, and in turn must work harder to support and open up prospects for the children. Or better, prospects for the family. For the willingness to subordinate short term personal pleasures to the long-term well-being of the family makes possible the supercharged feedback loop of education and growing productivity that have distinguished the contemporary heirs of the Confucian tradition.

Modern individualism, with its focus on the fulfillment of what is perceived as a "personal" life emerged largely in the western world, and most especially in America. Confucians paid great attention to inculcating a deep awareness of life as a transpersonal flow through a matrix of interdependent relationships. The family, with children being considered literally extensions of the existence of their parents, was the paradigm of such relationships.

But while Confucians may have articulated these ideas with more refinement, reflection, and emphasis than most, such familial relationships

1 Nicholas Kristof, "China's Winning Schools," *New York Times*, Jan. 15, 2011.

have in fact been more the norm than the exception through most of human history. What turns this relational structure into an incredible force for economic transformation is the channeling of energies into education, a distinctive and potent feature of the Confucian heritage. Children supporting their families by spending their days picking through garbage dumps outside a Latin American slum are no less examples of filial piety than a Korean child going from school to a private study institute to spend another three or four hours cramming for entrance exams. But the trajectories into the future from these filial practices could hardly be more different.

There is a deep irony in this situation. I have elsewhere argued that the Confucian (and especially the Neo-Confucian) heritage of East Asia constitutes perhaps the world's richest resource for contemporary humans seeking a deep self-understanding and sustainable fit within the interdependent community of life on earth. But that aspect of the tradition remains largely untapped. Meanwhile other aspects of the same heritage become in effect a kind of supercharger for the chainsaw of the global consumer economy as it slices deeply into the tree of life. Perhaps future technology will render this consumerism more benign. But at the present, the kind of self-augmenting feedback loop of production and consumption celebrated in double digit GNP figures by the fortunate heirs of Confucius is exactly the phenomenon we also recognize as a systemic "sustainability crisis" for the earth's biotic community.

The aspects of the Confucian heritage now regarded with such envy by pundits such as Kristof receive little attention from contemporary scholars of the tradition. Indeed, they have carried forward so powerfully in part because they call for no special scholarly attention, no reading of classical texts or attention to erudite sources. Rather they belong to the deeper layer of assumptions about the nature of life in society and about what it takes to survive and get ahead in that life. Confucian societies were so steeped in understanding the critical interdependence of human life, and so habituated to seeing education as the privileged path to worldly success, these basic assumptions carried forward to put a "Confucian" stamp on the East Asian engagement in the competitive world of the global capitalist market.

In the premodern Confucian world, the civil service exam system served as the primary framework for competing for prestige and economic success. In the eyes of Confucians such as T'oegye or Yulgok or Ki Kobong and Ugye, there were clearly two sorts of Confucians: their kind, practitioners of *tohak*, and those somewhat scornfully referred to as "*sogyu*" or 'worldly Confucians.' Worldly Confucians studied hard to pass the civil service exams and carry forward the reputation, status, and material success of their lineage. While they absorbed Confucian learning and values, their overriding engagement with the mundane project nowadays referred to as "getting ahead" earned for them the "worldly" label—a term of course no Confucian would use regarding himself. *Tohak* Confucians, in contrast, greatly prized intensive self-cultivation practices, deep reflection, and the kind of learning that transformed the character of the learner.

The civil service exam system was the anchor of Confucian societies. As the gateway to careers as officials in the all-important world of government service, it ensured that generations of the most capable and well-placed minds would turn to Confucian learning. And in turn this had the effect of giving Confucian discourse a hegemonic role in the shaping and functioning of government, which in turn supported the plausibility of Confucian examinations as the appropriate selector for admission to the circle of the elite.

Although they recognized this essential function of the exams, serious *Tohak* Confucians were under no illusions regarding the effects of this kind of system on both the motivation and the quality of learning of candidates studying for the exams:

> [Chŏng Sasŏng] was sitting in attendance in the study. The Teacher [T'oegye] said to those assembled there: "The meaning of the Confucian school is of itself something apart. Proficiency in literary skills is not Confucian; passing the civil service examinations is not Confucian." Then he sighed and said: "In the world a great number of men of excellent ability become completely absorbed in conventional studies. Who is there that is able to succeed in liberating himself from the mortar-bowl of the examinations!"[2]

T'oegye's comments are a commonplace in the writings of morally engaged Neo-Confucians. But the critique cuts both ways, for to families looking to secure their position among the social elite, *tohak* could seem an unnecessary distraction:

> Our Teacher [T'oegye] also said: "Fathers and elder brothers nowadays always regard expounding the *Classic of the Mind-and-Heart* and the *Reflection on Things at Hand* as wrong and criticize their sons and younger brothers [for engaging in such studies]. Scholars likewise are intimidated

---

2 *T'oegye sŏnsaeng ŏnhaengnok* 5.lla, B, 855.

> by public opinion and few expound this learning. In my lecturing on the *Classic of the Mind-and-Heart* I feel certain uneasiness, but I am unwilling to put aside our kind of learning and lecture on other texts."[3]

The texts mentioned by T'oegye were pillars in the edifice of Neo-Confucian self-cultivation practice, but they had little to do with the examinations. The distress of the fathers and elder brothers of T'oegye's time mirrors almost perfectly the feelings of contemporary families when their young might stubbornly want to major in humanities rather than business, engineering, law, or medicine. One must keep one's priorities straight!

Historically *tohak* practitioners and *sogyu* intertwined interdependently in complex and important ways. In the contemporary world, however, for the most part what continues and is flaunted with pride as the Confucian pedigree of economically robust East Asian societies belongs to the *sogyu*. Free market global capitalism has been shaped by western sources, but as we enter the digitalized age of information, knowledge becomes the supreme resource, and the Confucian tradition that always identified learning as the key to a worthy life (*sogyu* or *tohak*) has proved the most valuable cultural heritage a society can have. Combined with willingness to subordinate personal comfort to larger family well-being, it becomes an economic driver of unmatched potency.

The global market/consumer economy has arisen from western sources, and the Confucian tradition has had little to do with shaping

---

3 Ibid., 5.18b–19a, B, 858–859.

the dynamics or values of the system. But the heirs of *sogyu* worldly pragmatism now play a major role in the scale and speed with which that system grows and progresses, so East Asia and particularly the Chinese now play a major role in the sustainability crisis that is the shadow of capitalist consumer growth.

While *sogyu* thus exacerbates the sustainability crisis by accelerating capitalist growth, in its more integral form, the Confucian and especially the Neo-Confucian traditions potentially offer a penetrating critique of the excesses of consumerism. Further, they are deeply versed in forms of cultivation that might mitigate the illfit of contemporary human societies with the community of life on the earth. It was chiefly the *tohak* Confucians, with their deep cultivation practice and care for the resources of the tradition, who took responsibility for the ongoing creative maintenance, development, and application of the tradition to an always changing socio-economic milieu. And it is *tohak* Confucianism that has largely disappeared from the contemporary world.

CONTEMPORARY GRIDLOCK AND *SŎNGNIHAK*

The contemporary intellectual world has an odd disjuncture between those who most deeply analyze our environmental sustainability crisis and those who shape the human economy which is at the core of the crisis. Contemporary environmental studies discusses in detail the complex flow of nutrition through the living web of an environmental system and analyzes the flows of matter and energy through which life continually creates and recreates the conditions for its own existence. And the study of economics does much the same in understanding the flows of matter and energy that create and maintain the market through which contemporary consumer societies create and recreate their existence.

Oddly, the economists pay great attention to the human manipulation of those flows, but scarcely recognize the origins (sources) of those flows and their destination (sinks) in that larger system we share with all life on earth—the system studied by the environmentalists. This impossible separation of a human economy from the larger complex economy of the entire web of life (all living creatures must *make a living*, and therefore in a very real sense have an economy) permits the dream of unending economic growth and unmitigated consumption. Clearly the way we think scientifically about the system of life is woefully divorced from the way we frame and analyze the Market. But market thinking has become currently the paradigm that informs virtually every human organization and activity. An inclusive, holistic economics, such as espoused by the small group of Environmental Economists,[4] would bridge that gap, but in the economic world theirs is an almost invisible fringe position.

Sŏngnihak, in contrast, was deeply versed in thinking in terms of the holistic relational patterns that seem so difficult for the heirs of the modernist reductionist methodology that still dominates in most areas of scientific inquiry. Reductionism certainly has its place, but it becomes problematic when it causes people to overlook the implications of dynamic relational interdependence. Confucians long stressed such relational interdependence as the foundation for thinking about appropriate human

---

[4] See, for example, Herman Daley, *Beyond Growth*. Daley has long been one of the foremost representatives of those who insist on whole-systems thinking in economics.

relations, and nothing prevents a more contemporary reflection from extending the same modes of understanding inclusively to encompass the whole web of life. Ethics, inquiring into a fitting way of life, follows immediately from recognizing the relational matrix within which we exist and sustain our lives. Thus the *sŏngnihak* of T'oegye's masterful Ten Diagrams moves immediately from holistic analysis of the all-inclusive patterning Supreme Ultimate in the first diagram to a second diagram explaining the ethics of a necessarily relational existence described in the Western Inscription.

At first glance, the movement here from cosmos to ethos or way of life is typical of prescientific thought, which often begins with human concerns and then reads them into the nature of the cosmos. Neo-Confucian cosmology or metaphysics of *li* is in fact a moral cosmology. So not surprisingly it yields an account of the moral patterning of our minds-and-hearts that correlates wonderfully with the patterning of the life force throughout the four seasons. And from relating our own inner lives to the life-giving cosmic pattern exemplified in the four seasons, we can easily proceed into a discussion of the factors that distort the life-giving responsiveness of our inherently good natures and go on to an elaboration of effective forms of cultivation to lessen or remove the distortion. Seeing this easy interchange, one might well suspect that we have here a reading of the universe that is little more than a projection of conventional human moral concerns.

Modern thinkers in East Asia as well as in the West have been inclined to dismiss such premodern ways of thinking as prescientific. It seems self-evident to them that one should begin with science. A mode of thought that begins with moral concerns and works into statements about the cosmos is backwards and can yield only the pseudo-science of an artificially moralized universe. No matter that we have never figured out how to move from scientific analysis to meaningful discussion of how humans are to live (ethics), one cannot read ethics into the universe.

My argument, on the contrary, is that the particular character of Confucian thinking makes it an exception to this objection. The objection is only a half-truth. Moving from the human to the description of the non-human is invalid only if one is dealing with what is uniquely human and then projecting it into a realm that is not human. But observations regarding human physiology, for example, can well be used to understand non-human physiology. Where there is sufficient continuity on both sides, one can cross the bridge in either direction. Confucian ethics—and especially its Neo-Confucian formulation—is based upon a premise that applies equally to the whole system of organic life, the premise that we exist interdependently within a network of relationships. It is the entire relational network that conducts life. Hence life flows to us from those relationships and in return should flow back from us into the relational web surrounding us.

Contemporary systems science looks at all systemic phenomena in terms of networked relationships, for that is the very nature of a system. And of the dynamic relational network we call the earth, certainly life itself is the most spectacular systemic emergence, and organic life itself has woven through dynamic feedback loops the further dimensions of systemic complexity we call environments and social systems (the uniquely complex environment woven by humans). Neo-Confucians likewise thought in terms of a single pattern weaving everything into a performance relating to everything else. That is, the world as they imagined it, even without important scientific concepts such as evolution, amounts to a world easily in continuity with the understanding of contemporary systems science.

Revitalizing *sŏngnihak* is a worthy project because an updated *sŏngnihak* can show us how to bridge the world of systems science to the world of human ethics and self-cultivation. The central feature of that bridge is the question of life-conducing systemic relationships. Historically Confucians pursued their concern with life-givingness mainly in terms of inter-human social relationships in family and government, but in grounding that life-givingness in the life-givingness of the universe (earth) itself, they gave us a framework for seeing the necessary fit and continuity between the life-maintaining economy of the human community and the life-maintaining economies of the natural world. These are not two separate questions, but as they saw, a single, complex, interwoven dynamic in a single, whole, life-giving system.

That much, of course is already a common-place understanding among many contemporary environmental thinkers. But contemporary thought cannot push much further except to suggest a range of somewhat disparate and disconnected strategies. In the Neo-Confucian tradition, however, this was only the starting point for systemic thinking about the education and cultivation of the human mind-and-heart. We have thus far covered only the first two of T'oegye's Ten Diagrams! And because they assumed the essential cultivation challenge revolved around becoming a fittingly life-giving person in relation with others (仁), the core concepts and insights of their over two thousand years of reflection still have much to tell us.

To begin with, instead of the Greek fascination with ideation and rationality, Confucians saw human activity as essentially a response to our ever-present relational situation. Accordingly they saw inherent feelings and inclinations as the leading component of the way we respond. This may seem basic to any systemic understanding of sense-informed activity, but actually this understanding is just now being hailed as a cutting-edge new insight in the world of western psychology and ethical thinking.[5]

But what kinds of feelings, and how do they inform our responsiveness? On one level, Korea's famous Four-Seven debate went into this issue with unprecedented depth. And on another level the question has been explored in the controversy between the two major schools of Neo-Confucian thought, the Cheng-Zhu school and the Lu-Wang school. Obviously there is much to be understood here, and contemporary psychology, assisted by new brain-imaging technology, may make even further advances possible. But the broadly shared Confucian consensus picked up on a polar tension expressed in terms of the Dao Mind and the Human Mind. As the paradigmatic passage in the *Book of Rites* puts it:"The human mind is perilous, the mind of the Dao is subtle; be discerning, be undivided. Hold fast the Mean!"[6]

Recalling that the Dao is the relational pattern woven throughout all existence, it is no surprise that the Dao Mind refers to the relational or social side of our instinctive makeup. Thus the Dao Mind is commonly associated with what Mencius described as the "Four Beginnings," inherent inclinations that when fully developed become humanity, propriety, rightness, and wisdom. These feelings that equip us to act appropriately in all sorts of relationships are "subtle" in the sense that, unless carefully cultivated, they can easily be overshadowed by the equally inherent but

5 See, for example, "The New Humanism," By David Brooks, in the March 7, 2011 *New York Times*: http://www.nytimes.com/2011/03/08/opinion/08brooks.html?ref=opinion(accessed August, 28, 2011).

6 *Book of Documents,* pt. 2, 2.15.

stronger Human Mind. The Human Mind is comprised of feelings such as anger, fear, desire, and pleasure, that is, feelings that guide us to take care of our own well-being. This Human Mind is "perilous" in that it is forceful and easily triggered, so it can easily lead to an inappropriately self-centered mode of responsiveness that is in denial of the true relational flow of life.

Contemporary systems thinkers would agree that this analysis of the human condition picks up on some of the most basic system dynamics of being alive. Life exists only in terms of sources and flows that originate outside the individual organism. Evolution would soon deselect any organism that developed tendencies noxious to the relational environmental sources upon which it depends. Even competitive strategies must fit and complement the larger relational web, and selective pressure likewise rewards the emergence of overtly cooperative strategies and sociability. Contrary to the dominant economic image of humans as inherently self-centered profit maximizers, we have evolved as the most extreme example among primates of this sociability vector. We have been selected for and evolved responsive inclinations and abilities to work together that are so powerful our inter-human dependencies and prowess even obscure in the short term our continued dependence on the larger, inter-species web of relationships. Indeed, our systemic survival in the longer term depends upon the emergence of a form of Dao Mind again responsive to the encompassing web of life.

At the same time, we survive only as physically distinct, individual organisms. This demands an array of inclinations that will keep our individual selves intact—appropriately responsive feelings such as fear, anger, pleasure and desire. Insofar as these feelings guide often immediate situations of life and death importance, such as crossing a busy street or eating enough to maintain health, they are very strongly wired into our response system. Again, through natural selection and basic dynamics of life systems, the Human Mind is a fundamental feature of being human, but one we often find in tension with the Dao Mind.

So the environmentally educated and those versed in systems science share these insights with the Confucians. But only the Confucians made them the fundamental framework for understanding how human responsiveness gets distorted away from the deep life-giving dynamic that shaped our responsiveness in the first place. We must indeed take care of ourselves, but those inclinations easily run to excess and need watchful restraint; we spontaneously empathize with the difficulties and needs of others, but those feelings are easily overshadowed and need careful nurture and cultivation. This was the bedrock understanding upon which Confucians layered ethical reflection and self-cultivation practices for over two thousand years.

The special contribution of the *sŏngnihak* analysis was bringing this reflection to bear on the question of the appropriate, life-giving responsiveness of the mind-and-heart. They looked for a cultivation that could put the life of our feelings on a more spontaneously life-giving track. Though they were thinking mainly about inter-human responsiveness, the same question is systemically valid for our response to the whole community of life. And this, the question of sustainability, has become the central crisis of our era.

Sustainability is thus systemically the same question about life-giving re-sponsiveness asked by Neo-Confucians, though on a more massive and forbidding scale. We are all too aware that a species that undercuts the very web of relationships from which its life flows becomes extinct. But so far, we do not seem to be able to correct ourselves. The broad lines of the cultivation question are very similar, but the depths of the challenge are more difficult. We evolved over hundreds of thousands of years with strong interdependence among ourselves and relatively limited abilities to destroy other life on a large scale (although that too has been a problem). So the selectively evolved social inclinations the Confucians called "subtle" are perhaps super-subtle when we cross the line of our own species. How much we spontaneously empathize with or care for non-human life decreases rapidly as such life looks less and less like a human infant. Indeed, the potential shoots or sprouts of such inclinations may well be present (we see them actualized in more and more people these days), but they require even more careful nurture than our human-to-human sociability. And as many note, we have not even succeeded at the human-to-human very well much of the time.

THE CRISIS: ANY HOPE FOR A SOFT LANDING?

If there is any trove of wisdom, any lore of cultivation that might render humans more life-giving and responsive in their relation to their own systemic sources of life, it has never been more desperately needed than at present. Confucians aimed their cultivation at enhancing the sensitive responsiveness of the Dao Mind and habituating restraint regarding the inclinations stemming from the Human Mind. This Dao Mind/Human Mind window on the question of life-giving responsiveness casts the problem of contemporary consumer society in bold relief. The deepest scientific research on the responsive makeup of our minds-and-hearts proceeds today not from those concerned to deepen our cultivation but from those eager to sell us things. Human needs are inherently limited, but the consumer economy is premised on unlimited wants, and the advertising industry is indispensable as the tool to insure that ever growing production correlates with ever growing wants. Thus massive, coordinated global effort is spent cultivating and strengthening the Human Mind and its tendency to prioritize personal desires, pleasure, and comfort over other considerations.

We live immersed in a media world saturated with and shaped by the advertising money that supports it. We have even been persuaded to adorn our clothing with logos so we become walking billboards. Sports teams and their equipment are displays of what we might buy and consume. Simply put, the world of contemporary auditory and visual experience is shaped by the attempt to urge us to greater pleasure, convenience, relaxation, and stimulation. In a market economy, marketing becomes omnipresent. One can hardly appeal to the world of nature as an alternative, for nature too is marketed as an escape, a relaxation, a serene beauty for our eye and spirit.

Ease, pleasure, and convenience are not easily ratcheted back. They appeal deeply to our instincts for personal well-being. This Human Mind is already powerful even in the absence of massive efforts to strengthen its guiding role in our lives. Social or system-oriented motivation, the Dao Mind, seems weak by comparison. Indeed, the Tao Mind is subtle, the Human Mind perilous!

Thoughts about how we might transform into a more sustainable society reflect this difficult situation. We urge life-giving feeling and concerns for our fellow creatures, but these seem ineffectual in curtailing the dominance of convenience and comfort. Those who hope the Dao Mind will triumph most often anticipate some kind of new evolutionary leap in which life-giving concerns become predominant in our minds-

and-hearts. But explanations are lacking as to how such an evolution will happen. Thus many more people anticipate that we will need a sufficiently large global catastrophe to make us fear for our own well-being. That is, fear trumps pleasure in the Human Mind, and finally widespread and more or less immediate peril is the only motivation that can lead us to transform from our consumption maximizing ways. But by then it might be too late.

In the absence of some kind of magical transformation of the human mind-and-heart, perhaps the best we might hope for is some kind of "soft landing." Just as contemporary global culture fosters and strengthens the Human Mind side of our inclinations, so we would need the emergence of a global culture that is motivated to foster and strengthen the Dao Mind. Something would have to happen to motivate societies to give up dreaming of development as ever-growing production and consumption and instead encourage their populations to think of the enhanced flourishing of the entire community of life as the path to their own highest quality of life. If that "something" was sufficiently definitive to bring about a sustained cultural shift, but not so dire that it brings about systemic social collapse, we might have such a soft landing, an evolution that changes not the social-individual tension of the mind-and-heart, but changes rather the currents of culture which bring to the fore and prioritize some inclinations over others.

Few observers expect such a soft landing, though many would see it as a best hope. The problem is that consumer culture and the capitalist market system are so deeply entrenched it seems only a devastating downturn can dislodge them. What we need, however, is a softer catalyst that can nonetheless bring about a deep, long lasting, and eventually global cultural change. And for a softer catalyst to achieve that, there must be a society more sensitively or perilously on the brink of transformation, and that also systemically has ligatures throughout the global system. I propose that China is perhaps the only such society in the world today, that its Confucian heritage could facilitate a soft landing for the globe.

At present, for good reason, the eyes of the world are on China, which is undergoing phenomenal economic growth, rapid urbanization, and deep social change. It is the poster-child for the vision of development that sees capitalistic growth leading to a happy consumer society. The Chinese Communist government has in fact now openly premised its own legitimacy almost entirely upon such growth, and accordingly admits that social stability demands something like steady on-going 8.5% annual growth. If events make such growth not only unsustainable in the long run but impossible in the present, the situation would indeed become extremely unstable. Because the government of China is so perilously leveraged on legitimation by a form of economic growth that is highly vulnerable to conditions still far from catastrophic, it meets the conditions for responsiveness to a relatively softer catalyst of change.

Nationalism, always a potent force in the "Middle Kingdom," has been strongly reinforced by international awe drawn by recent economic performance. Even architects are required to incorporate some distinctive "Chinese" feature into the daring new buildings which mark out a new urban skyline. This sets the stage for the kind of strategic move typical of governments in trouble. If conditions take a turn that make it look like rapid economic growth is a thing of the past, the government will be desperate to wean people away from their expectations of growth and to redirect them to a new reason to support the government. Especially if environmental problems contribute to those conditions—as seems highly likely—what better strategy than a rediscovery of the centrality of systemic life-givingness that is such a deep part of "our own" heritage, accompanied by an all-out critique of the blindness and devastation wrought by misguided "western" capitalist values.

I do not mean to be cynical here: sometimes profound truth can also happen to serve very self-interested purposes! Neo-Confucian *tohak* insights can indeed be revitalized as better, deeper, and more relevant to the current state of affairs than the consumer ethic. A government seeking to redirect public thinking and expectations could well launch a cultural shift that would again support both efforts at personal cultivation and creative thinking in a twenty-first century *tohak* mode.

For the purposes of the global system, we should note China's role as the paradigmatic development dream. No matter that it would take three earths for the populations of China and India to live like Americans; this has been the shared vision of potential development that has been the stable underpinning of the entire international global order. But if China hits a wall, it makes the impossibility of this dream evident to all. In the search for a new vision, a new way of telling ourselves the deeper meaning of our societies, the moves that China makes are likely to have wide impact—especially as it will be seen as a radical critique of the unsustainable and unobtainable vision still represented by the United States. Neo-Confucian *tohak* is unlikely to sweep the world, but it is entirely possible that its revitalization in China as a response to waning capitalism could inspire the rediscovery or invention of similar dimensions in other major world traditions.

CONCLUSION

Sung dynasty Neo-Confucians did not just revive the Confucianism of Mencius, they thoroughly recreated it in terms of the problems and challenges of their time. In the same manner, a revived *Tohak* would find ready sources in life sciences, and in environmental and systems thinking to carry the fundamental insights of earlier Confucians/Neo-Confucians to new depths. As global human society wrestles with a sustainability problem that challenges basic structures and values we have long taken for granted, new thinking and vision coming from the *Tohak* heritage may have an audience reaching far beyond East Asia.

Whether what I have described regarding China will ever come to pass is an open question: this is perhaps the best or most optimistic of many possibilities. But we can say major cultural transformations typically emerge from just such a convergence of deep lying and historically contingent factors. Although richly life-giving orientations can be derived from virtually any of the world's great religious traditions, the heritage of *sŏngnihak* and its *tohak* practice has a unique symmetry with systemic environmental understanding and with the pressing needs of the contemporary world. That China might turn from its present deep embrace of market-oriented consumer values to revivify this heritage would be judged wildly improbable if it were just a matter of better ideas displacing less good ideas. In the short term, it is all too possible for blind and unsustainable notions to win out the real demands of the life system to which we belong. But at critical moments entire cultures can pivot on the exigencies of political survival, and conditions are such that such a juncture may bring about a "Confucian turn" in China. That might, in fact, be our best hope for a non-catastrophic transition to a more sustainable, life-conducting human presence on earth.

Michael C. Kalton (mkalton@u.washington.edu) *is a Professor Emeritus of Interdisciplinary Arts and Sciences at University of Washington, U.S.A.*

HUMAN FULFILLMENT AND LOVE OF THE UNIVERSE: A MEDITATION ON EMOTION IN KOREAN AND CHINESE SOURCES

By Philippe Thiébault

INTRODUCTION

When we think about it sincerely we recognize that human development is often not on a par with economic development which is accelerating together with all the materialistic acquisitions that go along with it. Although pertinent warnings were expressed about the weaknesses of the Enlightenment project,[1] strangely enough the Western pattern remains the exemplary way because it continues to fascinate due to its contribution to democratization and the freeing of people. However, emphasizing individualism, materialism, inequalities and also weakening values and emotions are not sufficiently considered to correct certain human behaviors and the abuse of the environment. These aspects are, furthermore, connected. If men do not discover their true identity and the depths of their mind-and-heart, how can they appreciate the

1 Cf. particularly Tu Wei-ming, International Conference on Universal Ethics and Asian Values, Seoul, October 1999, Korean National Commission for UNESCO. Korean Society for Future Studies, "A Confucian Perspective on the Core Values of the Global Community," 362–375, also Alasdair Macintyre, *After Virtue*, a study in moral theory, Duckworth, 1981/1996.

beauty of the universe and how can they even respect this universe? Besides, man needs the universe. The universe continues the awakening and the education received within the family, allowing us to go beyond narrow ambitions and to acquire a sense of the totality. The universe symbolizes by its infinity, its simplicity and its mysterious dimension what man is destined to achieve.

To come out of misery, be free and create comfortable surroundings are natural desires especially for those who have been oppressed for a long time. However, true development calls for considering deeply human fulfillment, especially on an internal level, and relating to the natural environment. An unbalance is created between our demands for our rights and material success and our human condition which is emotional and not just physical. In our search for well being something has escaped us. We did not achieve yet the "supplement of soul/*supplément d'âme*" that Bergson desired at the beginning of the twentieth century[2] and the true joy that would have resulted from it. Intelligence suffers from atrophied emotions. Activities are not balanced by an internal understanding.

Not respecting our environment is in fact working against ourselves and future generations; it is hurting ourselves. Struck by more and more huge accomplishments we play the demiurges who are blind to the consequences of their acts. We remember Mencius' words: "With those who do violence to themselves, it is impossible to speak. With those who throw themselves away, it is impossible to do anything."[3]

---

2 Henri Bergson, *Les Deux Sources de la Morale et de la Religion*, 1932, PUF, Paris, 2008.

3 *The Works of Mencius*, Dover Publications, 1970, Book IV, Part I, Chapter X, trans. James Legge, 301.

All the warnings, the rules and international declarations will not suffice to arouse a reaction and responsible involvement in people of all levels of society to avoid greater crises and more evil consequences. It seems that sometimes only catastrophes and suffering pull men out of their indifference and blindness. Mencius says: "Men for the most part err, and are afterwards able to reform. They are distressed in mind and perplexed in their thoughts, and then they arise to vigorous reformation. [...] From these things we see how life springs from sorrow and calamity, and death from ease and pleasure."[4]

This article aims at reacting to the distance and the fissure which have been created, especially since the eighteenth century, between nature and us; these are linked to a split which has also developed in us. Our decisions have led us to 'err' progressively. What we are today is above all the result of the cultural and philosophical evolution of the last two centuries which shaped our identity. During these centuries traditions were shaken and values were weakened. Man gave himself a more and more important position and pushed aside the ontological and spiritual foundations. The result produced a great disillusionment (disenchantment) which is very different from the wonderment of the beginnings of philosophy in the West and the Far East.

We are at a turning point in history. A dose of humility, clear thinking, courage and love is now necessary. Although Gabriel Marcel deplored "the decline of wisdom" and the lack of humility of some Western philosophical schools of thought, Paul Ricoeur was one of the few Western thinkers who together with Merleau-Ponty recognized the

---

4 Ibid., 447.

limits of Western philosophy in its initial movement and who spoke of the necessity of a meeting with Eastern thought (Chinese, Indian) for "mutual explaining/*explicitation mutuelle*" which he felt had never really taken place and which would allow the West to overcome its limitations and have a philosophy leading to a concrete universality.[5] Paul Ricoeur sensed this from the 1960s and was in fact aware of Far Eastern thought, having suffered the excesses of the movements of suspicion (based on Marx, Freud, and Nietzsche), structuralism and deconstruction. So much could be discovered today in a dialogue and a mutually authentic and courageous recognition between the Far East and the West for the good of the world; this Leibniz was aware of in the seventeenth century.

Only a deep rooted experience allows us to really glimpse who we are and what the universe represents and to act accordingly. Then we vibrate in wonderment at a reality which presents itself and gives itself to us with generosity for the fulfillment of everyone. This experience can take different forms according to the diversity of cultures and their complementary riches. This vision, anybody having experienced it once cannot forget. [...] The light which opened his eyes remains like a non changing light in the depth of the eyes and he quivers always remembering the sensation of that universal contact. [...] The liberating word is here: it is not enough for man, rejecting his egoism, to live socially. He needs to live with all his heart united with the whole world which carries him—cosmically.[6]

---

[5] Paul Ricoeur, *Philosophie de la Volonté* II, *Finitude et Culpabilité*, Aubier, Paris, 1960, 185.

[6] Pierre Teilhard De Chardin, *Ecrits du temps de la guerre* (1916–1919), Grasset, Paris, 1965, 17–18.

Nothing is insignificant in our universe. Teilhard made his first discovery with the density of a piece of iron and then studied stones and through a huge adventure opened up to what he calls "The Heart of the Matter/*Le Coeur de la Matière*." Plants and flowers, animals far from being just moving objects are a part of our education to become more human. When Confucius' dog died, Confucius was upset because he was unable to do more for the companion who had just left him.[7]

The cosmic environment is dependent on our responsible or irresponsible actions. Do we use the earth to dominate it or do we respect it? Do we think about how we pass on the earth to future generations? Are we only the conquerors or do we truly love the universe? Paul Ricoeur worried a lot because the West had not developed a philosophy of heart and emotion, a philosophy of mutual recognition and an ethics of gratitude. If we remain insensitive when forests are wiped out and animals tortured we are already vulnerable to the mutilation of our emotions in relating to other human beings. Ecology is more than a political strategy, a technical problem or an academic subject. It allows us to reconsider our relationship with beings, all beings.

This article hopes to reconnect with the beauty and meaning of the universe according to certain Korean and Chinese philosophers and sages who had great admiration for life and the universe in their changes during the day, the seasons, the year, and the generations. Since an extensive theoretical analysis is not within the scope of this article, we searched

---

7 Quoted by Jean Levi in *Confucius*, Albin Michel, Paris, 2003, 152 (Excerpts of the Tan-kong): "Alas, I am so poor that I do not even have an old blanket used for a carriage to wrap my dog in it and to put him in the ground. However I will give him a mat in order that his head does not rest on the bare ground."

only to discover a way for the spirit to open, a sensitivity and approach appropriate to certain Far Eastern sources like the *Book of Changes, T'oegye's Chasŏngnok* and Yulgok's *Sŏnghak chibyo*, among others, and in an incomplete way. This could help to ease the actual impoverishments of spirit and heart and to arouse this "*supplément d'âme*" for which Bergson was hoping. Thus overcoming the tendencies towards mechanization and functionalism, causes of the indifference which block our in-depth maturation and our connecting with the universe, we attempted to tune to a more adequate vision, an interiorization and new expressions of emotions and essential care concerning the future even of life which risks being unable to arouse in us the sense of wonderment and gratitude.

1. HUMAN FULFILLMENT AND LOVE OF THE UNIVERSE ACCORDING TO CHINESE SOURCES

From the first contact with Chinese sources like the *Yijing* we feel that the place of man in the universe is noble but modest, that it cannot get out of proportion. When man acts like Prometheus or Superman (*Übermensch*), it is because he has not developed a sensitive and authentic relationship with the universe. That is why working on oneself while studying the great texts of wisdom is vital, because they are not only texts but footprints, saved from past destructions, "sources" of thought according to the beautiful etymological expression. In fact the word "source" also reminds us of hidden places high up in the mountains from which springs spontaneously water which gives life; so it is with the major texts to which we return because they bring us to vibrant thinking and meaning together with authors who are known forever.

We need especially in uncertain times to stop, to temporarily stop writing, researching and thinking in order to look at what is around us, not to take advantage of it but to welcome it. To stop and reunite with the silence of the universe from which nevertheless emanates a music which we had not suspected. To stop ourselves. To get a glimpse of what man misses. To glimpse the sacred. Every instant awaits with a new experience, completely human and at the same time beyond human.

Although we look for shortcuts always quicker and more modern, the detours in research are far from being a loss of time and the strangeness of texts and traditions which are less familiar both historically or geographically opens for us other ideas in order to act more correctly. Certain pages of the *Yijing*, T'oegye or Yulgok disorient us today and at the same time "resource" us, paradoxically bringing us closer to ourselves.

Experts gave and continue to give their reports on the serious ecological situation of our planet. Humanity is confronted with an increase of natural disasters. Nevertheless scientists mention the capacity of the earth to regenerate; those responsible state that in the long term the great ecological evils can be overcome if men themselves change their attitudes and how they act. That is why if on the one hand effective intervention is necessary in certain situations, Far Eastern wisdom teaches us also the importance of stepping backwards, of "not acting" and contemplating in order to implement a richer human fulfillment connected to the love of this planet and this universe.

In their research to understand life the sages of the *Yijing* retired and even hid themselves, not because they lacked courage, but because they decided to prepare themselves. Before opening to the world, they wanted to have a correct spirit. The holy sages purified their hearts, withdrew, and hid themselves in secret.[8] These men did not worry about their opinions or their knowledge. They wanted to welcome reality in all its depths and harmonize with it. "They put themselves in accord with the Tao and its power (和順於道德), and in conformity with this laid down the order of what is right."[9] To harmonize with the Tao means that man, recognizing his condition, does not put himself forward because it is the Tao which is the reference and guides his actions.

Fu Xi, who is a symbol of Far Eastern sages, meditated deeply and saw the world: "Fu Xi looked upward and contemplated the images in the heavens; he looked downward and contemplated the patterns on earth. He contemplated the markings of birds and beasts and the adaptations to the regions."[10]

Far Eastern thought very early considered particularly the first look, the first emotion and the first thought. It is the passage from calm to movement, from silence to the beginning of sound, from non-action to action. "The seeds are the first imperceptible beginning of movement, the first trace of good fortune (or misfortune) that shows itself. The superior (profound) man perceives the seeds and immediately takes action."[11]

Drawing the first line of a hexagram symbolizes this beginning which is hardly perceptible. Our distance from the natural environment, industrialization and urbanization diminished the freshness of our first

---

8 "The Great Treatise," Part I, Chapter XI.2, trans. Richard Wilhelm, Princeton University Press, 1976, 316.

9 "Discussion of the Trigrams," Wilhelm, 262.

10 "The Great Treatise," Part II, Chapter II, trans. Richard Wilhelm, 328.

11 "The Great Treatise," Part II, Chapter V.11, trans. Richard Wilhelm, 342.

contacts with nature. It seems that our condition is getting worse and yet new starting points are possible as the Hexagram "Return" shows "Things cannot be destroyed once and for all. When what is above is completely split apart, it returns below. [...] Return is the stem of character. Return is small, yet different from external things. Return leads to self-knowledge."[12]

The consideration of this first imperceptible beginning or of this return which is hardly visible applies to all our experiences in relationships with others and with the universe: first meeting, first creative movement or first step to return. It is then that we have to search for the correctness of our emotions. We find in the *Doctrine of the Mean*:

> While there are no stirrings of pleasure, anger, sorrow, or joy, the mind may be said to be in the state of equilibrium (centred, 中). When these feelings have been stirred, and they act in their due degree, there ensues what may be called the state of harmony (和). This equilibrium is the great root in the world and this harmony is the universal path. Let the states of equilibrium and harmony exist in perfection and a happy order will prevail throughout heaven and earth, and all things will be nourished and flourish.[13]

Thus the centre of deep heart and the harmony of emotions when they begin to show themselves, as we come in contact with things, will bring about the fulfillment of all beings. The words of Arthur Waley are

---

12 *The Book of Changes*, Hexagram 24, "Return/The Turning Point," "The Sequence," "Appended Judgments," trans. Richard Wilhelm, 504.

13 *The Doctrine of the Mean*, Chapter I, 4–5, trans. James Legge.

known: "The Chinese were in love with nature"[14] since Antiquity and that showed itself in the early appearance of landscape painting, while in Europe we had to wait until the Renaissance. Furthermore the Chinese were very early excellent astronomers but in a particular way. Their observations were linked especially to the development of a calendar for the advancement of human activities. Thus the study of the universe or of nature was not centered on pure scientific knowledge but was centered on the deep comprehension of what moves the universe and on what helps the ful-fillment of man.

Thus this article wants to reread and interpret relating to our time certain Chinese source inspirations like the *Book of Changes, Yijing*, which have intrigued great Asian thinkers since their development. We want to go further than a structural logic or an attraction to foresee the future in order to join what Marie-Ina Bergeron called "The eternal wonder"[15] or "The great unity of the world [...] in the warmth of relating."[16] In fact to accompany our meditation it would be appropriate to approach our universe, to listen to a waterfall in the heart of a mountain or admire the glistening snow weighing down the branches of the trees on a winter's day. It would be appropriate through paintings to see the same landscape changing according to the seasons, spring, summer, autumn, winter as the artists depict with delicacy and poetry. A vast canvas of time and space

14 Arthur Waley, *An Introduction to the Study of Chinese Painting*, Grove Press. New York, 1958, 137.

15 Marie-Ina Bergeron, *L'Eternelle Féerie—L'image*, Guy Trédaniel Editeur, 1989.

16 Marie-Ina Bergeron, *La Chine et Teilhard,* Jean-Pierre Delarge, éditeur, Paris, 1976, 58.

where beings respond to one another trying to build relationships which hopefully will be fruitful.

Our hypothesis is that those who contemplated and observed the beings of the universe as mentioned in the *Yijing* did this out of love for the universe and out of concern for the well being and fulfillment of their fellow beings. These words seem too strong and utopian today because we are accustomed to using nature and even other human beings without feeling. The level to which we aspire is that of tolerance and civility. For the Chinese it does not mean a vague and sentimental love but a precise love in harmony with the rhythm of phenomena and of time. For example it means appreciating the song and habits of a particular bird at such and such a time of the day in a certain season. We find this passage: "Seeing the countenance, it instantly rises. It flies round, and by and by settles. The Master said: 'There is the hen-pheasant on the hill bridge. At its season! At its season!'"[17] We are constantly questioned in the *Yijing* by an internal logic: "A crane calling in the shade. Its young answers it. I have a good goblet. I will share it with you."[18] Confucius appreciated the *Yijing* so it is not strange that he chose as the central idea of his thought the ren which is found in the *Yijing* as one of the four fundamental attributes of the *kŏn/qian* (The Creative) (乾, first hexagram); those four attributes are the same in the kon/kun (The Receptive) (坤), whereas the pure Yang and the pure Yin are the two fundamental doors of the cosmic rhythm. The four attributes are difficult to translate. Richard Lynn calls them fundamentality (*yuan*), prevalence (*heng*), fitness (*li*) and constancy

---

17 *The Analects of Confucius*, 10.18, trans. James Legge.

18 *The Book of Changes*, Hexagram 61, "Inner Truth," "Nine in the second place," trans. Richard Wilhelm, 237.

(*zhen*).[19] Richard Wilhelm translates them by: «sublimeness, success, what favors, perseverance.» It is to be remarked that according to the commentaries on the first hexagrams, the attributes of the Creative and of the Receptive are in harmonious correspondence with Human Nature's attributes. We read: "Because the superior man embodies humaneness (*ren*), he is able to govern men. Because he brings about the harmonious working of all that is beautiful, he is able to unite them through the mores. Because he furthers all beings, he is able to bring them into harmony through justice. Because he is persevering and firm, he is able to carry out all actions."[20]

We see that according to the ancient Chinese vision, the universe and man respond to each other, are in "mysterious correspondence" to use the expression of Yulgok in his commentary on the *Yijing*.[21] And one of the essential centres is '*ren*': love, deep emotion. How can the universe only be a machine, no matter how sophisticated it is? And how is it that the West often considers that there is no moral dimension in the universe? Perhaps we concentrated too much on a narrow scientific analysis of the universe. The exclamation of Pascal surprises us: "The eternal silence of infinite space frightens me,"[22] which contrasts with the Teilhardin approach in the "Hymn of the Universe" which shows the joy of belonging to this universe: "The roots of our being? They plunge [...] to the most unimaginable

---

19 *The Classic of Changes*, Columbia University Press, 1994.

20 *The Book of Changes*, "The Creative," "On the Hexagram as a Whole," trans. Richard Wilhelm, 376.

21 *Yulgok chŏnsŏ,* Edition of the Academy of Korean Studies, IV, 1988, *Yŏksuch'aek, Book on the Changes and Numbers* [易數策], 14.49A.

22 Blaise Pascal, *Pensées*, Seuil, Texte établi par Louis Lafuma, Paris, 1962, fragment 201(206), 110.

past!" And the consequences of this discovery unfold in succession: " If we could but admit that all makes only one in the process which from top to bottom acts and directs the elements of the universe [...] Man has to build a work, an "opus" where something of all the elements of the universe appears [...] He has to collaborate in the world's fulfillment. "[23]

Thus man shares the life of the cosmos, "Man would not know how to see himself outside of humanity, nor humanity outside of life nor life outside of the universe. " [24]

The Far East expresses sometimes in a laconic way the mystic power of certain Western visionaries such as in these words of Mencius: "All things are already complete in us (me)"[25] and "benevolence, *ren*, subdues its opposite just as water subdues fire"; "The value of benevolence depends entirely on its being brought to maturity."[26] Thus the nobility of man for Mencius is that he contains within himself the universe, he meets in himself the benevolent heart of the universe and guides this benevolence to its fulfilment.

Beyond the complexity and certain realities difficult to explain, the universe allows us to sense the welcoming heart. We find in the *Yijing*: "The Changes show care and sorrow and their causes. Though you have no teacher, approach them as you would your parents."[27] Benevolence,

---

23 *Milieu Divin*, 48/49.

24 *Phénomène humain*, 28. Texts presented by Marie-Ina Bergeron, *La Chine et Teilhard, Parole d'homme*, Jean-Pierre Delarge, éditeur, 1976, 26.

25 *The Works of Mencius* Book VII, Part I, Chapter IV, trans. James Legge, 450.

26 *The Works of Mencius* Book VI, Part I, Chapter XX, trans. James Legge, 420–421.

27 *The Book of Changes*, "The Great Treatise," Part II, Chapter VIII, trans. Richard Wilhelm, 349; also Chapter VII, 345: "Those who composed the

care of parents in the depths of silence. To those who accused him of not speaking about subjects like human nature and Heaven[28] or just of not speaking Confucius said:

> Does Heaven ever speak? The four seasons pursue their courses, and all things are continually being produced, but does Heaven say anything?[29]
> Does the spring not return regularly after the winter? Do men lack water, air and fruits of the earth? And yet, affected by the temptation that this is ours, we have a right to it, how often are we grateful for these gifts? Nevertheless we realize from time to time that if we are without air for a few minutes or water for a few days our lives are in danger.
> We have the admiring depth of those who approached the Tao: "The kind man discovers it and calls it kind. The wise man discovers it and calls it wise. The people use it day by day and are not aware of it, for the way of the superior (profound) man is rare. The Tao manifests itself as kindness but conceals its workings. It gives life to all things, but it does not share the anxieties of the holy sage. Its glorious power, its great field of action, are of all things the most sublime."[30]

Changes had great care and sorrow."

[28] *The Analects of Confucius*, 5.12, trans. James Legge.

[29] *The Analects of Confucius*, 17.19, trans. James Legge.

[30] *The Book of Changes*, "The Great Treatise," Part I, trans. Richard Wilhelm, 298–299.

We do not reach the loving heart of the universe because we have a utilitarian mentality and we have not learned yet the language of modesty. Our ears are not yet well tuned. Tseu-k'i said to Yen: "Perhaps you have heard the music of man but not that of the Earth; perhaps you have heard the music of the Earth but not that of Heaven."[31]

The Chinese character for landscape (山水) in art is expressed by the characters mountain and water which we find among the eight trigrams at the base of the hexagrams of the *Yijing* and which contain a very rich symbolism. Two famous paintings come to mind: Ma Yuan's sage meditating near a waterfall and the Korean Kang Hui-an showing a sage contemplating the water of a river. Confucius's words are known: "The wise find pleasure in water; the virtuous find pleasure in hills. The wise are active; the virtuous are tranquil. The wise are joyful; the virtuous are long lived."[32] As T'oegye mentioned in one of his letters of the *Chasŏngnok*, to know what these joys mean, you have to understand the characteristics of the man of ren (virtuous) and of a sage (wise).

The disciple Hsu said "Chung-ni (Confucius) often praised water, saying, 'O water! O water!' What did he find in water to praise?" Mencius replied: "There is a spring of water; how it gushes out! It rests not day nor night. It fills up every hole, and then advances, flowing on to the four seas. Such is water having a spring! It was this which he found in it to praise."[33]

Here it is the life enriching activity which is stressed. We read in the *Yijing*: "Water flows uninterruptedly and reaches its goal. The image of

---

31 *Tchouang-tseu, Oeuvre Complète*, traduit par Liou Kia-hway, Gallimard, 1969, "La Réduction Ontologique," 35.

32 *The Analects of Confucius*, 6.21, trans. James Legge.

33 *The Works of Mencius* Book IV, Part II, Chapter XVIII, Legge, 324.

the Abysmal repeated. Thus the superior (profound) man walks in lasting virtue and carries on the business of teaching."[34] Man like water is not stopped by any obstacle, he develops his possibilities and helps others.

However this unceasing activity requires the other dimension of calm as the *Yijing* expresses in the symbol of the mountain: "Things cannot move continously, one must make them stop." and "Keeping still means stopping. When it is time to stop, then stop. When it is time to advance, then advance. Thus movement and rest do not miss the right time, and their course becomes bright and clear."[35] In the logic of development according to the *Yijing*, the harmony of two com-plementary dimensions is necessary such as development and decline, splitting apart and returning, standstill and progress. That is why moving back from activity is sometimes necessary.[36]

However, balance and the Mean are important for a righteous action. That is why Mencius reflecting on the notion of time, for example the time to stop, calls Confucius the sage who corresponds to the precise moment, the sage who knows the exact value of time in relation to the righteous action and to the fulfilment of being.[37] A whole meditation

---

34 *The Book of Changes*, "Hexagram 29," The Abysmal, "The Image," trans. Richard Wilhelm, 116.

35 *The Book of Changes*, "Hexagram 52," Mountain, trans. Richard Wilhelm, "The Sequence," 652; "Commentary on the decision," 653.

36 *The Book of Changes*, Hexagram 33, "Retreat," trans. Richard Wilhelm, "The Image," 130: "Mountain under heaven. The image of retreat. Thus the superior (profound) man keeps the inferior (small) man at a distance, not angrily but with reserve."

37 *The Works of Mencius* Book V, Part II, Chapter I, Legge, 371–372: "When it was proper to go away quickly, he did so; when it was proper to delay, he did so; when it was proper to keep in retirement, he did so; when it was

could be pursued on this notion of time, this time which sometimes seems to us too short and sometimes too long. It is easy to rush into feverish daily activities thinking that we are accomplishing a lot and often we are in agony having to wait for a response, a sign, the indication to advance. We feel we fail by waiting, but if we hurry we ruin what is most important. Here we remember the surprising saying of the *Yijing*: "Only through the divine (spiritual) can one hurry without haste and reach the goal without walking."[38]

The *Yijing* comes from men who not only contemplated the universe but who loved it; they became active in the universe to open a way for men to fulfill themselves. They knew how to combine retreating and action, silence and words, abnegation and joy. We find this reflection in the *Yijing*:

> Since man comes to resemble heaven and earth, he is not in conflict with them. His wisdom embraces all things, and his tao brings order into the whole world. Therefore he does not err. He is active everywhere but does not let himself be carried away. He rejoices in heaven and has knowledge of fate, therefore he is free of care. He is content with his circumstances and genuine in his kindness, therefore he can practice love.[39]

---

proper to go into office, he did so: This was Confucius."

38 *The Book of Changes*, "The Great Treatise," Part I, Chapter X. 6, trans. Richard Wilhelm, 316.

39 *The Book of Changes*, "The Great Treatise," Part I, Chapter IV. 3, trans. Richard Wilhelm, 295.

What progress would we make in all domains if these words became for us a source of inspiration and action! When man embraces all things and contributes to world order, he cannot err.

Although often modern thoughts insist on conflict, contradiction, the mask, falsehood, the spirit of the sages of the *Yijing* and those who practiced it shows a harmonious exchange between all life forms, a true goodness. Connected deeply to the universe, man embraced it in its totality. He rejoices in what is given to him for living. Having no worries, loving is enough. We see in this passage a balance in man's progress and his actions, in the connection between beings and the universe. Unity, order, joy, sincerity and love are the most important. These lines reached their apogee at a time when China went through moments of chaos, cruelty and misery often due to the ignorance of men who used power and sacrificed to their own earthly ambitions millions of innocent lives enduring unimaginable conditions. Although many became cynical and believed that nothing could break the rule of the most powerful, others, often retreating in silence, found the inspiration that the true universal principles are totally different. The violent fall in the end, and the weak reach true fulfillment. Meditating on the *Yijing* text today is like being called to overthrow false principles which we have allowed over time to slowly dominate our lives and our world.

2. HUMAN FULFILLMENT AND LOVE OF THE UNIVERSE ACCORDING TO KOREAN SOURCES

Different from China, Korean Thought sources are more hidden and less known but reveal their riches if we know how to be patient. At the beginning of the twenty-first century, after the tragedies of the nineteenth and twentieth centuries many people are turning towards Asian countries, Korea included, admiring it for its economic development. However, a greater effort has to be made to appreciate Korean cultural values.

During the second half of the twentieth century Korea became westernized and in the end forgot a lot of its own tradition as Professor Park Chong-Hong, who knew both Western and Eastern philosophies well, mentioned in the past. As we are confronted today to certain excesses of world modernization, the time seems to have come to reconsider development in the larger framework of human fulfillment and our relationship with the universe. Instead of decrees and slogans we need examples like the sages of the *Yijing* and Confucius. Are we taking the time like the sages to think about rivers, national protected spaces and the environment in general before taking on a project? Do we think of the flora and the fauna, or of a particular animal species? Do we think of repercussions on men's lives?

In this second part we want to meditate together with Korean philosophers. Our hypothesis is that, if the Koreans received a lot from the Chinese tradition, not only did they take it seriously and did their best to put it into practice, but they particularly enriched the internal dimension of emotion which we urgently need today to take care of ourselves, others and the universe.

Let us note that Korean Confucian Thought really flourished under Neo-Confucianism especially from the sixteenth century. That is why we are drawn to Yi Hwang, T'oegye and Yi I, Yulgok for this ecological reflection. It is necessary to emphasize as we set out that Neo-Confucianism, or precisely the study of human nature and principles, is not only a reaction to Buddhism but rather a return to Confucian Classical sources to re-appreciate the problems of that time in Korea and

China. In its original movement, Neo-Confucianism confronted the present without losing the inspiration of the Classics. One of the Classics which particularly enlightened this movement was the *Yijing*, which we mentioned in the first part of this article.

A. Reflections centered on Yi Hwang, T'oegye

When we consider the simple, self-effacing and deep love of nature, the example of Yi Hwang, T'oegye (1501–1570) naturally comes to mind. His penname includes the character 'retreating', not with the meaning of not acting, but in order to grasp reality and one's responsibility while enjoying nature. T'oegye encouraged his students to spend time near rivers, plants and flowers before become absorbed again in study or activities, sensing certainly an uplifting presence which inspired him.

> Thus in every day life (his wish was), that exchanging cups of wine be lessened, that taste and desires be controlled, freeing the heart so that each day is spent calmly and agreably. Whether in the appreciation of painting or writing, of flowers or of plants, whether in admiration of fish in the rivers or birds in the mountains, we should delight in thought and never refuse what the will needs. We should strive that the mind-and-heart is always in a mild state and not confrontational, confused or quick to anger.
>
> When reading we should not do so intensly to the point of burdening the spirit and if we read a lot we have to be absolutely prudent allowing ourselves to appreciate the 'taste' and to turn towards the mind-and-heart.

> Concerning the research of essential principles, (T'oegye says), go to simple bright ordinary life places to appreciate and become familiar with them. Sufficiently soaked in what we already know we feel comfortable with the knowledge that we have in a condition where 'the will is neither set nor non-set'[40] If we persevere in our efforts we reach understanding naturally. Also it is not good to look for quick results which are pleasant and to which we become attached.
>
> In the letter (which you sent) the points that you mentioned "deep culture" (*hamyang/hanyang*, 涵養) and discovering through experience (*ch'e ch'al/ticha*, 體察)[41] are fundamental Confucian ideas; heaven's principles and men's activities are not two essentially different things, all these are important.[42]

We feel in these lines how T'oegye found sources for his thought in contact with nature. Nature lived in him, calmed him, allowed him to find moderation, joy and gentleness guiding the clear-mindedness of his mind-and-heart and of his will. Rather than studying in a complicated way, what is necessary is to appreciate what is important. The essential

---

40 Expression used by the Master of Zhu Xi (1130–1200), Li T'ung (Li Yen-p'ing) (1093–1163).

41 These are two fundamental values of Neo-Confucianism for the cultivation of the Self. The former indicates more the widening of knowledge and of the development of human nature. The latter indicates more a deep consideration of the Self within experience.

42 T'oegye, *Chasŏngnok* (自省錄), Letter 1, "Answer to Nam Shi-po," presented by Ch'oe Chung-sŏk, Kugakcharyowŏn editions, 1998, Original, 37; translation into Korean, 42.

principles can be seen in ordinary life. Mildness,[43] peacefulness and simplicity in harmony with nature can help us today. In the *Yijing*, after the hexagram 'Gentleness' comes the hexagram 'Joyous/Lake'. T'oegye who loved the stretches of water surrounding his Tosan Sŏwŏn Academy leads us to think of the smiling calm of a lake. "To be joyous and with this to have perseverance furthers; thus does one submit to heaven and accord with men."[44] In this way in transforming ourselves by self-cultivation we discover the principles which govern the world. The activities of Heaven and the activities of men are linked. In this framework of natural beauty, T'oegye met those with whom he studied, his disciples or friends, but he was also the friend of all life in the universe.

We remember that T'oegye in his youth ruined his health studying the *Yijing* and that he wrote the *Kyemongjŏnŭi* in 1557 on this classic. Before anything else T'oegye practiced the wisdom which is discovered in the *Yijing*. His meditation on the first hexagram,[45] for example, shows how his character developed connected at the same time with the spirit of the sages and with the uplifting presence which he felt in nature:

> Enlightened men humbled themselves, were self effacing

---

43 *Yijing*, Hexagram 57, "The Gentle," "Appended Judgments," trans. Richard Wilhelm, 680: "The Gentle shows the exercise of character. Through the Gentle one is able to weigh things and remain hidden. Through the Gentle one is able to take special circumstances into account."; "The Judgment," "The Gentle. Success through what is small."

44 *Yijing*, Hexagram 58, "The Joyous, Lake," "Commentary on the Decision," 686.

45 *Yijing*, Hexagram 1, "The Creative," "Nine at the top," 10: "Arrogant dragon will have cause to repent."

> and were modest and respectful; they followed the Tao emptying themselves, "Arrogance means that we know how to progress but not how to retreat, we know how to exist but not how to die, we know how to win but not how to lose. Only the sage knows how to progress, retreat, exist and die without losing his righteous nature.[46]

It is not surprising that T'oegye chose as the first diagram of his study *The Ten Diagrams on Sage Learning*[47] written in 1568 for the young King Sonjo the "Diagram of the Supreme Ultimate" of Zhou Dun-I that mentions man's place in the universe returning all things to their original source. The *tai-chi/t'aeguk* appears also in the *Yijing*.[48] T'oegye comments with Zhu Xi:

> One who would learn to be a sage should seek the beginning here in this [diagram] and apply his efforts to the practice of [what is presented in] such works as the *Elementary Learning* and the *Great Learning*. When the day of reaping the fruits arrives and one completely returns to the Single Origin, he will have arrived at the condition described as having 'exhaustively comprehended principle, fully realized

---

[46] *Complete Works of T'oegye*, 3, T'oegyehak yŏn'guwŏn (1992), Original, 58, 48B.

[47] *To Become a Sage, the Ten Diagrams on Sage Learning* by Yi T'oegye, trans. and with commentaries by Michael Kalton, Columbia University Press, 1988.

[48] *Yijing*, "The Great Treatise," Part I, Chapter XI.5: "There is in the Changes the Great Primal Beginning, *tai-chi/taeguk*."

> his nature, and so completely fulfilled the Mandate'; he will have become 'the person of perfectly accomplished virtue who exhaustively comprehends the realm of the spirit and understands the transformations [of the universe].'[49]

It seems that one of T'oegye's joys was to strive to reach the unique fundamental principle between the Self and the things of the universe beyond the narrowness of the "I" as can be seen in his reflection on Zhangzai's *Western Inscription*:

> Breaking the self interested heart which includes the I and opening widely the general principle of no Self we harmonize and are able to penetrate the stony heart, making it so that there is no space between the other and the Self. If there is any little bit of self centered heart, harmony cannot be made. All the beings of the universe become one family, the whole country becomes like one person and if I consider with deep feeling the others' suffering, I can receive the tao of the *ren*.[50]

T'oegye made his own Zhangzai's approach according to which despite his littleness it is possible for man to enter into the cosmic dimension of self. As Tu Wei-ming mentions: "(In the immensity of the

---

49 *To Become a Sage, the Ten Diagrams on Sage Learning* by Yi T'oegye, "Diagram of the Supreme Ultimate," trans. and with commentaries by Michael Kalton, 42.

50 *T'oegye's Selected Works*, Minjok Munhwa Ch'ujinhoe edition, Seoul, 1979, 1, "Commentary of the *Western Inscription*," Korean Translation, 162, Original, 522.

cosmos) not only a place exists but an intimate place for each one of us. We are all, in fact, the guardians and co-creators of the universe. In this unitary vision of man, an Ontological chasm between the Creator and creature seems inconceivable."[51]

This unitary relationship within the cosmos is brought about by the '*ren*'. T'oegye meditates like this in Diagram two of his Ten *Diagrams*:

> The learning of the sages consists in the seeking of humanity. It is necessary to deeply inculcate in oneself the intention [of becoming humane], and then understand that one makes up a single body with Heaven and Earth and the myriad creatures. To truly and actually live this way is what is involved in becoming humane. One must personally get a taste [of this experience]; then he will be rid of the problem [of thinking that] it is something so vast as to be unobtainable and also will be free from the mistaken notion that other things are identical with himself, and the inner dispositions of his mind and heart will thus become perfect and complete.[52]

T'oegye was fascinated by the lofty *Li* of the universe which he found difficult to understand. He felt his insignificance and shortcomings and

---

51 Tu Wei-ming, "Neo-Confucian Ontology: A preliminary interrogation," *Journal of Chinese Philo-sophy* 7, 1980, 101.

52 *To Become a Sage, the Ten Diagrams on Sage Learning* by Yi T'oegye, trans. and with commentaries by Michael Kalton, Columbia University Press, 1988, 58.

yet he sensed that man participated deeply in this sublimity. In one of his letters he writes:

> To say that the mind-and-heart is the *taichi/t'aeguk* is to speak of '*renchi/ inguk*'.[53] According to this principle there is neither 'thing' nor 'I', there is neither interior nor exterior, there are no levels between things either nor distinction between directions. When really calm and possessing everything, this principle becomes the only foundation. At the beginning there was no difference between what was in the mind-and-heart and what was in things. When one moves and responds to activity, contacting things, the principle of each thing is the principle that my mind-and-heart originally possessed. The mind-and-heart is the only subject and all things respond following this rule."[54]

Life itself is a constant object of meditation for man who tries to make sense of it through symbols like the five trigrams in the *Yijing* or mountain and water. T'oegye meditates like this:

> Concerning the saying of the Ch'eng brothers "he heart of compassion (惻隱之心)[55] is the living tao of man (人之生道)." [...] In general with the Chinese character '*saeng/cheng*, life

---

53 *In'gŭk* (人極), means that the *tai-chi* (太極), is reflected in man.

54 T'oegye, *Chasŏngnok*, Letter 5, "Answer to Chŏng Cha-jung," presented by Ch'oe Chung-sŏk, Original, 65, translation into Korean, 69.

55 Reference to *The Works of Mencius*, Book II, Part I, Chapter VI.

(生)' we want to say 'what begets all begetting without being exhausted (生生不窮)'[56] in the sense of 'life of life (生活之生).' This means that to be in total unity with the heart of Heaven and Earth which gives life to all things is expressed by the one character 'life'. Zhu Xi responded thus to the question of someone who asked him what was the heart of Heaven and Earth which gives life to all things: "The heart of Heaven and Earth is just life. All things have life, thus they exist. The reason that men and things have a non ending life is because they have 'life'. If we do not exist through life, soon we dry up and die."[57]

Reflecting on ecology is not only discussing about ideas and planning but rediscovering the deep meaning of life, changing oneself in contact with men and women who lived taking full responsibility for a higher good. Thus Gandhi helps us with these words: "Be the change that you want to see in the world" and Albert Schweitzer is an example in having embodied what he designated as fundamental : The Teaching of Reverence for Life.[58]

---

56 This makes us think of *The Book of Changes.* "The Great Treatise," Part I, Chapter V. trans. Richard Wilhelm: "The Tao possesses everything in complete abundance: this is its great field of action. It renews everything daily: this is its glorious power. As begetter of all begettings, it is called changes (生生之謂易)." Richard Lynn in the Columbia University translation puts: In its capacity to produce and to reproduce we call it "change."

57 T'oegye, *Chasŏngnok,* Letter 8 "Answer to Chŏng Cha-jung," presented by Ch'oe Chung-sŏk, Original, 78–79, translation into Korean, 82.

58 Albert Schweitzer, *The Teaching of Reverence for Life*, Holt, Reinehart and Winston, 1965: "The elemental fact, present in our consciousness every

However human tasks in this world are difficult to accomplish as T'oegye often complained:

> If we look at the ordinary relation with others (reception) of these days, we see that falling into wrong habits and losing the Self represent six or seven times out of ten. You mentioned in your letter: "I understood the difficulty of finding one's way in society." or "I feel sorry for not being able to be stricter in proprieties." Or "If the external appearance is slackened, the heart within also changes." For us these are not small deficiencies, they should of course be corrected, which is not easy. [...] Through reverential respect we should not lose the fundamental mind-and-heart and should avoid taking superficially daily relations by enriching deep culture [...][59]

T'oegye attached great importance to reverential respect (mindfulness) in order to solve the complex problems of the human condition.[60]

---

moment of our existence, is: I am life that wills to live, in the midst of life that wills to live. The mysterious fact of my will to live is that I feel a mandate to behave with sympathetic concern toward all the wills to live which exist side by side with my own. The essence of Goodness is: Preserve life, promote life, and help life to achieve its highest destiny. The essence of Evil is: Destroy life, harm life, hamper the development of life."

59 T'oegye, *Chasŏngnok*, Letter 9, "Answer to Chŏng Cha-jung," presented by Ch'oe Chung-sŏk, Original, 85, Translation into Korean, 88.

60 *To Become a Sage, the Ten Diagrams on Sage Learning* by Yi T'oegye, trans. and with commentaries by Michael Kalton, op.cit., "The Diagram of the Great Learning," quotation of Zhu Xi, 85: "Mindfulness (*kyŏng*) is the mastery of one's entire mind and the foundation [of correctly dealing with]

Following Zhu Xi, he considered that the ten diagrams that he presented held reverential respect as essential. This major concept for T'oegye is the opposite of the models of "Prometheus" and of "Superman" with which modernity has burdened us and which disturb the genuineness of our relationships with others and the universe. In a time when we have lost to a great extent the sense of the sacredness of life, of our activities and of our relationship to the universe, T'oegye's attitude moves us. Although his scholarship was one of the most advanced in his time and although he invested a lot of energy in administrative positions in his country, he hardly dared to speak,[61] asking that people reprimand his inaccuracies and he worried about his limitations. "Beginning early in my life I feared more the heart's anxiety than the danger of tigers. [...] If we understand that the heart is misled and lost, that is where the heart is found."[62]

In his letters T'oegye often speaks of 'an illness' of the mind and heart which he cannot undo. Thus for him one of the guiding threads between all beings on a cosmic level is the mind-and-heart, the fundamental human emotion which springs up in diagrams six, seven and eight. This feeling has weakened today. It is a surprising reality that emotion connects beings while reason separates because it analyses. Paul Ricoeur speaks even of a 'mystery of emotion', knowing the unbreakable link of my existence to beings and to being through desire and love.[63] We remember T'oegye's

---

all affairs."

61 *Chasŏngnŏk,* Introduction, first sentence of T'oegye: "The ancients did not speak lightly because they were concerned that their words would not match their actions." This refers to *The Analects of Confucius*, 3.22.

62 T'oegye, *Chasŏngnok*, Letter 11, "Answer to Chŏng Cha-jung," presented by Ch'oe Chung-sŏk, Original, 95/97, Translation into Korean, 100/103.

63 Paul Ricoeur, *Philosophie de la Volonté/The Philosophy of the Will*, 105: "The

reflection, "The mind (heart) of each person is the mind (heart) of heaven and earth. And the mind of the self is the mind of thousands of people. Originally there is no distinction between the inner and the outer or the here and there."[64]

How is that possible? Through emotion. Thus when a part of my body suffers, my whole body suffers and when an element of the universe is damaged, the whole universe feels it. Thus T'oegye urges us through diagrams six, seven and eight to develop the heart which is our weak point compared to our intellectual brilliance.

Depth expresses itself sometimes in certain lines of poems which crystallize the experience of a whole life[65] as we see in Gaston Bachelard's inspiration. T'oegye exclaims: "The eye is like a clear mirror and the mind-and-heart is like the sun (眼如明鏡 心如日)."[66]

Seeing is linked with brightness and purity; feeling and understanding are linked with luminosity and heat. Hence the symbol: "The heart is like the sun."

We cannot develop here the study of this symbol of a mirror usually used for the heart which Paul Demiéville explained in depth through

universal function of emotion is to connect; it connects what knowledge divides; it connects me to things, beings, being; while the whole movement of objectivism aims at confronting a world; emotion unites the intention which puts me outside myself and the affection by which I feel I exist. Thus emotion is always below or above the duality of subject and object."

64 Quoted by Tu Wei-ming, "Yi Hwang's Perception of the Mind," The T'oegyehak Study Institute, no. 19, Seoul, 1976, 462.

65 Gaston Bachelard, *L'Intuition de l'Instant*, Stock, 1931/1992, 103. "Poetry is an instantaneous Metaphysics. A short poem has to give a vision of the universe and the secret of a soul, a being and objects—all at the same time."

66 *T'oegye chŏnsŏ,* T'oegyehak Yŏnguwŏn, Seoul, 1998, 101 (no. 161).

different facets of Taoism, Buddhism and even Christianity. Commenting on Zhouang Zi, Demiéville writes:

> For the spirit (mind) to be the mirror of the universe it is important, according to Zhouang Zi, to be calm, to reduce oneself to a state of non feeling: thus the spirit identifies itself to the 'virtue of Heaven,' which is its true nature; pure and calm, one and unchanging, without feeling and inactive the spirit (mind) is like water. Water is a mirror but on condition that it is calm and that nothing external moves it.[67]

According to T'oegye: "The eye is like a clear mirror (眼如明鏡)." To really see is difficult. We know from experience that because of our activities and our preoccupations we often do not see the beauty of nature or the goodness of human actions. Only when we stop do we see the magnificence of the orchid or the greatness of an act of forgiving. In the *Chasŏngnok*[68] T'oegye meditates on what Mencius and Confucius say. Mencius: "To the mind (and heart) belongs the office of thinking. By thinking it gets the right view of things; by neglecting to think, it fails to do this. These—the senses and the mind—are what Heaven has given to us."[69]

---

67 Paul Demieville, *Choix d'Etudes Bouddhiques* (1929–1970), Leiden, 1973, "Le Miroir Spirituel/ The Spiritual Mirror," 137.

68 T'oegye, *Chasŏngnok*, Letter 12 "Answer on the discussion concerning the joy in encountering the mountain and the joy in encountering water according to the writings of Kwŏn Saeng-ho-mun," presented by Ch'oe Chung-sŏk, Original, 105, Translation into Korean, 107.

69 In T'oegye, *Chasŏngnok*, Letter 13 "Answer to Kim Ton-sŏ, Puryun,"

Confucius: "In regard to the use of his eyes, the profound man is anxious to see clearly. In regard to the use of his ears, he is anxious to hear distinctly."[70] Thus there is in the Confucian tradition exercising the spirit and the senses to come into a higher vision. We find in Teilhard an echo: "To see! You could say that all life is there."[71]

"The mind-and-heart is like the sun (心如日)"—a surprising expression of T'oegye. T'oegye criticized Wang Yang-ming and Buddhism and yet in the framework of Neo-Confucianism he gave an important place to Heart and to the culture of Heart. There is one sun which shines on and gives life to our planet. There is one Heart rooted in Heaven's Heart which allows the relationships between all beings. The closer we get to the purity of the Tosim (道心), the Heart of the Tao, the more we overcome the limits of the human condition and the more we are capable through this heart[72] to transform relationships with men and the universe. We think here of the diagram made by Ch'en Chen-sheng (1410–1473) called "The Diagram of Heaven, Earth and Wisdom" where the heart is placed in relationship

---

Original, 110, Translation into Korean, 123. *The Works of Mencius,* Book VI, Part I, Chapter XV.2, trans. James Legge.

70 *The Analects of Confucius*, 16.10, trans. James Legge.

71 Words of the *Phénomène Humain/Human Phenomenon*, 25, quoted by Marie-Ina Bergeron, *La Chine et Teilhard,* Jean-Pierre Delarge, éditeur, 1976, 65.

72 *To Become a Sage, the Ten Diagrams on Sage Learning* by Yi T'oegye, trans. and with commentaries by Michael Kalton, "The Diagram of the Admonition on Rising Early and Retiring Late," 194 : "The foundation being established, as day breaks... sitting erect, compose your body and recollect your mind, making it as luminous as the rising sun." We find also this poetic verse in *T'oegye's Selected Works*, Minchok munhwa ch'ujinhoe edition, Seoul, 1979, 1, Original, 478; Korean translation, 54: "The paper window shines in the sun, its brightness is like my heart."

with the universe represented by the dynamism of the Changes, the center of which is the *tai-chi*.[73] Teilhard thought that humanity still lacked heart in the intelligent planetary development which accelerates, that which was producing itself in the Noosphere on the level of reason had to enter the sphere of emotion.[74]

The longing of T'oegye is to get back to daily practical life where everything is finally decided because in the Confucian spirit[75], what counts is refining, realization and fulfillment. If we think again about the *Ten Diagrams* we see that the first part of this work deals with metaphysical and ontological questions while the second part speaks of the practical application of the mind-and-heart going as far as daily actions. However, the name of the work "Study of Wisdom" means it intends to guide toward a full human fulfillment. Thus chapters nine and ten deal with the details of daily life, but we know how often what appears like a detail plays a crucial role in life.[76]

---

73 Introduced by WM. Theodore de Bary in *The Message of the Mind in Neo-Confucianism*, Columbia University Press, 1989, 69.

74 Pierre Teilhard De Chardin, *Réflexion et Prière dans l'espace-temps*, Seuil, 1972, 9 et 17: Evoking the cosmic God he said: "Vast and enveloping like matter but warm and intimate like a soul, God is the center that exists everywhere" [...] "Center in which everything meets and that expands in all things to bring them back to itself."

75 *The Analects of Confucius*, 7.3: "The leaving virtue without proper cultivation; the not thoroughly discussing what is learned; not being able to move towards righteousness of which a knowledge is gained; and not being able to change what is not good: these are the things which occasion me solicitude."; *The Analects*, 15.29: "To have faults and not to reform them, this, indeed, should be pronounced having faults."

76 Throwing a glass bottle in a forest seems an insignificant action but if many people do this in a dry summer the sun can set this forest on fire. The forest

T'oegye shows us that from the beginning of a day the real direction of our action is involved:

> When the cock crows and you awake, thoughts gradually increase their pace; at this time how can one but compose himself and bring order to them. Sometimes reflect on your past faults; at others follow out what has been newly apprehended. With proper order and sequence, lucidly ponder this matter in silence. [...] Over the cyclic alternation of activity and quiet, the mind presides; it should be possessed in quiet and discerning in activity. Do not allow it to become divided into two or three. In the time left over from reading, from time to time take a swim (stroll) to relax your mind and refresh and nourish your feelings and nature."[77]

Meeting T'oegye, who is in himself representative of Far Eastern wisdom, we cannot but humbly recognize that we have let down our original nature and that we have to learn to renew the link of fraternity with all things. We have insisted so much because of the modern world on the rights and individual freedom that sympathy for people and things has faded and moved by diverse ideologies we have become insensitive to the beauty and the unique value of life, of all life.

---

is threatened with destruction by an irresponsible attitude.

77 *To Become a Sage, the Ten Diagrams on Sage Learning* by Yi T'oegye, trans. and with commentaries by Michael Kalton, Chapter 10, 194.

B. Reflections centered on Yi I, Yulgok

Yulgok's approach is complementary to that of T'oegye, T'oegye embodying more the example of retreating when it is time to retire and Yulgok (1536–1584) embodying more the example of committing oneself when it is time to get involved. T'oegye philosophized and acted calmly, in a gentle way; Yulgok confronted obstacles energetically. However, they were equally courageous, clear-minded and sensitive to man's suffering and the injustice of situations, although in different ways. In fact, despite the age gap, each saw the other's value because of their depth and their cosmic vision.

To approach the texts of Yulgok or T'oegye is to set out on a hermeneutic task of relearning to read and to "taste", it is working on rediscovering the meaning of these texts. This work is even more complex than for Chinese texts. We wonder: "What have these Korean Neo-Confucian texts of the sixteenth century to do with the modernization of the twenty-first century and with the serious ecological questions which are today endangering man's future?" If these texts are presented as museum pieces they will remain dumb, but if we discover the key to reading them, their message will become precious.

Our hypothesis is that as in the case of T'oegye the texts of Yi I, Yulgok not only pass the test of time, but they guide us as we mature, confronting the complex challenges of humanity's global evolution. However, an intensive exploration of Yulgok's work is necessary. Yulgok was not an ordinary Neo-Confucian as an old Buddhist monk he met in the Kŭmgang Mountains said to him. Yulgok, then still young, was considered to be a living Buddha (生佛). He was, moreover, in harmony with the spirit of Laozi, whose *Daodejing* he commented on in his essay

Sunŏn(醇言). He appreciated Wang Yang-ming at a time when the Koreans hesitated about introducing his thought. Yulgok was a risk taker, which is why he died early. Just as he climbed high mountains to reach the summit, he challenged complex political situations, was in an advisory position to the king for daring reform projects like organizing a competent army but also, among other works, improving education. Besides, his reflection on governing in *Sŏnghak chibyo, Compendium of Sage Learning* inspired *Sirhak* thinkers such as Yi Ik and Chŏng Yag-yong.

In a clear and concise way, Yulgok gave his all not only on the level of thought but also through action. For him the reason for the success of an accomplishment was to invest all his energy from the moment of setting his will to the attainment of the highest level of wisdom that was possible. He still fascinates and inspires us because he not only worked out a particular kind of thought that could develop into orthodoxy, but his vision embraced rich aspects of diverse thoughts. His motivation was creativity, the quest for truth and relationships between researches which seem to differ. He succeeded in this comprehensive approach because he embodied Confucius' words: "My doctrine (Tao) is that of an all-pervading unity."[78] Yulgok guides us to the depths of unity having probably understood Zhuang Zi, who said that the schools debate opinions endlessly because they have left the original unity with the Tao.[79]

---

78 *The Analects of Confucius*, 4.15, trans. James Legge.

79 "There ensued great disorder in the world, and sages and worthies no longer shed their light on it. The Tao and its characteristics ceased to be regarded as uniform. Many in different places got one glimpse of it, and plumed themselves on possessing it as a whole. [...] The case was that of the scholar of a corner who passes his judgment on all the beautiful in heaven and earth, discriminates the principles that underlie all things, and attempts to estimate

The tradition on which Yulgok leaned was not dried up but dynamic and open-minded: "The wise and spiritual personalities of ancient times having made a connection with Heaven established standard norms for humanity and from there they passed on the Tao tradition."[80]

Yulgok understood the intention of the sages who wrote the *Yijing* saying that King Wen, the Duke of Zhou and Confucius expressed the same heart and concern.[81] He quoted in the *Sŏnghak chibyo* an important reflection of Confucius on the *Yijing*: "The Changes, what do they do? The Changes disclose things, complete affairs (controversies) and include all conditions on earth—this and nothing else. For this reason the holy sages used them to (discern) all wills on earth, to determine all fields of action and to settle all doubts (fears) on earth."[82]

Showing thus how much he responded with enthusiasm to the all embracing vision and the depths of the *Yijing*.

Having reached the heart of the dynamic of the *Yijing*, Yulgok was

---

the success arrived at by the ancients. Seldom is it that such an one can embrace all the beautiful in heaven and earth, or rightly estimate the ways of the spiritual and intelligent; and thus it was that the Tao, which inwardly forms the sage and externally the king, became obscured and lost its clearness, became repressed and lost its development. [...] The students of that later age unfortunately did not see the undivided purity of heaven and earth, and the great scheme of truth held by the ancients. The system of the Tao was about to be torn into fragments all under the sky." based on James Legge's translation: http://oaks.nvg.org/zhuangzi31-.html#33 (accessed May 21, 2011).

80 *Yulgok chŏnsŏ*, Edition of the Academy of Korean Studies, V, 1985, *Sŏnghak chibyo, Compendium of Sage Learning* (聖學輯要), 26.2A.

81 *Yulgok chŏnsŏ*, Edition of the Academy of Korean Studies, IV, 1988, *Yŏksuch'aek, Book on the Changes and Numbers* (易數策), Original, 14.49A: " 三聖一心"

82 *Yijing*, "The Great Treatise" Part I, Chapter XI.1, trans. Wilhelm, 316.

also able to harmonize with Laozi's spirit whose way was one of decreasing, humbling oneself, appreciating the fruits more than the flowers[83] and the responsibility of governing came to the one who dealt with the lowest problems—being able to deal even with garbage.[84] We are usually drawn to being famous, but it is more difficult to work for the common good in obscurity. The *Yijing* brings down what is high and lifts up what is low. The *Daodejing* emphasizes the symbol of water which flows downward and calls us paradoxically to consider the vulgar and the dregs of humanity. Who can take responsibility today for world pollution in all its aspects?

The ordinary way of the world is elevating. We are drawn to position, honours, and famous names. But Laozi says that the Tao does not have a name. Yulgok by his life gave the example of voluntary deprivation through his admiration of the Classical sages, his Buddhist experience and his appreciation of Taoism evident in his poems. For him it was not a question of words but of putting into practice and a true fulfillment in harmony with the cosmic reality. That is why he used the character *shil/shi* (實), together with sincerity *sŏng/cheng* (誠), which became a leitmotiv in his work, showing the correspondence between true principles *silli/shili* (實理), the true heart *silsim/shixin* (實心) and true fulfillment *silhyo/shixiao* (實效). So we have the famous passage:

---

83 *Daodejing*, Chapter 38, translated by Victor Mair, Bantam Books, 1990: "The great man resides in fruitful reality not in blossom ornament."

84 *Daodejing*, Chapter 78.
"He who bears abuse directed against the state
Is called 'lord of the altars for the gods of soil and grain';
He who bears the misfortunes of the state
Is called the 'king of all under heaven.'"

> Heaven's work is nourishing and transforming all things through true principles. Man can touch others through true heart. True principles and true heart are none other than sincerity. That is why he who adheres truly to Heaven's principles and receives sincerity totally is a sage and he who fulfills a part of the principles and receives partially sincerity is an enlightened man. The essence is very subtle, the application is evident. That is why we can move Heaven and earth, we can move the spirits and we can arouse men's admiration.[85]
> 天以實理而有化育之功人以實心而致感通之效所謂實理實心者不過曰誠而已矣純乎天理而得誠之全者聖人也實其一端而得誠之偏者賢者也其體其微而其用甚顯故天地可以格鬼神可以動人心可以服矣

Yulgok did his best to explain the most difficult questions of the human condition without cutting off from the entirety of the cosmos and society. The future of the cosmos and that of man are deeply linked. Yulgok expressed this relationship of a mysterious exchange between Heaven and men:

> The Tao of the Master (Confucius) was in correspondence with Heaven (夫子之道 合乎天).[86]
> Ah! Heaven and men are one, there is no distinction

---

[85] *Yulgok chŏnsŏ*, Edition of the Academy of Korean Studies, IV, 1988, *Sŏngch'aek, Book on Sincerity* (誠策), Original, 6.15A.

[86] Yi I, Yulgok, *Kongmaeng ŏnsŏngdo kunnyŏŭi* (孔孟言性道軍旅疑) *Complete Works,* Academy of Korean Studies, IV, Original, 14.61B–63B.

between them but only Heaven and Earth are disinterested while men are self seeking. That is why men cannot identify with the greatness of Heaven and Earth.
嗚呼天人一也更無分別惟其天地無私而人有私故人不得與天地同其大.[87]

Meditating on the *Yijing* Yulgok spoke of the correspondence between Heaven and man: "There is a natural correspondence between Heaven and man, a mysterious dimension of exchange between the two (自然之應而天人交與之妙也)."[88] He also says in a reflection on the Tao of Heaven and human undertakings:

> Heaven is nothing if not close. It helps those who are virtuous, gives good fortune to him who follows virtue and bad fortune to those opposing. We can understand here the principle of correspondence between Heaven and man. [...] Heaven sees through the eyes of the people. Heaven hears through the people's ears. The place of return for man's heart is where we find Heaven's will."
> (人心之所歸 天命之所在.) 皇天無親 惟德是輔 順德者吉 逆德者凶 天人感應之理 斯可知矣[...]天視自我民視天聽自我民聽人心之所歸 天命之所在也.[89]

87 Yi I, Yulgok, *Kongmaeng ŏnsŏngdo kunnyŏŭi* (孔孟言性道軍旅疑) *Complete Works,* Academy of Korean Studies, IV, Original, 14.61B–63B.

88 Yi I, Yulgok, *Kongmaeng ŏnsŏngdo kunnyŏŭi* (孔孟言性道軍旅疑) *Complete Works,* Academy of Korean Studies, IV, Original, 14.61B–63B.

89 *Yulgok chŏnsŏ*, Edition of the Academy of Korean Studies, V, 1985, *Sŏnghak chibyo*, *Compendium of Sage Learning* [聖學輯要], 22.5B.

And also

> One who acts without artificiality is Heaven. He who acts artificially is man. If we understand that Heaven starts nothing which is not for man and man undertakes nothing which is not for Heaven, we can say that we understand the will of Heaven.
> 莫之爲者天地有所爲者人也知天之未始不爲人知人之未始不 天則始可謂知命矣.[90]

The point of departure of Yulgok's thought and actions is nature and the cosmos but not in the sense that he had a materialistic tendency or an aesthetic affinity. If man cuts off from his ontological and cosmological roots, he cannot enter into the full comprehension of his condition nor into the process of his transformation. Confucius already said: "Without recognizing the ordinances (will) (of Heaven), it is impossible to be a superior (profound) man (不知命 無以爲君子也)."[91]

The cosmos is for Yulgok a place to experience, to meditate on, a place for a unique discovery where man can open his mind to the diversity, the depth and the value of principles and also to the dynamics and maturation of life. It is a place we approach with great expectation but also with great respect. It is at the same time a place where we come and we go, and which

---

90 *Yulgok chŏnsŏ,* Edition of the Academy of Korean Studies, IV, 1988, *Yŏksuch'aek, Book on the Changes and Numbers* [易數策], Original, 14.49A.

91 *Yulgok chŏnsŏ*, Edition of the Academy of Korean Studies, IV, 1988, *Chŏndoinsa, Book on the Tao of Heaven and on Human Activities* [天道人事策], IV, 6.9B–6.10A.

we do not own.

> Looking as far as the horizon, we grasp the greatness of the Eastern sea. [...]
> I try to perceive where the sun rises but I do not succeed.[92]
> 極目始知東海大
> [...]
> 欲看出處知無奈

The rising of the sun, the appearance of things, energy, primordial energy. These poetic lines were found in a letter he sent:

> The original *qi/ki* , where does it begin?
> What is formless is found within what is formed.
> We search for the source but from the beginning it is an integral part.[93]
> 元氣何端始
> 無形在有形
> 窮源知本合

Like the sages who composed the *Yijing*, Yulgok examined intensely the forces of the universe to discover its mysteries because as he just said the source that moves all things is at the heart of these things. The

---

92 *Yulgok chŏnsŏ*, Edition of the Academy of Korean Studies, IV, 1988, *Kidoch'aek, Book on Prayer, Original*, 5.7B.

93 *The Analects of Confucius*, 20.3. trans. James Legge.

imperceptible *ji/ki* (幾) of the *Yijing*,[94] the first Yang movement fascinated him.

Some Deep Thoughts on the Night of the Winter Solstice
At midnight a Yang started to move,
It is difficult to speak of the mysterious Heart of Heaven
Discovering what exists (*yu*, 有) from what is not visible (*mu*, 無).
When the thunder rolls, the earth shakes,
In one night a new fire lights up. [...]
In this night of pure energy,
Let us think silently about the mysteries of hidden principles. [...]
Closing and opening, who arranges all that?
I am moved by this return determined by Heaven.
When we think about the mind-and-heart we feel fear.
I also participate in the three Ultimates.[95] [...]
The truth of Heaven (innocence) may become depraved and false. [...]
Henceforth in my pain I promise willingly.
Heaven responds to what I hear and what I see. [...]
If I concentrate on reverential respect
Where can the defiled heart invade? [...]
Observing calmly the changes and transformations of Heaven and Earth,
We see how they contribute to the health of all beings.

---

94 *Yulgok chŏnsŏ*, Sŏnggyun'gwan University Press, Seoul, 1958/1986, 1, Poetry, Original, 1.22B.

95 *Yulgok chŏnsŏ*, Edition of the Academy of Korean Studies, III, 1987, *Tap Sŏng Howŏn, Letter to Sŏng Ho-wŏn,* Original 10.22A.

If men do not take this cosmic transformation as a model,
It is like they give up on themselves.
Like you are sweeping away the dust and you stop.
The water and a mirror, originally they are without stain.[96]

子半一陽動
天心妙難議
若識無中有
雷聲殷大地
中宵點新火 [...]
及此夜氣清
默念玄機秘 [...]
闔闢誰汝使
感彼天運復
省心還惴惴
感披天運復
省心還惴惴
噫我參三極 [...]
天眞汩私僞 [...]
我今痛自誓
昊天應聽視 [...]
若使敬爲主
染心安所自 [...]
冥觀天地化
至健功乃施
爲人不法此

96 "The Great Treatise," Part II, Chapter V.11, trans. Richard Wilhelm, 342.

有身乃自棄
但使泥塵盡
水鏡元無累

Yulgok was fascinated from an early age by the beauty of the universe: "the mountain crests covered with snow", "the waterfalls which rush down shaking the earth", "the sea in its vastness." How to respond to this majesty, to nature's power? Although there was a time when Yulgok was tempted to live as a hermit, he decided to return to society. "I still have not finished my relations with the world." Even if he was absorbed in action, he kept the vision of vastness, mystery and the reality of the universe-cosmos. What is special about Korean and Chinese cosmology is that it is not just about passive contemplation where you reach an indifference to the troubles of the world but it is an active cooperation with the creative forces of nature, which are not only natural physical forces but also the manifestation of an internal spiritual energy acting in man and the cosmos. Energy at the heart of things. Unity of a reality where phenomena are real. "I also participate in the three Ultimates." Yulgok wrote. Astonishing expression: "If men do not take as their model this cosmic achievement it is like they give up on themselves."

The cry of Yulgok who often expressed how man can so easily be corrupted ("polluted heart") aspires to an original purity symbolized by 'stainless water', 'pure energy', 'mysterious heart of Heaven', 'Heaven's truth may become depraved and false.' In the thought of Yulgok everything converges towards the mind-and-heart and springs from it. Man is at the heart of the universe and (becomes) the heart of the universe. He reflects the mysterious heart to which he is inextricably connected. The desire of the heart for the original source in all its beauty and its purity is often an inexpressible suffering.

There is a heart wrenching in Yulgok between the absence of light and maturity in society and the fulfillment of man which he called *Ingansŏngch'wi* (人間成就). This world is waiting for fulfillment. One of the essential ways to achieve this for Yulgok is with sincerity which we cannot go into in this essay. Yulgok was familiar with the *Zhongyong/Doctrine of the Mean*: "Sincerity is the way (tao) of Heaven. The attainment of sincerity is the way (dao) of men (誠者 天之道也 誠之者 人之道也);"[97] "Sincerity is the end and beginning of things; without sincerity there would be nothing (誠者 物之終始 不誠無物)."[98] Also Yulgok knew of the work of the Neo-Confucian Zhou Dun-I: "Sincerity is the foundation of the sage (誠者 聖人之本也)."[99] Through becoming more and more sincere we come closer to the cosmic heart, to the essence of things and to the Dao. Through sincerity we touch at the same time higher spirits and men.

Touched by the internal beauty seen through the cosmic experience, Yulgok found in himself the capacity to set his will in order to accomplish fully his destiny as a man. Correcting oneself, cultivating oneself, constant practice, perseverance are necessary to go in the direction of what was glimpsed: "There is this saying from of old: He who wills it will succeed in what he undertakes (古語曰 有志者 事竟成 [...])" and:

> The study of wisdom means giving all to reach in reality
> the sincerity of the will and the correction of the heart.

---

97 Heaven, man and earth.

98 *Yulgok chŏnsŏ*, Sŏnggyun'gwan University Press, Seoul, 1958/1986, 1, Poetry, 8.

99 *Zhongyong*, Chapitre XX.18.

> Even though you set up a strong will, it has through study to become substantial and thus unite word and action and when the interior and the exterior respond to each other in harmony you cannot go against the will."[100]
> 聖學克盡誠正之功者大志雖立必以學問實之 然後言行一致表裏相資無負乎志矣.

Unavoidable foundation of:

> Without sincerity you cannot establish the will, without sincerity you cannot attain the deep understanding of principles and without sincerity you cannot change the physical disposition."[101]
> 如志無誠則不立理無誠則不格 氣質無誠則不能變化.

Yulgok's work which allies the internal treasures of a whole tradition of wisdom and the ardent concern of the most down to earth realities can inspire new expressions of wisdom and noble culture to confront the considerable challenges of our time like that of the environment. Yulgok is an example of decision, of courage, of perseverance combined with a lofty vision and a profound feeling for all beings, accepting hard effort, suffering and thinking only of fulfilling.

---

100 *Yulgok chŏnsŏ*, Edition of the Academy of Korean Studies, II, 1984, *Manŏn pongsa* [萬言封事], *Ten-Thousand Characters Memorial,* 5.26A–B.

101 *Yulgok chŏnsŏ*, Edition of the Academy of Korean Studies, V, 1985, *Sŏnghak chibyo, Compendium of Sage Learning* [聖學輯要], 21.6A.

CONCLUSION

Experts from numerous disciplines agree that the ecological situation of our planet is very serious and that it is important to act quickly as we do not have a lot of time.[102] Although we know these problems, we are changing very little. Why? According to these experts, it is because we have decided on progress at any cost, on a certain form of economic development and consumption, on the continuation out of habit of a system which uses and wastes non renewable energy and produces waste which is sometimes uncontrollable and harmful.[103] Other forms of energy are possible; solar energy would suffice for our needs. A new economic conception, freed from greediness would slow down pollution and other disasters. Although we change constantly in order to be more up to date in technology, ideas and fashions, we do not change our mistakes about certain essential problems. In fact we are hardly allowed to speak about these weaknesses.

Contrary to what we might think, experts unanimously point out that the solution to this deadlock is in becoming aware of our irresponsibility and our attachment to our own interests. We have cut off our relationships with nature, which is not only material to be exploited. We believe ourselves to be superior to it. The great majority of environmental problems are caused by man, so the solution is in man. "We have to become more human, more caring, more kind, slower and smarter, more frugal, treating

---

102 Scientific Documentary, "The 11th Hour—Turn Mankind's Darkest Hour into its Finest," produced and narrated by Leonardo DiCaprio, 2007.

103 For a long time chemical, plastic and nuclear waste, among others, still remain a serious problem not yet resolved.

life with humility and respect," some say. So it is the scientists who are calling us to rediscover ancient wisdom!

Care, authenticity, humility, frugality are unchangeable values to relearn and to live today. This article is limited to certain aspects of the teaching of the *Yijing*, T'oegye and Yulgok, which can inspire us to discover once again a relationship with nature (and with ourselves) which is rich and full of sense so that we choose options which stop damaging our planet and give all beings a place of dignity and the possibility of fulfillment. Especially essential are modesty and humility[104] at which Nietzsche scoffed, convincing many that they meant mediocrity and cowardliness. Thus, as Paul Ricoeur showed, modern man fell from the arrogant Cogito inherited from Descartes to the humiliated Cogito caused by the masters of suspicion but the consequences were harmful and behind his apparent technological success man hides a poverty, especially of spirit and emotion. Therefore, it is necessary to look for a balanced approach.

We are humiliated today by the civilization that we have developed and which in many ways turns against us. It is not a loss of time to stop and evaluate what needs to be corrected and to be accomplished in a positive way. We are far from "the opus" about which Teilhard spoke which ought to include the dimension of heart[105], we are far from "the co-

---

104 *Yijing*, Hexagram 15, "Modesty," "Commentary on the Decision," trans. Richard Wilhelm: "It is the way of heaven to make empty what is full and to give increase to what is modest. It is the way of the earth to change the full and to augment the modest. [...] It is the way of men to hate fullness and to love the modest."

105 Teilhard De Chardin, Pierre, *The Future of Man*, translated by Norman Denny, Harper & Row, 1964, 178: "Humanity is building its composite

creation" spoken of by Tu Wei-ming[106] linked to a sense of sanctity and the sacredness of man and the universe.

We cannot fulfill ourselves at the cost of nature and the cosmos but in harmony with them. We act impulsively as if the earth was our property. We give nature no rights legally. In fact the earth is entrusted to us. It prospers if we love and respect it and deteriorates if we treat it badly. Only a conscience that is more acute allows us to find again a sense of wonderment and a feeling of gratitude towards nature. The deforestation and the expanding of deserts actually reflect the dryness of our souls. We have in our hands the power to make life more fruitful or to bring about death.

The universe is not only a source of wonder but education. We have a lot to learn from the universe, infinitely vast and infinitely minuscule,

---

brain beneath our eyes. May it not be that tomorrow, through the logical and biological deepening of the movement drawing it together, it will find its heart, without which the ultimate wholeness of its powers of unification can never be fully achieved? To put it in other words, must not the constructive developments now taking place within the Noosphere in the realm of sight and reason necessarily also penetrate to the sphere of feeling (emotion)?"

106 Tu Wei-ming, International Conference on Universal Ethics and Asian Values, Seoul, October 1999, 369: "The sanctity of the earth, the divinity of the body, the beatitude of the family and the sacredness of the community are encoded in human nature anthropocosmically defined. There is spirituality in all matter because any matter (Sun, moon, star, animal, tree, or rock) is a specific configuration of the vital energy. There is, therefore, consanguinity between us and all other modalities of being. Self-cultivation, intended for the full realization of our nature, is none other than the transformation of our earthly, bodily, familial and communal realities into all-embracing expressions of ourselves as the co-creators of the cosmic process."

in order to put in place forms of energy and techniques which reflect the marvelous achievements that are taking place under our eyes in the vegetal and animal kingdoms where neither robot nor machine exist; but perhaps more urgent than finding new forms of energy is to work on ourselves in order to become more "human."

At this turning point of history when we are faced with the complexity of the world and its innumerable challenges, we need more than ever to rediscover the fundamental sources of being and of life, sources of the conscience, moral sources. We consider too often as treasures transient things and pay very little attention to the real treasures.

The real treasures are this universe which has been given to us and mind-and-heart of which we become aware a little more each day. We can contemplate untiringly a water source which begins in the depth of a mountain because it symbolizes the mystery of this gift of life. It is only when there is a lack of water that we can really feel its value.

It is even more difficult to appreciate the sources of the mind-and-heart which are easily neglected and presented as utopian, outdated and irrelevant to the contemporary issues. The sources make us hear the voices of courageous men.[107] They are one of the important keys of our culture and of our capacity to cope with the challenges of our time. That is why the Korean and Chinese sources which were preserved by many sacrificial and visionary men are for us today treasures if we know how to receive them and rediscover their meaning to complete our present task.

---

107 *The Analects of Confucius*, 16.8, trans. James Legge: "The superior (profound) man stands in awe of the words of the sages. [...] The mean man makes sport of the words of sages."

Philippe Thiébault (pthiebault@hotmail.com) *is a professor at Sejong University, Korea.*

THE ECOLOGICAL DIMENSION IN KOREAN LITERATI PAINTING: THEORY AND ART

By Cheeyun Kwon

INTRODUCTION

Korean artists tackled subjects inspired from nature since ancient times, evident in Bronze Age (1500–300 BCE) artifacts decorated with birds, duck-shaped earthernwares from the proto-Three Kingdoms Period (300–57 BCE), and tiger-shaped bronze belt buckles and horse harnesses inspired by the Northern Steppe cultures.[1]1 During the subsequent Three Kingdoms period (57 BCE–668), Daoist-inspired art such as the sixth-century Paekche incense burner in the shape of mountain peaks, Koguryŏ tombs decorated with the four cardinal animalistic deities, and seventh-century brick tiles with landscape scenes demonstrate the impact of sinicized cultural traditions on Korean artistic production.[2] The practice

---

1 For further discussion on this subject, see Kukje Han'guk Hakhoe, *Silk Road wa Han'guk Munhwa* (The Silk Road and Korean Culture), Seoul: Sonamu, 1987.

2 For illustration, see the catalogue from the *National Museum of Korea*,

of painting natural subjects among the Korean literati class became an established tradition during the Koryŏ (918–1392) and Chosŏn (1392–1910) dynasties. Landscapes of mountains and rivers, birds set in idyllic natural surroundings, puppies napping under a tree, fish meandering in water, and the four noble plants, namely the plum, bamboo, orchid, and chrysanthemum, were among the favorite themes painted by the educated elite during those times. This paper will examine the impact of Chinese art theoretical treatises on the Korean literati and the ways in which ecological subjects were adopted as a means of self-cultivation of sage-hood by the Korean literati.

THE INTRODUCTION OF CHINESE ART THEORY ON NATURE AND LANDSCAPE PAINTINGS

The adoption process of natural subjects in the painting repertoire of the Korean literati was probably greatly enhanced by the introduction of the well-articulated Chinese art treatises in the Koryŏ dynasty (918–1392). Perhaps the most significant was the introduction of the *Lidai minghua ji* (歷代名畵記 : Records of Famous Paintings through History), a ninth-century compilation by Zhang Yanyuan of pre-Tang and Tang artists in the twelfth century. This art historical treatise made its way to Korea as part of the *Taiping yulan* (太平御覽 : Imperial Writings of the

---

Seoul: Tongchon Publishing, 1998.

Taiping Era),[3] making an unprecedented impact on the Korean literati circles thereon. These books were first introduced by an emissary named O Yŏn-ch'ong (吳延寵) dispatched to Song in 1100 to congratulate the emperor's accession. When emissary O failed in vain to purchase a copy of the Taiping yulan during his visit, he evidently wrote a pleading letter to the emperor, who then granted him a copy to take back home.[4] O was greatly awarded by the Koryŏ king for his successful procurement of the rare book. Another copy of the books was dedicated by a Song merchant to King Myŏngjong in 1192, for which he was awarded 60 kun of silver.[5]

The introduction of the *Lidai minghua ji* is significant because as a detailed record of the biographies, works, and writings of pre-Tang and Tang artists, it included well-articulated theories on landscape painting and natural subjects. Earliest among these was the *Introduction to Landscape Painting* (Hua shan shui xu, 畵山水序) by Zong Bing (宗炳, 375–443), who proclaimed the pivotal role of landscape painting in attaining the Dao. Zong asserted that the beautiful physical existence of landscapes had "the ability to reach out into the realm of the spirit," and that past worthy notables such as the Yellow Emperor and Confucius insisted upon roaming in the famed mountains as part of the pleasures of the humane and wise.[6] Zong also advocated the creative process of

---

3 Hong Sŏn-p'yo (洪善杓), "Koryŏ sidae ŭi hoehwa iron (高麗時代의 繪畫理論: Art Theory in Koryŏ period)," *Kogo misul* (『考古美術』) 187, 1990, 9.

4 *Koryŏ-sa* (『高麗史』), vol. 96, yŏlchŏn (列傳), O Yŏn-ch'ong (吳延寵).

5 *Koryŏ-sa* (『高麗史』), vol. 20, Myŏngjong (明宗), 22:8.

6 *Hua shan shui xu* (畵山水序: Introduction to Painting Landscape); cited in *Lidai minghua ji* (歷代名畵記: Records of Famous Paintings through History), book 6, *Chungguo hualun leibian* (中國畵論類編 : Chinese Painting Theory by Categories). Ed. Yu Jianhua (兪劍華). 2 vols., Beijing: Chungguo

painting landscapes as a way to purify the mind. An artist himself, he painted images of landscapes on the walls of his home when he was no longer able to travel, and in the process, was impressed at the power of the artist to recapitulate a vast scenery of mountains within a small piece of silk. When this was well executed, he said, "the verisimilitude will stir the spirit and as the spirit soars, truth will be attained.[7] As such, Zong advocated the creative process of recreating a landscape painting as an ultimate exercise to cultivate one's spirit and a way to attain the Dao.

The *Lidai minghua ji* also contained writings by a younger scholar Wang Wei (王微, 415–443), who purported that paintings should not limit their role to mere capturing of appearances of specific localities or delineating the boundaries of cities, mountains, and watercourses, but must correspond to a deeper universal law of the *I Ching* (易經, Book of Changes).[8] As symbolic images, he argued, landscape paintings should be fused with soul and be activated with movement through the mind. Just as the sight of autumn clouds inspired his spirit and the spring winds expanded his thoughts in fluidity, he expounded that the inspirational power of natural scenery superseded that of music and treasured objects.[9] The spiritual and symbolic dimensions of landscape painting and their role to inspire the viewer were thus further emphasized.

---

gudian ishu, 1957, pp. 583–584; translated in Acker, William, *Some* 36–38. *T'ang and Pre-T'ang Texts on Chinese Painting*, Leiden, E.J. Brill, 1974; also in Bush, Susan, *Theories on the Arts of China*, Harvard-Yenching Institute, 1985, pp. 36–38.

7 Ibid.

8 *Xu hua* (Discussion of Painting); cited in *LDMHJ*, Book 6. *CGHLLB*, p. 584; Bush, pp. 38–39.

9 Ibid.

The transmission of *the Lidai minghua ji* provided a theoretical grounding to a cultural soil already duly exposed to Chinese landscape paintings of the highest caliber. Eleventh and twelfth century accounts on the Koryŏ missions to China describe how Koreans explicitly sought out Chinese paintings in great quantity.[10] In 1074, ambassador Kim Yang-gam (金良鑑) evidently purchased some three-hundred Chinese paintings while on mission there,[11] and two years later in the winter 1076, the eminent Koryŏ scholar-official Ch'oe Sa-hun (崔思訓) was sent to China with several painters to copy in detail the wall paintings of Xiangguosi (相國寺), a most prominent imperial temple at the time in the capital city of Kaifeng.[12] Included on the wall of Xiangguosi was a "level distance view of a stream in a valley" by Guo Xi (郭熙, ca. 1001–ca. 1090), one of the greatest landscape painters then serving as painter-in-attendance under Emperor Shenzong (神宗, r. 1067–1085).[13] Koryŏ painters, according to Guo Ruoxu, "made the completest possible copies [of Xiangguosi

---

10 See Ko Yusŏp, "Koryŏ sidae hoehwa ŭi oegukgwa ŭi kyosŏp (Foreign interaction of Koryŏ dynasty painting)," *Hanguk misulsa kŭp mihak nonsu*, Seoul: T'ongmun-sa, 1972, pp. 69–81.

11 Guo Ruoxu (郭若虛), *Duhua jianwen zhi* (圖畵見聞誌 (compiled after 1076)), in *Songren huaxue lunzhu* (宋人畵學論著), Taibei: Shih chiai shuchu, 1967, chapter 6, pp. 258–260; translated in Alexander Coburn Soper, *Kuo Jo-hsu's Experiences in Painting* (Washington, D.C.: American Council of Learned Societies, 1951).

12 Guo Ruoxu, Ibid.

13 *Linchuan Gaozhi* (『林泉高致』), section 6, Huaji (畵記), in *Songren huaxue lunzhu* (『宋人畵學論著』), Taibei: Shijia shuzhu, 1967; translated in Susan Bush and Hsio-yen Shih, *Early Chinese Texts on Painting*, Harvard-Yenching Institute, 1985, p. 187; Suzuki Kei 鈴木敬, "Rinsen kōchi shu no Gaki to Kaku Ki ni tsuite (林泉高致集の<畵記>と 郭熙について," Bijutsushi (『美術史』), 30 (1981), pp. 1–11.

walls] to carry home," and they "showed a good deal of refinement in their methods of working.[14] These were copied onto the walls of the royal temple Hŭngwang-sa (興王寺) in the capital city of Koryŏ, and greatly treasured and admired by the Koryŏ people.[15]

Figure 1. Guo Xi (1001–1090), *Early Spring*, 1072; Hanging scroll; ink on silk. H. 158. 3 cm National Palace Museum, Taibei

---

14 Guo Ruoxu, *Ibid*.

15 Xu Jing (徐兢), Gaoli Tujing (『高麗圖經』: Illustrated Account of Koryŏ), vol. 17; *Koryŏ Tokyŏng* (『高麗圖經』), *Kochŏn kukyŏk ch'ongsŏ* vol. 119, Seoul: Minjok munhwa ch'uchinhoe, 1978, p. 43 and p. 111.

Guo Xi was the most prominent of landscape painters in the Northern Song court, who also expounded his views on landscape painting in *Lichuan gaozhi* (林泉高致), or *Lofty Ambition in Forests and Streams*[16]. Guo emphasized that artists should study nature with meticulous detail, convey the seasonal and timely aspects, impart movement water and clouds, and arrange the motifs in a symbolic fashion reflecting social principles. The mountains should be "calm and luring" in spring, "moist and green" in summer, "clear and bright" in autumn, and "melancholy and withdrawn" in winter.[17] Symbolic parallels were drawn between the landscape motifs and the social order, the designs being arranged around a central mountain flanked by subordinate peaks, just as an emperor is attended by his subordinates. Guo's landscape paintings embody multiple experiences in time and space beyond the limits of the painting, while reflecting the ever-present laws of the universe and social order (fig. 1). While he was still active in the Emperor Shenzong's court, two of his paintings, Autumn Scenes and Rising Mist, were given as gifts to the Korean envoys, attesting to the direct transmission of current Chinese landscape paintings of the highest caliber to Koryŏ.[18]

Although no Northern Song paintings survive from the Koryŏ period, evidence of Koryŏ's knowledge of the Northern Song landscape styles can be found in the eleventh-century illustrations of the woodblock edition of Ŏje bijangchŏn (御製秘藏詮), or *Imperially-composed Explanation of the Secret Treasure*. Vast scenes of landscapes are illustrated in the thirty-

---

16 *Linchuan Gaozhi, Ibid.*; trans. by Shio Sakanishi, An Essay on Landscape Painting, London: John Murray, 1935, p. 54.

17 *Linchuan Gaozhi, Ibid.* p. 634.

18 *Linchuan Gaozhi*, Huaji, Ibid.

volume set surviving in Nanzen-ji temple, Kyoto, Japan, and in one volume in Sŏngam Archives, Seoul.[19]

Figure 2. *Landscape from Imperially-composed Explanation of the Secret Treasure*, Vol 10, woodcut 1. 11thC., 28X54.4cm. Nanzen-jitemple, Kyoto

These images show Koryŏ's well-acclimated knowledge of early Song monumental landscape styles, with scenes filled with tall overlapping peaks, deep gorges enveloped in mist, and vast expanses of water receding

19 For a discussion on these landscapes, see Max Loehr, Chinese Landscape *Woodcuts-From an Imperial Commentary to the Tenth-Century Printed Edition of the Buddhist Canon*, The Belknap Press of Harvard University Press, 1968; Yi Sŏng-mi (李成美), "Koryŏ ch'ojo taejangkyŏng ŭi Ŏjebijangjŏn p'anhwa – Koryŏ ch'oki sansuhwa ŭi ilyŏngu (高麗初造 大藏經의 御製秘藏詮 - 高麗初期山水畵의 一硏究: The Woodblock prints of the Imperially-composed Explanation of the Secret Treasure—A Study of Early Koryŏ Landscape Painting)," *Kogo misul* (『考古美術』), 169–170, 1986, pp. 14–70.

into the far distance.[20] A trove of Northern Song landscape painting styles, including those of Jing Hao, Guan Dong, and Li Cheng, attests to the deep infiltration of the genre into Koryŏ. As such, the transmission and adoption of Chinese landscape painting styles including those by the greatest masters, paired with the introduction of important art theoretical treatises, provided Koryŏ scholars with both the theoretical foundation as well as tangible examples to emulate.

THE KOREAN LITERATI'S ADAPTATION OF THEORY AND ART OF NATURAL SUBJECTS

Evidence of a Korean scholar's literacy of Chinese philosophical views on art can be already detected in the case of Kim Pu-sik (金富軾, 1075–1151), author of the earliest extant historical account of Korea and one of the most prominent scholars of the twelfth century.[21] When he visited the Northern Song court, he was evidently shown many paintings by Emperor Huizong (徽宗, r. 1100–1125) who bestowed a score of paintings including one by the emperor himself.[22] He thanked the emperor with a

---

20 For a complete illustration of the Nanzen-ji woodcuts, see Egami Yasushi (江上綏) and Kobayashi Hiromitsu (小林宏光), *Woodcuts in the Nanzenji Bizangquan* (『南禅寺所藏 秘藏詮の木版畫』), Tokyo: Yamakawa Publishing Co., 1994.

21 The *Samguk Sagi* (『三國史記』).

22 For a list of these paintings, see Hong, Sŏn-p'yo, *Chosŏn sidae hoehwasa-ron* (『朝鮮時代繪畫史論』: Discussion on the History of Chosŏn Dynasty Painting), Seoul: Munyech'ulp'an-sa, 1999, p. 164.

letter saying: "Your highness' many inborn talents that emanate through benevolence and frolic in the arts respond intuitively to objects and sceneries, reaching the far depths of meaning. As they take form on torn silk, the essence of purified beauty is rendered in five colors.... The works shine brightly, indeed created by a sage.[23] This letter reflects the belief in the refined quality of painting that is anchored in virtuous character and leisurely pleasure, emphasizing the non-professional context of the painting activity.

Duhua jianwen zhi (圖畵見聞志: Account on Experiences in Painting), a Song art historical treatise compiled by Guo Ruoxu (郭若虛) in 1074, most clearly states the relationship between social standing and art.[24] Guo wrote: "Rare works of the past were mainly those by talented notables of high position or superior gentlemen in retirement, who cleaved to loving-kindness and sought enjoyment in the arts or explored the abstruse and plumbed the depths, and their lofty and refined emotions were all lodged in painting.[25] Such respect for the leisurely artistic practice connected to intellectual activity by those of deep learning became the very axiom of literati painters in Korea, attaching great meaning and value to paintings by amateur scholar-artists.

The association between scholarship and art further influenced the choice of subject matter and their expressive manner. In addition to landscapes, subjects with symbolic associations such as the four noble

---

23 *Tongmunsŏn* (『東文選』), vol. 35.

24 Reproduced in Yu Jianhua (兪劍華), ed., *Chungguo hualun leibian* (『中國畵論類編』: Chinese Painting Theory by Categories), vol. 1, Beijing: Chungguo gudian ishu, 1957, pp. 52–63.

25 *Ibid.*, p. 59; Bush, pp. 95–6.

plants—bamboo, plum, orchid, and chrysanthemum—were greatly favored as they embodied qualities of integrity, moral rectitude, and sagely virtue. The Northern Song scholar Su Shi (1037–1101), who was highly venerated by Koryŏ scholars, was a great admirer of bamboo paintings, and proposed the idea of becoming one with bamboo in the process of painting it:

> To paint bamboo, one must first obtain a complete one in one's breast. One grasps the brush and looks thoroughly. Then, when one has seen what one wants to paint, one rises rapidly to follow it, moving the brush in direct pursuit to close upon what one has seen. It is like a rabbit starting as a hawk dives: a little looseness [of concentration] and [the rabbit] gets away. Thus [Wen Tong] instructed me. Though I knew the nature of bamboo, I could not convey it to paper. Now, when one knows an object's nature but cannot achieve the true effect, inner and outer are not one. The mind and hand are not mutually responsive. This is the result of not studying. If one is not well practiced at grasping whatever one has noted within, what one ordinarily fully comprehends will suddenly be lost at the crucial moment.[26]

---

26 Su Shi, *Jing jin Dongpo wenji* (『經進東坡文集』), comp. Lang Ye (郎曄) (*SPTK* edition) 49, 1a–b; cited in Michael A. Fuller, "Pursuing the Complete Bamboo in the Breast: Reflections on a Classical Chinese Image for Immediacy," *Harvard Journal of Asiatic Studies* 53:1, June 1993, p. 10.

Figure 3. Wen Tong (1019–1079), *Bamboo*. Hanging scroll; ink on silk; H. 132. 1 cm National Palace Museum, Taibei

As such, he emphasized studying the subject of painting carefully, to the effect of transferring its nature unto oneself in order to recreate it in painting. Only with utmost concentration one would succeed in rendering the true essence of the painted subject. A great admirer of the bamboo painter Wen Tong, Su described how Wen painted bamboo:

> When Wen Tong painted bamboo,
> He saw bamboo and not himself.
> Not simply unconscious of himself,
> Trance-like, he left his body behind.
> His body was transferred into bamboo,
> Creating inexhaustible freshness.
> Zhuangzi is no longer in this world,
> So who can understand such concentration?[27]

Su Shi saw in Wen Tong's bamboo paintings the perfect realization of one's transfusion with the forms and principles found in the painted subject, during which one's heart and mind were cleansed of impurities to rediscover one's innate goodness. He considered such realization an ultimate aim in painting, an idea that had long-lasting reverberations among later scholar-painters.

Many Koryŏ scholars admired and followed Su Shi,[28] including Kim Pu-sik and his son Don-jung(敦中, ?–1170) who are known to have

---

27 Translated in Bush, p. 212.

28 Yi Kyu-bo, *Tongguk Isanggukjip* (『東國李相國集』), vol. 21; Hong, 1999, p. 166.

painted bamboo.[29] Their political rival Chŏng Chi-sang 鄭知常(?–1135) was known for his ink plum paintings. Chŏng Sŏ (鄭敍, ?–?), a scholar-official also known for his ink paintings, wrote the following inscription on a bamboo painting:

> Frolicking with brush and ink stone in leisure,
> A bamboo stalk has been painted.
> Glancing occasionally at the pasted painting on the wall,
> Its peaceful demeanor reveals its true loftiness.[30]

Chŏng Sŏ lived a life in exile in his late years finding consolation in his qin instrument, composing tunes expressing his unwavering loyalty to the king and his deep-felt sorrow. The tunes were apparently so uniquely melancholic that they acquired the name "Chŏng kwa chŏng gok (鄭瓜亭曲). The above inscription reflects a Koryŏ scholar's adoption of the bamboo subject to perhaps allude to his lonely disposition in exile, and the lofty spirit of a scholar who finds pleasure in the painting activity.

Yi Kyu-bo (李奎報, 1168–1241), a noted connoisseur of paintings in the late Koryŏ,[31]31 left several inscriptions on bamboo painting. Like his predecessor Chŏng, he is focused on the symbolic associations of the plant and its metaphoric use for a scholar's disposition. He wrote the following

---

29 Yi In-ro 李仁老, *P'ahanjip* (『破閑集』), 上.

30 *Tongmunsŏn* (『東文選』), vol. 19; Kim Dae-won, "Koryŏ hwaron ŭi mun'kijŏk hoehwagwan yŏn'gu (高麗畫論의 文氣的 繪畫觀 研究 : A Study on the Literary Views on Painting in Koryŏ Art Theory)," *Sŏyehak yŏngu* (書藝學研究) 18, 2011, p. 85.

31 Hong, Sŏn-p'yo, "Yi Kyu-bo ŭi hoehwakwan (Yi Kyu-bo's Views on Painting)," *Misul Charyo* (『美術資料』), vol. 39, 1987, 6, pp. 28–45.

inscriptions on a four-panel bamboo screen by Chŏng Hong-chin 丁鴻進, whose bamboo paintings reputedly surpassed those by Wen Tong:[32]

The peculiar and lonely bamboo
Is difficult to grow
Regarding it with mercy
Heaven wet it with dew
Understanding heaven's intentions
It should not fear even when met with snow.[33]

This was a poem written on a painting entitled Dew-laden Bamboo. On another panel entitled *Windlbown Bamboo*, he commented:

The most precious in you
Is the moral rectitude
The uncontrollably shaken body
Is due to the wind
That which is also empty
What is it then that shakes the bamboo?[34]

On the panel entitled *Old Bamboo*, he wrote:

It may break with old age

---

32 Yi Kyu-bo, ibid., vol. 5.

33 Yi Kyu-bo (李奎報), *Tongguk Isanggukjip* (『東國李相國集』), vol. 4; Kim Dae-won, Ibid., p. 97.

34 Ibid.

But not alter its moral rectitude
Just as jade retains its essence while it is abraded
The unwavering spirit remains untouched
The large leaves do not fall
Only bring in clear breeze[35]

On the last panel, entitled *New Bamboo*, he wrote:

Sprouting above the ground
Flowery base, silky husk
Who has pulled its neck?
Its spouted forms are beautiful
While piercing toward the sky is good
Height is also bound to be perilous[36]

As such, by the thirteenth century in Yi Kyo-bo's writing, we find the varied metaphoric use of the bamboo motif by a Koryŏ scholar to describe a person's disposition or convey a didactic message. The scholar Yi In-ro (李仁老, 1152–1220) is also recorded to have received a screen painting of bamboo from his friend An Ch'i-min (安置民) that he apparently displayed prominently and practiced emulating until he reached a similar level[37]. By the thirteenth century, the subject of the four noble plants must have come into vogue among the elite. They can be found painted even on tomb murals such as the royal tomb of Hyŏnnŭng (顯陵) in Kaesŏng,

---

35 Ibid.

36 Ibid.

37 Yi In-ro (李仁老), *P'ahanjip* (『破閑集』).

where bamboo is painted with plum (fig. 4).[38] Although no actual paintings attributed to the literati painters on these subjects survive, their reflection may be detected in the details of Buddhist paintings,[39] and an entire silk hanging scroll of the Three Friends of Winter in Myōan-ji, depicting a pair of tall pines flanked by plum bushes and stalks of bamboo (fig. 5).[40] The so-called "three friends of winter" was a frequently painted subject by Zhao Meng-jian (1199–before 1267) in the advent of the fall of the Song dynasty to the marauding Mongols, epitomizing the spirit of resilience in the face of hardship.[41] These three plants became very popular among the Korean literati painters in the subsequent centuries, acting as metaphors for the upright spirit of the scholar.

---

38 Illustration in Hong, 1999, p. 140.

39 See Kikutake, Junichi and Chŏng, Woo-taek, *Koryŏ sidaeŭiPulhwa* (『高麗時代의 佛畵』 : Koryŏ Buddhist Painting), Seoul: Sigong-sa, 1998.

40 The seal in the upper left reads Hae-Ae (海崖), who is believed to be the painter of this painting, but nothing further is known of him. See Ahn, Hwi-joon (安輝濬), *Han'guk Hoehwa-sa* (『韓國繪畵史』 : History of Korean Painting), Seoul: Ilchi-sa, 1987, p. 64.

41 For an example of Zhao's painting, see Barnhart, Richard M., et al, *Three Thousand Years of Chinese Painting*, New Haven: Yale University Press, 1997, p. 141.

Figure 4. Plum and Bamboo (detail), Hyŏnnŭng, 13th C., Kaesŏng (Hong, p. 140)

Figure 4. *Three Friends of Winter*, 14thC. , inkonsilk. 131. 6X98. 8cm. Myōan-ji temple, Japan(Yi Tong-ju, p. 235)

By the late thirteenth century, with the introduction of Zhu Xi's Neo-Confucianism and its growing influence on Koryŏ scholars, painting became an essential means to cultivate one's mind and spirit. This is already evident in Yi Sŭng-hyu's (李承休, 1224–1301) inclusion of painting as one of the six arts (六藝) a scholar should acquire.[42] Under the growing influence of Neo-Confucian philosophy, scholars such as Yi Che-hyŏn (李齊賢, 1287–1367) who was a long-term resident in Yuan China, was responsible for further introducing the Chinese literati tradition into Koryŏ. Under the auspices of King Ch'ungsŏn's (1275–1325) study hall Mankwŏn-dang (萬卷堂) in Yanjing (present-day Beijing), he freely interacted with the most cultured men at court including Zhao Meng-fu (1254–1322), and had his portrait painted by a Chinese painter. His lofty spirit is evident in an inscription he wrote on a portrait of a man named Kim Chŏng-sŭng:

> Oblivious of self-interest considering short and long life on equal terms,
> His spirit frolics outside the universe.
> He rambles where nothing resides
> This is Chukhŏn [Kim Chŏng-sŭng] himself.
> Who should be able to render his image
> Or describe him in words?[43]

He expressed the difficulty of transmitting the spirit of a high mind in portrait painting, challenging the boundaries of image and words in transmitting the spirit of a person.

Yi Saek (李穡, 1328–1396) was most prominent among the literati

---

[42] Yi Sŭng-hyu (李承休), *Tong'an Kŏsajip* (『動安居士集』), vol. 2; Hong Sŏn-p'yo, Chosŏn sidae hoehwa-sa ron, Seoul: Munye ch'ulp'an-sa, 1999, p. 167.

[43] Cited in Kim, Ibid., pp. 101–2.

painters of the late fourteenth century, leaving many commentaries on landscape and other paintings of natural subjects. Full of poetic flair, he wrote the following inscription on a painting of bamboo:

> He is truly otherworldly
> Pure and dignified
> As he only thinks of writing poetry
> How can he think of untying his belt?
> The autumn winds blow into Xiegu
> The night rain is thick in the Xiao and Xiang Rivers
> Resisting the endless windblown rain
> He will occasionally immerse into poetry.[44]

This inscription makes references to Chinese localities, thus showing his knowledge of popular Chinese landscape subjects. Most likely landscape paintings of these subjects were also painted by the Koryŏ scholars.

By the early Chosŏn dynasty, scholar Sin Sukju (1417–1475) considered the stature of painting equal to poetry, as evident in this writing:

> One who contemplates on a painting with true essence pleases one's innate nature through clarity and loftiness; nurture one's spirit with rectitude and restraint. How could one belittle its benefits? Painting stands in par with poetry

---

44 Yi Saek (李穡), *Mok'ŭn Chip* (『牧隱集』), vol. 16; Kim, Ibid., p. 102.

in its informed knowledge and detailed investigation of a subject's principle.[45]

Figure 5. Kang Hŭi-an (1419–1464), *Scholar Gazing at Water*, 15thcentury. Ink on paper, 23. 5 X 15. 7 cm. National Museum of Korea, Seoul

45 Sin Sukju (申叔舟), *Pohan Chaejip* (『保閑齋集』), vol. 4, Hwagi (畫記); Hong, ibid., p. 202.

Kim Sisŭp (金時習, 1435–1493), the disillusioned early Chosŏn scholar who retired as a monk, described the creative painting experience inspired by nature as such:

> Steeping the brush into ink, thinking of the far infinity, I have forgotten all I know viewing the trees; not only my knowledge, but all of myself. While I sit calmly oblivious of the stream and myself, in a split instance transpires the limitless transformation. The miraculous takes place in absolute stillness. When the heart has obtained this and transmitted it to the hand, the brush reaches harmony and the spirit its highest loftiness.[46]

As such, by the fifteenth century, the complete appropriation of Chinese philosophical tenets on the creative process of painting natural subjects as advocated by preceding art theorists appears to be grounded among the Korean literati. Perhaps Kim's spirit is best encapsulated in the fifteenth century painting by Kang Hŭian (1419–1464) of a Chinese scholar reflecting over water (fig. 5), where a scholar sits with arms folded on a rock, engrossed in thought while contemplating the stream. He is perhaps experiencing that moment of complete oblivion, losing oneself in nature undergoing a limitless spiritual transformation. As such, becoming one with nature by recapitulating its true essence and in the process purifying and elevating one's spirit, a theory first proposed by Zong Bing in the fifth century and elaborated by later art theorists, took firm root

---

46 Kim Sisŭp (金時習), *Maewŏl dangjip* (『梅月堂集』), vol. 4; in Hong, p. 209.

among the Korean literati in both theory and practice by the early Chosŏn dynasty as shown above.

The subsequent centuries saw a profusion of literati painters in Korea, aided by the proliferation of provincial academies in the sixteenth and seventeenth centuries.[47] Steeped in philosophical learning and surrounded by nature, the sarim, or provincial scholars, were rightful practitioners of this genre. In the process, they began to produce uniquely Korean renditions of the original Chinese subjects, such as the bamboo paintings by Yi Chŏng (李霆, 1541–1622) (fig. 6), grape paintings by Hwang Chip-chung (黃執中, 1533–1593) (fig. 7), plum paintings by Ŏ Mong-ryong (魚夢龍, 1566–?) (fig. 8), and bird paintings by Cho Sok (趙涑, 1595–1668) (fig. 9). By maximizing the expressive power of monochrome ink in a concentration of minimum motifs, Korean literati painters captured into the true essence of the matter devoid of superfluous distractions. The outcome was a microcosm of nature captured in its essential elements, the spirit-resonance embodied in a capsule form. Yi Chŏng expressed the spirit of resistance through the resilient stalks of windblown bamboo, while Hwang Chip-jung captured the essence of grapes through a few twigs and grape clusters in dashing calligraphic strokes. Ŏ Mong-ryong rendered a striking image of moonlit plum branches with their acute branches shooting straight up to the dark sky, while Cho Sok embodied a hopeful message in a unique iconographic combination of a magpie and a blossoming plumb branch.[48] As such, by the mid-Chosŏn dynasty,

---

47 Ch'oe Yŏngho, "Private Academies and the State in Late Chosŏn Korea," in Haboush and Deuchler, eds., *Culture and the State in Late Chosŏn Korea*, Cambridge, Mass.: Harvard University Press, 1999, pp. 15–45.

48 For further discussion on these artists, see Paik, Insan (白仁山), "Sŏnjo

Korean literati painters rendered their ideals, moods, and emotions in most evocative and stark images of natural subjects uniquely their own.

CONCLUSION

Although ecological themes were subject of artistic production since early times in Korea, their appropriation by the literati class in Korea was propelled by the introduction of Chinese art theoretical treatises which provided the philosophical grounding for these subjects. The influx of Northern Song landscape paintings and writings into Koryŏ, including the great masters of monumental landscape painting and writings by Su Shi, coupled with the transmission of the *Lidai minghua ji* and others, made a concerted impact on the literati to adopt painting and natural subjects as means to attain sage-hood and the Dao. The settling of these views among the Korean literati is evident in the surviving painting and literary materials. By the Koryŏ dynasty, painting was already considered one of the six arts for a scholar-gentleman to acquire, and as a practice for self-cultivation, painting became widely popular among the literati circles in the Koryŏ and Chosŏn dynasties. Closely following the highest artistic developments in neighboring China, Korean scholars were current with contemporaneous landscape styles, natural subjects laden with literary symbolism, and similar to Chinese scholars, practiced the word-and-

---

nyŏn'gan muninhwa samchŏl (宣祖年間 文人畵 三絶 : Three Literati Masters from the Reign of Sŏnjo)," *Kansong Munhwa* (『澗松文化』), vol. 65 (2003), pp. 103–127; Yi Ŭn'gyŏng, *Ch'anggang Cho Sok ŭi Hoehwa* (『滄江 趙涑의 繪畵』 : Paintings by Ch'anggang Cho Sok), M.A. Thesis, Seoul: Ewha Women's University, 1999.

image conversation by adding commentary inscriptions on paintings. In this manner, painting together with poetry, became an important vehicle for self-expression and self-cultivation, a way to become one with nature and ultimately attain the Dao.

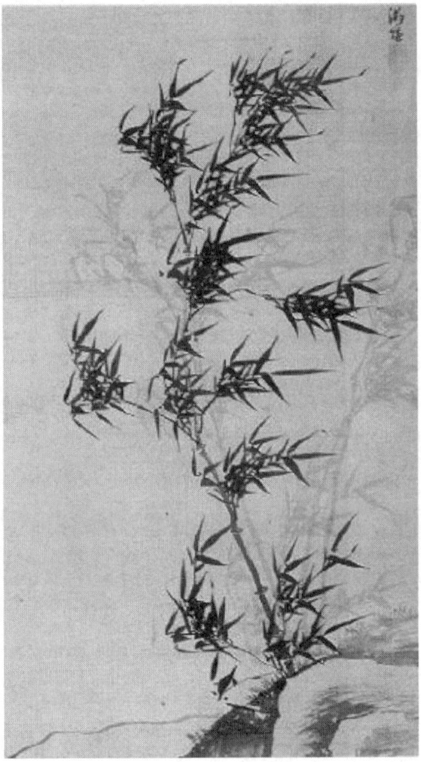

Figure 6. Yi Chŏng (1541–1622), *Windblown Bamboo.*
Ink on silk, 127.5 X 71.5 cm, Kansong Museum of Art

Figure 7. YHwang Chip-jung (1533–1593), *Grapes.*
Ink on ramie, 27 X 22.1 cm. National Museum of Korea

Figure 8. Ŏ Mong-ryong (1566–?), *Plum Branch Under Moonlight.* Ink on silk, 119.4 X 53.6 cm. National Museum of Korea

Figure 9. Cho Sok (1595–1668), *Magpie on Plum Branch*. Ink on paper, 100 X 55.5 cm. Kansong Museum of Art

Cheeyun Kwon (cykwon@gmail. com) *is a professor at George Mason University, USA.*

YI T'OEGYE ON REVERENCE (KYŎNG) FOR NATURE: A MODERN NEO-CONFUCIAN ECOLOGICAL VISION

By Edward Y. J. Chung

I. CONFUCIANISM AND ECOLOGY: PRELIMINARY REFLECTIONS

The spiritual traditions of the world are addressing the question of ecology. The current literature on religion and ecology presents several aspects of the Confucian contribution. In this section, I first explore how scholars in the West have developed Confucian ecological perspectives. The second and final sections continue with T'oegye's thought in order to articulate Korean Neo-Confucian and global perspectives.

A major challenge for today's world is how to deal with the ecological crisis. Our earth is suffering from unprecedented assaults, such as polluted water, species extinction, increasing air pollution, unnatural climate change, massive oil leakage to ocean water, nuclear radiation exposure, and so on. These environmental problems are fuelled by materialism, unlimited industrialization, technological manipulation, unrestricted urbanization, etc., especially in those societies influenced by the modern West. As a result, the human-earth relationship is significantly threatened. This problem is also related to the old belief that nature is a material thing to be mastered by humankind for the glory of God. The first major conference on Confucianism and Ecology was held at Harvard University in 1996 (May 30–June 1). This was one of The Religions of the World and Ecology Conference series hosted by the Harvard Center for the Study of World Religions over a three-year period (1996–98). It was fully agreed that the modern ecological crisis requires a fresh review of Confucianism which is essentially a nature-friendly tradition; other groups at this conference series including Taoist and Buddhist groups arrived at similar conclusions.[1] Mary Evelyn Tucker and John Grim, co-editors of the Harvard Religions of the World and Ecology book series, pointed out that all religions including Confucianism are encouraged to contribute to global ecological awareness and environmental ethics by exploring divine-human-earth relations in a comprehensive way (1998:xxiv).

No doubt, today's world is considering various aspects of ecology: e.g., personal, social, scientific, political, ethical, religious, environmental, and so on. In particular, "the essential function of our belief systems" influences certain ways of perceiving ourselves with a growing "ecological awareness" (Bergmann and Eaton 2011, a new interdisciplinary study of ecological awareness). Modern Confucians are interested in connecting nature, philosophy, and religion; Tu Weiming, Tucker, and others were instrumental in establishing the Forum on Religion and Ecology (FORE) which became affiliated with the Center for Religion and Ecology at Yale. In their introduction to *Confucianism and Ecology*, Tucker and Berthrong (1998:xxxv) stated:

---

1 See Girardot, Miller, and Liu 2001 (*Taoism and Ecology*) as well as Tucker and Williams 1998 (*Buddhism and Ecology*), both of which belong to the Religions of the World and Ecology book series by the Harvard Center for the Study of World Religions.

> Confucianism has significant intellectual and spiritual resources to offer in the emerging discussions regarding attitudes toward nature, the role of the human, and environmental ethics. Its dynamic, organismic worldview, its respect for the vast continuity of life[...]its emphasis on holistic, moral education, and its appreciation for the embeddedness of life in interconnected concentric circles are only some examples of the rich resources of the Confucian tradition in relation to ecological issues.

Tu led the initial discussion of a Confucian ecology in his article "The Continuity of Being: Chinese Visions of Nature" (1985a, 1998). Confucian self-cultivation has an ecological dimension that relates the natural and moral character of the self to Heaven and Earth. As Tu said during his keynote speech at the 2011 Keimyung International Conference on Ecology and Korean Confucianism, the *Doctrine of the Mean* teaches a basic "Confucian cosmological vision" that the cultivated self can "form a trinity with heaven and earth" by fully understanding human nature and the nature of things (2011:17). The teaching about "forming one body with all things" is frequently mentioned in discussing Confucian ecological thought. Other modern scholars have highlighted similar points.

In the opening lines of the famous *Western Inscription*, Chang Tsai (張載, 1020–1073), a Sung Chinese Neo-Confucian, identified the human with the universe through a cosmological and spiritual union:

> Heaven is my father and Earth is my mother, and even such a small creature as I find an intimate place in their midst.

> Therefore that which fills the universe I regard as my body and that which directs the universe I consider as my nature. All people are my brothers and sisters, and all things are my companions. (Chan1963:497)

In other words, the true human being is best understood in terms of the network of connections between the self and the universe. The contemporary significance of Chang's cosmology may be an ecological view of the "anthropocosmic self" (Tu 1989, 1998): human beings form a triad with Heaven and earth that underlies our interconnectedness to all reality. Chang's *Western Inscription* emphasizes respect for human beings as well as respect for nature; regarding this sense of reverence, self-cultivation is said to be "deeply rooted in the ecological thinking of why human beings are not only observers (and) appreciators, but participants and co-creators" of the cosmic transformation (Tu 2011:20). So the Confucian tradition of self-cultivation is a resource for "moral ecology."

Tucker (1991, 1998) pointed out that self-cultivation enables Confucians to participate in "an anthropocosmic worldview." The reciprocal unity between the microcosm of the self and the macrocosm of the universe also reveals an ecological interest as manifested in cosmological orientation and moral-spiritual practice. Confucian ecology as a whole therefore covers a good range of philosophical and spiritual resources in the tradition for discussing human-earth relations. As Tucker and Berthrong wrote, "Its (Confucian) organic holism and dynamic vitalism give us a special appreciation for the interconnectedness of all life-forms" (1998:xxxviii). In other words, contemporary Confucians have begun to articulate this holistic, moral-spiritual view in relation to the doctrine of self-cultivation. Neo-Confucianism in particular is said to be suitable for developing an environmental ethics. In the next sections, I discuss a related topic by focusing on T'oegye's thought and experience.

From a contemporary perspective, the goal of saving the earth requires a "collective green shift" with an international religious intensity. Some scholars like Kearns and Keller (2007) have dealt with "Eco-Spirit: Religions and Philosophies for the Earth" by discussing traditional beliefs and contemporary practices and issues: for example, "a garden of green doctrines, rituals, and liturgies" is desired for new thinking and acting. In the Confucian context, nature is an area of pursuing the goals of self-cultivation. This task is therefore described as attaining the harmonious unity of Heaven, Earth, and human beings; for contemporary Confucians, it is not just a teaching about the unity of the universe, but may also be a call for environmental actions. As Berthrong has commented, "... self-cultivation must be expanded to embrace... a sustainable and balanced ecosystem" (1998:257).

Korean Confucianism is potentially capable of playing an active role in global dialogue on religion, ethics, and ecology, but I think that it should first learn how to address new issues beyond its own traditions. In the following section, I discuss a Korean Neo-Confucian ecological vision out of T'oegye's experience and insights.

II. T'OEGYE ON SELF-CULTIVATION, REVERENCE (KYŎNG), AND NATURE

We need to consider what aspects of T'oegye's religious thought are suitable for articulating Confucian ecology.[2] This section of my paper presents T'oegye's biography and nature poems, especially those covering his interpretation of self-cultivation and its ecological implications. His major writings include *Sŏnghak sipto* (聖學十圖, Ten diagrams on sage learning) and other philosophical essays and letters.[3]

Sung Chinese Neo-Confucians—such as Chou Tun-yi (周敦頤, 1017–1073), Chang Tsai, the Ch'eng brothers, and Chu Hsi (朱熹, 1130–1200)—all took nature seriously indeed. They saw the universe as a unitary structure in harmony with human existence. For example, Ch'eng I (程頤, 1033–1107) said that the person of *jen* (benevolence; human-heartedness) sees "Heaven and Earth and all things as one body." And the opening section of Chang Tsai's *Western Inscription* gives a poetic, mystical insight about uniting the human, natural and transcendent realms of the universe. As I outlined in the first section, it is often cited by modern scholars because of its significance for envisioning a Confucian ecology.

---

2 Books on the religious dimension of Chinese Confucianism include: Berthrong 1994; Ching 1977, 1997, 2000; Lee 1992; Neville 2000; Taylor 1991; Tu 1989; and Tu and Tucker 2004. For the Korean case, see Kalton 1988; Ro 1989; Chung (as indicated in note 1).

3 Consult Kalton 1988 for a full English translation of T'oegye's *Sŏnghak* sipto. The "Four-Seven letters" are another magnificent source of T'oegye's thought, which presents a sophisticated Neo-Confucian discourse on the mind, human nature, and feelings, as well as its implication for ethics and spirituality; for details, see Chung 1995, 2004.

In T'oegye's view, the true human being manifests the idea of "forming one body with the universe" by accomplishing the highest stage of self-cultivation as an embodiment of Heaven and Earth. As taught in the *Doctrine of the Mean* and also reaffirmed by T'oegye, the Confucian sage fulfills such a sacred rhythm with the natural and spiritual world. This is said to be the basic Confucian cosmological standpoint (Tucker and Berthrong 1998; Tu 1998, 2011).

T'oegye frequently mentioned Heaven's Principle (*ch'ŏlli/t'ien-li*, 天理), a key Neo-Confucian belief. In Sung China Chu Hsi talked about it as the transcendent li (理) full of moral principles, as well as the Great Ultimate (*t'ai-chi*, 太極) which is immanent in self-cultivation.[4] According to T'oegye's *Sŏnghak sipto*, self-cultivation is essentially to "preserve (hold fast to) Heaven's Principle (*chon ch' ŏlli/ts'un t'ien-li*, 存天理)."[5] One should clearly see it as distinguished from "selfish cravings (*sayok/ssu-yü*)."[6]

Here T'oegye's philosophy of principle (*li*) is also relevant. He basically followed Chu's system of *li* (理) and *ch'i* (氣), a well-researched topic that does not need to be rehearsed here.[7] *Li* (principle) is the universal principle

---

4 5 For this subject in English, see de Bary 1981; Chan 1963, 1967; Gardner 1990; and Chung 1995.

5 TC 7:29a (v. 1, 208). See also Kalton 1988:160–64. Also cited in Letter to Yi Pyŏngsuk, TC 37:28b (v. 2, 259).

6 Four-Seven Letter, TC 16:12a (v. 1, 407).

7 In short, *li* is the metaphysical "ground of being" present in each thing in its fullness of truth and goodness, whereas *ch'i* refers to the active physical energy that actually brings each phe-nomenon into concrete particular existence, resulting in good or evil. *Li* also means the omnipresent ground of being present in each phenomenon. By contrast, *ch'i* means vital energy, or "material force," which is thought to be the actual physical agent that brings everything into concrete existence; it determines the individuality and

of existence and the ultimate truth of human nature. The way of wisdom, therefore, means studying principles and cultivating the self. In short, he emphasized the transcendent and moral reality of *li* (Chung 1995, 2004). Human beings ought to form a harmonious unity with Heaven and Earth through realizing the metaphysical oneness and ethical continuity of principle in the human and natural world. Ecological thinking about the relationship between human beings and nature was a significant topic in Korean Neo-Confucianism.

According to T'oegye, Heaven's Principle is to be experienced as the ultimate truth of humanity in self-cultivation. His *Simhak to* (心學圖, Diagram on the learning of mind cultivation) concludes that the way of sagehood is "to transcend ordinary cravings and to preserve Heaven's Principle."[8] The way of transcending selfishness follows our moral-spiritual mind (*tosim/tao-hsin*, 道心).[9] T'oegye emphasized that its success depends on whether "the self governs emotions and desires properly."[10] As

transformation of phenomena that may lead to either good or evil. For Chu Hsi's philosophy of *li* and *ch'i*, see Chan 1967, 1986 and other relevant sources.

8 *Sŏnghak sipto*, TC 7:29a (v. 1, 208). As I have discussed elsewhere (Chung 2004, 2010), T'oegye's ethics and spirituality offers what Julia Ching calls a religious "model of self-transcendence" in the Confucian tradition (1977:10, 1993).

9 In his *Simhak to*, the eighth of his *Sŏnghak sipto*, TC 7:29a (v. 1, 208), T'oegye gave a major interpretation of Chu Hsi's doctrine on the "human mind" and the "moral mind." The *Hsin-ching* (*Classic of the mind-heart*) by Chen Tu-hsiu (1178–1235), Chu Hsi's leading follower in late Sung China, also influenced T'oegye's practice of mind cultivation and his religious thought.

10 See T'oegye's Four-Seven letters, TC 16:11a (v. 1, 407) and 7:24b (v. 1, 205), as well as his letter to Yi Koengjung, TC 36:2b (v. 2, 226). See also

I have discussed elsewhere (Chung 2009, 2010), he also recommended quiet-sitting (*chŏngjwa/ching-tso*, 靜坐) because of its effectiveness in "re-collecting the dispersed self" and experiencing one's interiority in a peaceful atmosphere.[11] In other words, contemplation facilitated T'oegye's continuous effort at spiritual cultivation.

The *ecological implication* of T'oegye's experience may assist our discussion of Confucian ecology. For example, by first controlling and harmonizing one's own emotions and thoughts properly, one truly respects all forms of life and maintains reverential attitudes toward nature.

REVERENCE AND NATURE:

Accordingly, T'oegye's spirituality of reverence (*kyŏng/ching*, 敬) is not just a significant development in the entire Neo-Confucian tradition, but also has a good deal of ecological meaning. The locus classicus for the teaching of reverence includes the *Book of Changes, Book of Rites,* and *Analects*.[12] Chinese Neo-Confucians also cited these classics in

---

The Doctrine of the Mean, chap. 1.

11 T'oegye's biography, *Ŏnhaeng rok* (Collected record of T'oegye's words and acts), 1:16b and 1:23a; *TC*, v. 4, 176 and 180. See also *Ch'ŏnmyŏng tosŏl* (天命圖說 Diagrammatic treatise on Heaven's Mandate), TC, vol. 3, p. 144. T'oegye emphasized quite-sitting, although it alone was not the primary choice of the Chu Hsi school. It occupied a prominent position among certain Ming Neo-Confucians such as Wang Yang-ming (王陽明 1472–1529), as discussed by Taylor 1991 and 1988:140–144.

12 According to *the Book of Changes*, "The authentic person applies reverence in order to straighten the inner life and righteousness in order to square the outer life" (cf. J. Legge, trans. Yi King, 426 and Chan 1963:264). The *Book of Rites* states: "The authentic person never lacks reverence" (see Legge,

emphasizing reverence in moral practice; for example, Chu Hsi taught it as a reverential attitude toward Heaven and Earth, as well as seriousness (or attentiveness) in learning and self-cultivation.[13]

In his *Sŏnghak sipto*, T'oegye intensified the spiritual cultivation of reverence as the key to Confucian sage learning. His famous *Ch'ŏnmyŏng tosŏl* (天命圖說, Diagrammatic treatise on Heaven's Mandate) also states:

> If one does not take reverence (*kyŏng*) to be the first principle of learning, how can he establish the original mind? Hence, before the mind is aroused, the learning of authentic persons is to take reverence as the first principle and to give full effort to preserving (nature) and nourishing (the mind-heart). After the mind is aroused, it is to give full effort to self-reflection. This is the reason why the cultivation of reverence completes the beginning and end of sage learning (*sŏnghak/sheng-hsüeh*, 聖學).[14]

As recommended in T'oegye's Four-Seven thesis as well, this means to harmonize daily feelings, desires, and thoughts. The term *kyŏng* also

---

trans. Li Ki, v. 1, 61). And Confucius emphasized: "Be reverent in handling all affairs" (*Analects*, 13:19; Lau 1970:121).

13 Chu Hsi also said that "one must do mind cultivation with reverence." See *Chu Tzu yü-lei* [Classified conversations of Master Chu Hsi] 95:41a, 96:2b. Furthermore, Ch'eng Hao (程顥 1032–1085) said: "Reverence simply means a way of managing oneself" (*I-shu* [Surviving works], 18:19a; Chan 1963:560); when one lacks it, "thousands of selfish desires arise to injure one's humanity" (*I-shu*, 15:9a). As Ch'eng I also said, "self-cultivation requires reverence" (*I-shu*, 18:5b).

14 *TC*, v. 3, 144.

means "mindfulness" (Kalton 1988:188) conveying an inner motivation for self-realization. T'oegye emphasized reverence before the universe:

> In order to abide in reverence (*chigyŏng/ch'i-ching*, 持敬), you have to remain at the center of the myriad things and make sure that reverence does not deviate from the myriad things[...] Even for a single moment, we cannot neglect reverence.[15]

For T'oegye, reverence is absolutely "the master of one, united mind-heart" (*ilsim chuje/yi-hsin chu-tsai*, 一心主宰).[16] His *Sŏnghak sipto* therefore articulates it as that which enables us to reach "the sacred mystery of the harmonious oneness of Heaven and human nature" (*ch'ŏnin habil/t'ien-jen ho-yi*, 天人合一).[17] I basically agree with Keum Jang-tae (Kŭm Changt'ae), a leading Confucian scholar in Korea, that "the distinctive nature of T'oegye's life and thought" centers around his religious interpretation of *kyŏng* (1998b:180).[18]

For T'oegye, harmonizing the self with nature is a way of cultivation involving reverence. We may call this "the reverential self," which becomes

---

15 *Ŏnhaeng nok*, 1:16a; TC, v. 4, 176.

16 *See Simhak to*, the eighth diagram of *Sŏnghak sipto, TC* 7:29a (v. 1, 208). See also Kalton 1988:160–164.

17 Introduction to the Sŏnghak sipto, TC 7:9a (v. 1, 198). See also *Kyŏngje kam* (Diagrammatic essay on *kyŏng*), *Sŏnghak sipto*, TC 7:31a–b (v. 1, 209).

18 Prof. Keum also explained in Korean that T'oegye assimilated the classical notion of "revering Heaven" (*kyŏngch'ŏn* 敬天) with the Neo-Confucian doctrine of Heaven's Principle (Keum 1998b:181–183). This is said to be an important part of T'oegye's philosophy.

important for Confucian ecological thinking. In "The Relevance of Chinese Neo-Confucianism for the Reverence of Nature," Tucker (1991) explained the Neo-Confucian way of "envisioning the universe as interconnected and inter-penetrating." For T'oegye, this would mean that the true human being is not merely a physical and rational self, but also a self-transforming person who harmonizes the transcendent and immanent realities of human existence. This defines us in cosmological and spiritual terms as well: uniting the cultivated self with the natural world.[19] In other words, the search for our ultimate being follows reverence (*kyŏng*) in unity with Heaven, Earth, and the myriad things. According to T'oegye's biography, this belief became important for his self-cultivation.[20]

Commenting on ecology and T'oegye's thought, Lee Dong-hee said that we may see T'oegye's notion of reverence "as a religious matter of self-cultivation" together with its "cosmological aspect" integrating the unity of human beings and nature (2011:120).[21] T'oegye's ethics and spiritual practice resonate with our contemporary views of Confucian ecology. As Tu pointed out, Confucian thought is a "comprehensive, spiritual humanism" because its self-cultivation remains "naturalistic and a spiritual project" (2011:18); this view is indeed compatible with T'oegye's case. As

---

19 In this regard, I am indebted to Tu Weiming, who also said that: "The sense of awe and reverence before the universe is prompted by our aspiration to respond to the ultimate reality that makes our life purposeful and meaningful" (2004:498).

20 *TC* v. 4, 209.

21 In this regard, I can quote Lee's comment that it is necessary to develop the Confucian ecological view consisting of a "cosmological religious awareness," and Korean Confucian thinkers may seek out "a way to revive its cosmological religious awareness for ecological protection actions" (Lee 2011:123).

I emphasized above, a *cultivated* life of reverence is to be in harmonious unity with the universe; the *reverential self* therefore appreciates the natural beauties respecting all beings. Accordingly, we also have to consider the poetic and aesthetic part of T'oegye's thought.

T'OEGYE'S POETRY AND ECOLOGICAL IMPLICATION:

Like some other great Neo-Confucians of the past, T'oegye often withdrew from his public career to a private scholarly life in his beloved home in T'ogye (Andong, Kyŏngsang province). He actually liked such a life in the countryside; his biography and letters indicate that retiring to his home and the Tosan Academy during his later years (fifties and sixties) really inspired him to advance his study and writing and, more important, to intensively practice self-cultivation. This also enabled his love of nature and informs us about his poetry and aesthetic experience.

T'oegye enjoyed composing poems, many of which were done during his retreat or retirement years. He composed over 2,300 poems, including the famous *Tosan sibigok* (Twelve songs of Tosan, 陶山). This is a well-researched topic by Korean scholars in Korean literature and poetry, so it does not need to be rehearsed here in terms of different types and meanings.[22] I focus more on its philosophical and ecological dimensions.

---

22 Korean scholars' research areas are associated with general poetry studies, Neo-Confucian poetry, traditional Korean poetry, comparative poetry and literature, etc. They basically agree that T'oegye's works may be grouped into several kinds: nature poems, self-cultivation poems, history-reflection poems, doctrine-explanatory poems, journey poems, mourning ritual

For example, T'oegye composed a short poem when he was fifty years old in 1550. He entitled this poem "T'oegye" (退溪):

> Being foolish yet comfortable after withdrawing (*t'oe*, 退) my body,
> Also worried about my last years because my study is lagging behind.
> After deciding my shelter at a place over this steam (*gye*, 溪),
> I practice self-reflection every day like this flowing water.[23]

This poem is about returning (*t'oe*) to his home after resigning from a high official position in Seoul. In revealing his feeling of intimacy with a *gye* stream, he entitled this poem identical to his pen name, T'oegye (退溪). Despite some regret over the lack of time he had for study and self-cultivation during his public career years, he expressed a good deal of pleasure with cultivating himself like a restless, "flowing stream" through self-reflection. Furthermore, T'oegye's two *Tongam ŏnji* poems also show a similar appreciation of the natural scenery around the Tongam site, such as mountain hills and rocks, clouds and fog, and streams.[24] In other words,

---

poems, society-related poems, etc. For this topic, consult Korean sources especially Kwŏn 1992, Yi and Chang 2007, Kim 2009.

23 See *T'oegye sŏnsaeng munjip* (Collected literary works by Master T'oegye), 1:47.

24 *T'oegye sŏnsaeng munjip*, 1:28. Each Tongam poem consists of eight lines, each of which has seven Chinese characters (hancha). I also note that the term gye used in this poem is identical to the second character of his pen name, T'oeg*ye* (退溪), and the first character *t'oe* (退) is also relevant here because of its meaning, "to retire/withdraw/return." Furthermore, examples of natural beauties and living beings used in his poetry include: mountain

returning to home encouraged in him a genuine reverence for nature, and we can see its ecological meaning as well.

Some of T'oegye's poems are about self-reflection on the unifying principle (*li*, 理) of human existence and natural beings. The ecological significance of this idea is the relationship between nature and human beings to be realized in terms of the metaphysical oneness and moral harmony of principle (*li*) in the human and natural world. Another group of his poems informs us about his sense of awe before the universe. For example, at age sixty he composed *Imgŏ siboyŏn*, a famous fifteen-piece poetry.[25] One particular poem reveals his practice of reverence (*kyŏng*) and mind cultivation in relation to natural creativity and aesthetic experience. For T'oegye, then, the creative and aesthetic power of nature becomes a source of inspiration for philosophical contemplation and spiritual cultivation.[26]

In my view, T'oegye integrated contemplation and *kyŏng* spirituality with his reverence for nature.[27] Forming one body with the universe

---

hills and rocks, rivers and streams, green fields and farmers, trees and blossoming flowers, moving clouds, spring sunlight, morning fog, flying or singing birds, moonlight, small sand islands in rivers, garden ponds, swimming fishes, and so on. The *aesthetic-ecological* implication of these examples is worthy of our consideration.

25 *T'oegye sŏnsaeng munjip*, 3:4. Each poem in the *Imgŏ siboyŏn* has four lines, each consisting of seven Chinese characters.

26 From a similar angle, Tu's latest view could be helpful here: Korean Confucianism emphasizes "human sensitivity" to be "aesthetically significant" and how this relates the naturalistic world to one's "self-cultivation and self-understanding" (Tu 2011:21–22).

27 I suggest that T'oegye did so to a greater degree than Chu Hsi did. The former put more emphasis on the self-cultivation part of Chu's philosophy of *li* in such a way. As I discussed elsewhere (Chung 2009, 2010), T'oegye

inspires continuous effort at self-cultivation while practicing reverence toward Heaven and Earth. As Tu interpreted the ecological and religious meaning of Confucian self-cultivation,

> For spiritual self-realization, the human should become the steward, guardian, and protector of nature in an aesthetic, ethical, and religious sense... We live with reverence and a sense of awe for the fecundity and creativity of nature as we open our eyes to what is near at hand. (2004:490)

T'oegye's nature poetry is closely connected to Neo-Confucian ethics and his spirituality. It may also represent a deeper spiritual and aesthetic dimension of Chu Hsi's thought. Furthermore, I note that the ecological implication of T'oegye's experience is noteworthy; it is compatible with, for example, a new study by Bergmann and Eaton (2011) which presents ecological awareness integrating "religion, ethics, and aesthetics." What we learn from T'oegye's poetry is: his aesthetic experience of intimacy with nature resulted from his dedicated and solemn effort at self-cultivation.

In the concluding section, I suggest that this will contribute to our development of a Confucian ecology, so as to benefit Korea and the world

---

developed a spirituality of reverence establishing a Confucian role model for it, probably for the first time in East Asia. In other words, T'oegye advanced his philosophy assimilating it with his aesthetic experience of nature-humanity harmony. Liu (2009:329) pointed out, in his article on the spiritual foundation of T'oegye's poetry, that: "The high quality of T'oegye's poetry resulted from his spiritual practice of reverence. Accordingly, the study of T'oegye's thought may be contributed actively by our recognition of his understanding and cultivation of reverence."

community in their shared quest for a sustainable green future.

III. CONCLUSION: TOWARD A GREEN CONFUCIAN VISION FOR KOREA AND THE WORLD

Overall, T'oegye's *kyŏng* spirituality, his love of nature, his nature poetry, and his metaphysics are deeply rooted in Confucian self-cultivation, thereby offering aesthetic and ethical implications for Confucian ecology from an integrated standpoint. This is significant for the study of ecology and Confucianism including the Korean topics. At the heart of T'oegye's life and thought is a profound belief in the harmonious oneness of human, natural, and spiritual realities. As I mentioned before (2009, 2010), T'oegye's experience and insights point to "holistic spirituality." A special feature of his philosophy is therefore about "holistic" thinking and practice. In this regard, I agree with Tu Weiming that

> ...the understanding of nature as an integral part of human self-reflection make(s) Korean Confucianism not only ecologically sound, ecologically significant, but also in itself a kind of deep ecological vision... And this close interaction between the human on the one hand and nature on the other hand helps us to understand the holistic interactive mode of Korean humanistic thinking. (2011:21)

Today's Confucian intellectuals discuss ecology by covering Confucian resources drawn from the Chinese, Korean, Japanese, or international traditions. They may preserve the best of Confucian ideas, and "advance it into a new area of contemporary concern for nature and environmental ethics" (Berthrong 1998:237–239). I also note that we need to continue interreligious dialogue. In his *Religion and the Order of Nature* (1995), the leading Islamic scholar Nasr pointed out that the Confucian tradition provides "essential teachings" about nature and universal wisdom, so the West has to learn more about these Eastern perspectives.[28]

I suggest that those of us Confucian intellectuals in the West and those at Korean or other East Asian universities or Confucian organizations can work together in order to develop a well-integrated framework that can handle the ongoing ecological issues. This framework would be Confucian yet pluralistic, but it also has to collaborate with global science, economy, and political leadership that are *ecologically friendly*. The 2009 Parliament of the World's Religions (Melbourne, Australia), in partnership with The Forum on Religion and Ecology, addressed its central theme, "Healing the Earth with Care and Concern." Its key environmental concerns and actions were discussed from various religious and spiritual perspectives. The Parliament also renewed the Earth Charter and its commitment to the future of the green planet by emphasizing an urgent need to cultivate our awareness of "global interconnectedness." In light of Confucian ecological thinking, I support this renewal and commitment.

---

[28] For Nasr (1995), this is partly because one problem with modern Western thought is its lack of interest in dealing with nature properly or sympathetically, due to the rising popularity of mathematical scientism and secular humanism. The Judeo-Christian-Islamic traditions were interested in developing anthropocentric worldviews, so they basically viewed the earth as "secondary" or "inferior" to human beings; in the West this was also influenced by a theological sense of the absolute transcendence of God.

To T'oegye, self-cultivation is a way of wisdom uniting the person of reverence with the natural world. This resonates well with our discussion of modern Confucianism and ecology. The *cultivated self* develops its ultimate harmony with Heaven and Earth by transcending the separation between the self and others and by extending his/her *reverential mind-heart* to embrace nature and all living beings. In order to promote an ecological value system, I therefore emphasize T'oegye's holistic ecological awareness from a Korean Confucian and global perspective.

As a living tradition, Confucianism has to deal with the new ecological crisis as a matter of ethical principle and sociopolitical action as well. Can the Korean tradition become a major contributor to global dialogue on this matter? My answer is cautiously yes. I say so partly because Confucian leadership in South Korea has been rather quiet about the ecological problem or their potential contribution to confronting it. As Lee Dong-hee pointed out, Confucianism in Korea is not actively interested in any public movements for protecting the earth, so "ecological awareness is stronger among Buddhists and Christians in Korea" than Confucians (2011:123).[29] Korean Confucian leaders and organizations need to play active roles in discussing the environmental problem and Confucian ecological ideas nationally or globally. Hopefully, T'oegye's ecological awareness will inspire them, so that they can promote reverential attitudes toward nature and new ecological values.

I am envisioning a modern Neo-Confucian ecological perspective

---

[29] From a comparative perspective, we may find Lee's critical observation helpful in motivating Korean Confucian leaders to become more active and engaging about the ecological issues. Also note that I previously discussed Confucian identity, ethics, rituals and religiosity in modern Korea elsewhere (see References).

on the basis of T'oegye's experience and insights. I applaud T'oegye for his reverence for nature as well as his holistic vision for human-ecological harmony, which may help Korean Confucianism to strengthen its modern ecological thought; this is potentially an important message for the global enterprise of religion, philosophy, and ecology. In this regard, we may also look forward to the development of what I call a "green Confucianism" that will protect the earth and preserve the healthy future of the world.

To conclude, T'oegye's thought is a leading legacy of Korean philosophy and spirituality, as well as a highly interconnecting and engaging resource for Confucian ecology.

Edward Y. J. Chung (chung@upei.ca) *is a professor in the Department of Religious Studies and Director of Asian Studies at the University of Prince Edward Island, Canada.*

ECOLOGY AND COSMOLOGY: A KOREAN NEO-CONFUCIAN APPROACH

By Young-chan Ro

INTRODUCTION

The title of this article touches upon three major topics, ecology, cosmology, and Korean Neo-Confucianism. How are these three subjects to be related to each other? All these three are serious topics and each requires substantial discussion. What I attempt to do in this article, however, is to discuss each topic in the context of the others to elucidate the theme of "Ecology and Korean Confucianism." I shall first discuss the relationship between ecology and cosmology in general, and then explore the Korean Neo-Confucian cosmology of Yi Yulgok (1536–1584) in expounding its ecological implications. My approach in this article is to argue that the ecological issues are profoundly cosmological issues and the ecological crisis is fundamentally a cosmological crisis. Often we think of environmental issues and ecological crises in terms of the moral and ethical sense of "care" or "action." The root of this ecological crisis and the degree of its seriousness, however, require us to search a deeper level of this problem. We can no longer look for a temporary remedy to deal with this crisis. We have to search for a deeper cause of this problem in light of the history of human civilization especially in the West. Furthermore, the ecological issue is neither a mere moral and ethical issue nor simply a political or public policy issue, but it is fundamentally a cosmological issue. The March 11, 2011 earthquake in Japan was a powerful reminder of the fact that we can no longer afford the idea that human beings are the center of all beings and the measure of all things (Protagoras). I do not intend to minimize the significance of human responsibility nor disregard the place of human beings in the cosmic order. Rather, what I intend to do is to explore and interpret Yulgok's understanding of the universe as a foundation in developing an "eco-cosmology," or an ecologically-conscious-cosmology by inter-preting Yulgok's Neo-Confucian philosophy, especially his two seminal essays, i.e., the *Treatise on the Way of Heaven* (*Ch'ŏndoch'aek*, 天道策) and the *Treatise on Numerical Changes* (*Yŏksuch'aek*, 易數策).

ECO-COSMOLOGY

The word ecology stems from the Greek word *oikos* and *logos*. The word *oikos* means "house" or "dwelling," and logos means "reason," "rationality," and "theory" among others. In this sense, ecology is a rational and theoretical study of the universe in which we live. The universe is the "house" of all beings. Since the Reformation, the Renaissance, the Enlightenment in the West, ushering in the dawn of the modern age, the perception of the *oikos* and the universe has shifted profoundly in making human beings, not the cosmos or the *oikos*, as the center of all beings. Moreover, as Lynn White, Jr., one the foremost medieval historians, has stated, we considered our planet was the center of the universe:

> Despite Copernicus, all the cosmos rotates around our little globe. Despite Darwin, we are not, in our hearts, part of the natural process. We are superior to nature, contemptuous of it, willing to use it for our slightest whim.[1]

Ecological issues are closely connected to worldviews and worldviews are also shaped by our understanding of the universe, cosmology. On the other hand, the way we understand the universe also affects the way we relate to the universe. The universe or cosmos is not to *objectively* be defined but to *subjectively* be comprehended and appreciated by us. The way we comprehend and understand the universe is very much part of our *being* in the universe. In this respect, the "modern mentality" or as Professor Tu Weiming put it, "the Enlightenment mentality," has become an acute problem for elevating the human as superior to all other beings, "anthropocentrism." To counter this "Enlightenment mentality," Tu Weiming, for example, proposed the term "anthropocosmic"[2] in emphasizing the unity of human beings and the universe. Cosmology, in this respect, is no longer an intellectual and scholarly study of the cosmos as an *object*, but a form of human *subjective* self-understanding

---

1 Lynn White, Jr., "The Historical Roots of Our Ecological Crisis," in Western Man and Environmental Ethics: Attitudes toward Nature and Technology, ed. Ian G. Barbour (Reading, Mss.: Addison-Wesley, 1973, 27–28). Originally published in Science 155 (March 1967): 1203–7.

2 Tu Wei-ming has expounded the fundamental unbroken continuum of the human and the heaven in his earlier interpretation of the Doctrine of the Mean, Confucian Thought: Selfhood as Creative Transformation and Centrality and Commonality: An Essay on Confucian Religiousness (Albany: State University of New York Press, 1989).

in relationship with the cosmos. In this sense, cosmology is not a mere intellectual discipline using "scientific" analysis of the universe as an object of our investigation. Rather, it is a form of "self-awareness" or "self-understanding" as a way of being in the cosmos or the *oikos*. In this case, human beings as a subject, also must be included in the process of understanding the universe. This requires a change of our attitude, a change of the habit of heart, a radical conversion or a spiritual metanoia. It requires a different mode of being in the universe as a form of spiritual experience.

From a methodological point of view, we need a fresh understanding of the universe from the point of view of *ecology*, we consider the universe as our "house" (*oikos*) or "dwelling." The ecological concern has to do with a unitary vision or an integrated view of reality. As we have seen above, the proper ecological perspective is a unitary vision of the human and the cosmos. To investigate the intrinsic relationship between human beings and the universe from the ecological point of view, it is necessary to investigate the meaning of the term *ecology*. Is ecology in the domain of the *logos*? Is ecology our human logical or ideological analysis of the universe, thus, an exercise of human *logos* on the cosmos? If so, the nature and characteristics of this *logos* are the same as the *logos* that created the modern contemporary problem and crisis in the first place, namely the Enlightenment mentality that shaped the "modernity," in elevating our human *logical* and *rational* thinking, and making the scientific method the absolute norm. Furthermore, the concept *logos*, as formulated and developed in Western civilization, has an unmistakable anthropocentric thrust. The modern scientific worldview was one of the results of anthropocentrism. We need a new way of thinking, turning from the anthropocentric and the *logos* oriented way of thinking to the "cosmocentric" thinking: from an aggressive and intrusive way of reducing the mystery of the universe to a way of understanding and appreciating the mystery of the universe without reducing it into a mere human *logos*, the "cosmocentric" worldview. This is a radical change of thinking, a *metanoia*. This new way of thinking is not entirely "new" but a rediscovery or a reinterpretation of the premodern wisdom found in our own traditional spiritual and religious traditions. In this respect, my attempt is to go back to the Neo-Confucian idea of the universe for a source of inspiration to develop a cosmocentric worldview, not an anthropocentric but a cosmocentric cosmology, or I submit "cosmoanthropic" cosmology. By "cosmoanthropic," I mean to think of the universe not from the human centered, the anthropocentric perspective, but from the perspective of the cosmos as the *oikos* of human beings, and human beings *within* the universe. This attitude requires us to open our heart-mind, to listen to the sound of the cosmos, and attune to the rhythm of the universe, not an aggressive and invasive way of penetrating the cosmos but a receptive and responsive way of following the flow of the cosmos. My concern in this attempt is neither to seek the *nomos* or the laws and the rules of the *oikos* nor to reduce the mystery of the *oikos*, or the universe, into the realm of *nomos*. The cosmos is not an object to be *apprehended* but a subject to be *appropriated* and *appreciated*. This attitude allows us to open to the irreducible, inexhaustible, and unexplainable cosmic phenomena containing the mystery of the universe.

NEO-CONFUCIAN COSMOLOGY

In the course of Neo-Confucian cosmological development, human beings, and Heaven and Earth, were placed within the proper context of th e universe. Confucian cosmology concentrates not only on the earth but, more importantly, on the universe. In order to develop an ecology which will truly take care of the earth, we have to shift our perspective from an "anthropocentric," or even a "geocentric," view of the earth to a "cosmocentric" one. The earth has to be understood in relation to the universe, as expressed in the term, "Heaven and Earth" in the Neo-Confucian tradition. Human beings are in harmony with Heaven as expressed in the Neo-Confucian terms, "making one with Heaven and the human" (*tianrenheyi*, 天人合一). This Confucian assumption provided the foundation for Yulgok to develop his deep understanding and a profound appreciation of the cosmos as expounded in the *Treatise on the Way of Heaven* (*Ch'ŏndoch'aek*, 天道策) and the *Treatise on Numeric Changes* (*Yŏksuch'aek*, 易數策).

Neo-Confucian cosmology as expounded by Yi Yulgok implies the significance of a "cosmoanthropic" view of the universe and the world. I use the term "cosmoanthropic" in describing Yulgok's cosmology rather than "anthropocosmic" because the term "antrhropocosmic" still implies that human beings, rather than the cosmos, are the center, but the "cosmoanthropic" worldview begins with the cosmos, not with humans. One of the significant transformations found in the Neo-Confucian tradition, compared to Classical Confucianism, was not only the Neo-Confucian interest in cosmology but, more importantly, the shift of emphasis from "anthropocentric" cosmology to "cosmo-anthropic" cosmology: The Neo-Confucian ideas such as *taiji* (太極), *yin-yang* (陰

陽), *wuxing* (五行), and *li* (理)and *qi* (氣), all started with cosmological concepts and ontological principles before they were applied to explain human beings. Classical Confucianism, on the other hand, developed an "anthropocosmic" vision by starting with the human and expanding to the cosmos as found in the following quotation:

> Only those who are absolutely sincere can fully develop their nature. If they can fully develop their nature, they can then fully develop the nature of others. If they can fully develop the nature of others, they can then fully develop the nature of things. If they can fully develop the nature of things, they can then assist in the transforming and nourishing process of Heaven and Earth. If they can assist in the transforming and nourishing process of Heaven and Earth, they can thus form a trinity with Heaven and Earth.[3]

This statement from the *Doctrine of the Mean* (*Zhongyong*, 中庸) demonstrates the unity and interaction between the cosmos and human beings. Furthermore, the idea of "sincerity (*cheng*, 誠)" plays a critical role in relating human beings to Heaven and Earth. The *Zhongyong*, together with the *Great Learning* or *Daxue* (大學) were most influential on Yulgok's Neo-Confucian philosophy, especially in developing the idea of "sincerity" or "*cheng/sŏng* (誠)" as the key concept in integrating the human, and Heaven and Earth. In the *Zhongyong*, the process of relating human beings to Heaven and Earth starts with and relies on individual self-cultivation. In

---

[3] A Source Book in Chinese Philosophy, trans. Wing-tsit Chan (Princeton: Princeton University Press, 1963), 107–8.

this regard, the idea of "*cheng/sŏng*" is crucial as an integrative principle of the human and "Heaven and Earth" in understanding the *anthropological dimension of the universe*. On the other hand, however, Yulgok was deeply concerned about the *cosmological dimension of human beings*. Yulgok's two most important essays on the cosmos, namely, the *Treatise on the Way of Heaven* (*Ch'ŏndoch'aek*, 天道策) and the *Treatise on Numeric Changes* (*Yŏksuch'aek*, 易數策) were written as parts of his civil service examinations. Yulgok started the series of his civil service examinations when he was twenty-three, and took first place in each examination. The *Treatise on the Way of Heaven* was his first essay written for the exam. The other one, the last of the state exam series, was taken when he was twenty-nine, and this essay was the *Treatise on Numeric Changes*. In both essays, Yulgok constructed his cosmology in a comprehensive manner by interpreting the basic Neo-Confucian cosmological and ontological ideas and concepts in a fundamental relationship with human beings and affairs.

Unlike Classical Confucianism, including Confucius himself who stated, "It is man that can make the Way great, and not the Way that can make man great,"[4] Neo-Confucianism explicitly explored the intrinsic unity of the way of human beings and the way of Heaven and Earth. Yulgok, while fully appreciating the role of the human in the trinity of the human, and "Heaven and Earth," was also deeply engaged in the cosmological idea of *taiji/t'aegŭk* (太極), *yin-yang/ŭmyang* (陰陽), *wuxing/ohaeng* (五行) and *li/yi* (理) and *qi/ki* (氣), and he was equally fascinated with the *Book of Changes* (*Yijing*, 易經) in understanding the symbolic representation of the universe. In other words, Yulgok understood the

---

[4] Analects, 15:28, in Chan, A Source Book in Chinese Philosophy, 44.

universe as a symbolic system engaged in a process of dynamic change. "Symbolic system" means neither a sheer "formality" nor "without substance," but a way of human self-understanding: a dynamic mutual participation and interpenetration between the cosmos and the human. In other words, for Yulgok, the universe is neither an unintelligible object nor a mere mechanical system, but a living dynamic *being* in which we, human beings, participate as our "house" or the *oikos*.

Based on the notion of "sincerity" as the unitary and the integrative principle not only in relating the human to the cosmos but also in forming the trinity of the human, and "Heaven and Earth, Yulgok developed a broader implication of the interrelationship between the human and the cosmos. Yulgok developed the intrinsic ontological unity between the human and the cosmos by stating the fundamental *yin-yang* movement that generates, maintains, transforms, and harmonizes all beings in the universe. His essay, the *Treatise on the Way of Heaven* or *Chŏndoch'aek* (天道策) is one of the most explicit and elaborate explanations of how the *yin-yang/ŭm-yang* (陰陽) movement governs and unites the human and the universe, and how *li/yi* (理) and *qi/ki* (氣) are the underlying "principle" and "vital force" of all beings in the universe. In this treatise, Yulgok emphasizes the unbroken ontological unity of the human and the cosmos, and mutual co-responses between the human phenomena and the cosmic phenomena.

Here we may clarify the function of the *yin-yang* phenomena and the role of the *li-qi* theory of the Neo-Confucian tradition in general and Yulgok in particular. As is the case with most Neo-Confucian scholars, Yulgok used the *yin-yang* movement as the most fundamental of two distinctive yet related forces of the universe, the *mutation* of *yin* and *yang* is expressed in the symbol of *taiji/t'aegŭk* (太極). As Yulgok asserted, *taiji/*

t'aegŭk (太極) is not an ontological entity that exists apart from *yin* and *yang*, and taiji is not an independent being from which yin and yang are generated or produced. Instead, *taiji* for Yulgok was a powerful symbol manifesting the mystery of the subtle yet profound process of "change" and "transmutation" of the two forms of the vital force, namely, *yin* and *yang* of the universe. Human beings also share the same *yin-yang* vital force with all other beings in the universe. For this reason, human beings share the unbroken unity with "Heaven and Earth." In this sense, human beings must be understood in a fundamental unity with the cosmos. Yulgok's cosmology, thus, begins with the cosmic force of yin and yang and is then also applied to human beings. In this regard, for Yulgok, human beings also are governed by the cosmic flow of the *yin-yang* mutation. On the other hand, however, Yulgok also understood that human beings possess a transformative power in relating to the cosmos. In this respect, while Yulgok accepts the fundamental unity of the human and the cosmos due to the basic ontological principles such as *li/yi* and *qi/ki*, it does not mean that he would consider that human beings are entirely subjected to the cosmos. Rather, for Yulgok, human beings have a unique capacity to relate to "Heaven and Earth." This relationship is neither deterministic in the sense that the human is under the complete control of the cosmic forces and determined by the cosmos, nor entirely independent from the cosmos, but is a mutual interaction between the human and the universe.

Yulgok's other essay, the *Treatise on Numeric Changes* (*Yŏksuch'aek*, 易數策), also expounds the dynamic changes of the universe and human relationship to the cosmic phenomena. Yulgok, like many other Neo-Confucian scholars of his time, took the *Book of Changes* (*Yijing*, 易經) seriously and studied it very carefully. *The Book of Changes* or *Yijing*, was understood primarily as a book of divination, but it became the primary source for the Neo-Confucian scholars in developing a Neo-Confucian cosmology. It is also known that Confucius himself reportedly studied the *Book of Changes* so thoroughly that the binding strings of his copy of the *Yijing* were broken three times as Yulgok himself mentioned. In his response to the question given to him by the civil service examiner, Yulgok tried to establish the three fundamental frameworks for understanding the cosmos and its relation to the human as follows:

1) The symbolic structure as shown in the *Yijing* and the numbers employed in it indicate that the universe is neither a fixed physical object nor a mere mechanical entity; rather, it is a living, dynamic, and changing reality.

2) The universe is not a mere physical reality but, more importantly, a *herme-neutical* reality: human understanding and interpretation of the universe, through images, numbers, and hexagrams, play a critical role in comprehending the universe. In this sense, Yulgok's interpretation of the *Yijing* had become the prime model through which he understood the cosmos and the human. The human is an active agent in the interpretive process of understanding the symbolic structure of the universe. This is the case especially with Yulgok's cosmological construction. According to Yulgok, the *Yijing's* symbolic structure was interpreted or clarified by the three sages: Wen, the first king of the early Zhou period, Zhougong, the Duke of Zhou, and Confucius and, thus, the knowledge of the *Yijing* was passed on to later generation.[5] The sage as a true human being is able to listen to the sound of the universe, attune to the cosmic flows, and

5 Yulgok chŏnsŏ [栗谷全書], vol. 1 (Seoul: Sungkyunkwan University Press, 1971), 308 (kwŏn 14:48b).

interacts and communicates with the universe:

> Heaven and Earth wait for sages, with numbers, to show [the meaning of the universe] to the world. Sages wait for the clue of written character to show the principle to the world. Heaven has to beget sages; sages have to produce the clue of the written character to show to the world. This is the response of nature and the mutual interaction and mysteries of Heaven and human beings.[6]

It was also crucial for a sage to interact with the universe: "The virtue of a sage is to coincide with Heaven and Earth. Their brilliance is like the sun and the moon. Their order coincides with the four seasons."[7]

3) The universe is an open system with a certain principles, patterns, and regularity. The Sixty-four Hexagrams, for example, appear to be a limited number of variations, but when taken in a symbolic form, they can provide unlimited possibilities of being in the universe: "In general, we know the limited variations of the Sixty-four Hexagrams but we know the inexhaustible functions of the Sixty-four Hexagrams."[8] These possibilities and variations, however, are governed by the patterns, the norms, and the principle (*li/yi)* inherent in the cosmos. The principle and the patterns of this dynamic process are called the Way (*Dao*). Thus, every being in the universe, and the universe itself, are governed by a certain principle (*li/yi*). In this sense, the universe for Yulgok is an open system, not total chaos but

---

6 Ibid., 14:49a.

7 Ibid., 14:50b.

8 Ibid.

a cosmos: it is an orderly universe with openness for a new possibility, not a closed system.

CONCLUSION

Yulgok believed that the universe could not be completely comprehended by human intelligence or through human thought processes alone. He believed that the universe is a "mystery" not to be reduced to the rational or conceptual framework of an intellectual system. That this dimension of mystery was irreducible to any fixed form of intelligence was very keenly appreciated by Yulgok.

It can be understood as the "sacred" dimension of the universe. We have a sense of "awe" toward the universe. The universe as a "symbol system," as understood by Yulgok, "manifests" itself to us as much as it "conceals" itself from us. This is the power of symbol, which *reveals* without *defining*, or delimiting, itself. The universe reveals and the humans (sages) decipher the meaning of the universe or try to understand the workings of the universe.

A Confucian sage must not be understood as an astrologer or a diviner but the one who understands the Confucian cosmological assumptions and discerns their human implications. For this reason, often, even sage kings made use of sorcery or divination, not because of their blind trust in the practice, but because of the acceptance of their intellectual limitations and their willingness to listen to the mysteries of the universe.[9] Yulogk,

---

9 Ibid., 14:51a.

in both *Chŏndoch'aek* and *Yŏksuch'aek*, tried to show his understanding of the universe in avoiding two extremes: a fatalistic or a deterministic view on one hand, and an intellectual reduction on the other. The former indicates that human beings are not mechanically dictated to by the universe, the latter shows that the universe preserves the dimension of mystery so it appears "sacred" to us. For Yulgok, the *Yijing* was not a mere book of sorcery or divination but a book of cosmology illuminating the relationship between the universe and the human through the symbolic system of the Sixty-four Hexagrams.

Yulgok can be a rich resource for inspiration in recognizing and rediscovering the cosmological dimension of Korean Neo-Confucianism in developing an ecocosmology, a new cosmology in emphasizing the interrelationship of human beings and the universe. This new ecocosmology, in turn, will become a foundation for understanding ecological issues from the cosmological perspective.

Young-chan Ro (yro@gmu.edu) *is a professor in Religious Studies at George Mason University, U.S.A.*

THE TRANSFORMATION OF CONFUCIANISM IN CONTEMPORARY KOREA: HOW IT HAS LOST MOST OF ITS METAPHYSICAL UNDERPINNINGS AND SURVIVES TODAY PRIMARILY AS ETHICAL RHETORIC AND HERITAGE RITUALS

By Donald Baker

South Koreans like to brag that their country is the most Confucian nation on earth (though Singapore might challenge that claim). Yet only around 0.2% of South Koreans, a little over 100,000 out of a population approaching 50 million, say they are Confucians when they are asked their religious affiliation.[1] Moreover, there is much about traditional Confucianism that is no longer relevant in contemporary Korea. Koreans no longer need to memorize the Confucian Classics or pay much attention to debates over the relationship of *li* and *ki* to the Four Fonts and the Seven Emotions. Nor does the government in Seoul need to promote official Confucian rituals, except as cultural heritage. So why do some Koreans brag about the importance of Confucianism in contemporary Korean culture?

To determine the actual role of Confucianism in contemporary Korea, we need first to define what we mean by "Confucianism," beginning

1 National Statistical Office, 2005 *Census in'gu chut'aek ch'ongchosa: chŏpsu chipgye kyŏlgwa [in'gu pumun]* [the broad results from the 2005 census of the population and housing: The results of the compilation of the overall totals, population section], Seoul: T'onggyech'ŏng, 2006, p. 32.

with Confucianism during the Chosŏn dynasty. What are we referring to when we talk about Confucianism, or when we describe something as Confucian? After we have come up with a definition of Confucianism, then we can ask what, if any, elements of Chosŏn dynasty Confucianism are still visible and relevant in Korea today, over a century after the fall of the Chosŏn dynasty.

DEFINING CONFUCIANISM

Let's begin by noting that traditional Confucianism embraces a family of many mutually-reinforcing components. The label "Confucianism" is applied to a particular metaphysical philosophy, to a particular political philosophy, to a particular type of social structure, to a particular approach to cultural production, to particular types of rituals, and to particular types of moral rhetoric. Let's flesh out those six categories one by one.

1) First of all, when we put "Neo" in front of "Confucianism," we are talking about the metaphysical system that dominated intellectual discourse during the Chosŏn dynasty. Neo-Confucianism provided a comprehensive nontheistic worldview, one that didn't clearly distinguish between the material and the spiritual but instead distinguished between *ki* (dynamic matter-energy) and *li* (the patterns of appropriate interaction within the realm of *li* and *ki*), both of which are inseparable from the world in which we spend our everyday lives. Because of the core role played by li, Neo-Confucianism assumes a moral metaphysics in which the "is" and the "ought" collapse into one, such that when the "is" is not as it should be, when something appears to be going wrong in the natural world, the assumption is that there is a problem with the "ought" as well

(i.e., someone important has not behaved properly. Moreover, human beings and other things are defined not just in terms of what they are but also in terms of what they should be and do. In other words, in the Neo-Confucian universe nothing truly is unless it is what it should be. Because of this joining of the "is" and the "ought," Neo-Confucian philosophers assumed that human beings were born virtuous (The "ought to be" of a human being was part of what a human being was). However, they also recognized that education was necessary for people to maintain their original good nature. This led to moralistic education, intended more to cultivate a moral character than teach facts or skills.

The Neo-Confucian universe was not a universe in which there is a sharp division between humankind and nature, though human beings were clearly seen as the supreme element in the natural world, and nature was seen as existing for the use of human beings. Moreover, human beings were supposed to live in harmony with nature (hence the popularity of geomancy), even when they did not see nature as having value in its own right but only valuable in as much it was a part of the cosmic network of which human beings were also a part.

In a broad sense, this is an ecological philosophy, if ecology is understand as referring to more than the understanding of how natural objects depend on each other but also to how natural objects, including human beings, should interact with each other. In other words, Neo Confucianism treats human beings as part of the natural environment, albeit the most important part, so in that sense Confucian can be described as "ecological" in orientation. Nevertheless, the relationship between Confucianism and the Korean traditional ecological science par excellence, geomancy, was somewhat ambiguous. As Yoon Hong-Key has noted in a recent book, Confucianism both supported geomancy and criticized it. A filial son should try to find a geomantically auspicious site to bury parents, but should not let a good burial site obviate the need for virtuous behavior.[2]

2) Second, we can talk about a Confucian social vision. Confucianism assumed a social hierarchy defined by both mutual responsibilities and differences in status. The hereditary nature of the social hierarchy during the Chosŏn was not Confucian, but the assumption that those who work with their minds and have a broad "liberal arts" education are superior to those who have technical expertise or work with their hands is Confucian. This is one reason Confucians preferred a broad education that did not provide much in the way of specific skills, other than skill at writing and reading Classical Chinese.

Equally genuinely Confucian is the patriarchal assumption that there is a sharp division of labor between men and women, and that men should dominate the public sphere. This is probably one of the reasons Confucianism has a negative image in many quarters today. Women, for obvious reasons, don't like being told that men should make all the important decisions. Moreover, many men today have recognized that it hurts society overall when half the adults in that society are denied the right to play a meaningful public role.

3) Third, we often use "Confucian" to label the dominant political philosophy of the Chosŏn dynasty. Confucian political philosophy privileged a monarchy in which a king governed with the assistance of Confucian-trained officials, and promoted a political culture in which both the military and the commercial sector were not highly valued. Also,

2 Yoon, Hong-Key, *The Culture of Fengshui in Korea: An Exploration of East Asian Geomancy* (Lanham, MD: Lexington Books, 2006), pp. 201–213.

under Confucian political philosophy, Korea accepted a subordinate role within the Sino-centric world order.

Moreover, in a sharp departure from contemporary democratic political theory, Confucian political philosophy leaves no room for a "loyal opposition." In Confucianism, by definition the policy of the ruling group at the time is the only policy that is based on the good of the entire country overall. Anyone who opposes that policy is therefore trying to benefit only a segment of the national community at the expense of the rest. By definition, that is selfish and therefore immoral. This is why the term we use now for "political party" is usually best translated as "faction" in a Chosŏn dynasty context.

4) Fourth, we also use "Confucian" to distinguish the cultural ideals of the Chosŏn dynasty from the way we think culturally today. In Confucian culture, nonfiction prose was valued over fiction, and poetry was valued over prose, or at least considered as essential as prose. Moreover, philosophy and history ranked over other subjects.

In the arts, muted colours were supposed to be used in paintings, sculpture was not highly valued, and music was supposed to calm the emotions, not excite them. In other words, cultural products were supposed to serve a moral purpose, at least by calming the mind in order to make clear selfless thinking more likely. Moreover, cultural products should be didactic and edifying, stimulating us how to behave properly.

5) Fifth, "Confucianism" also refers to a ritual system, in which the ritual hegemony of the state was employed to privilege Confucian rituals over shamanic, Buddhist, and, later, Christian rituals. What were these Confucian rituals? They were family rituals to honor ancestors, some Confucian village rituals, rituals to honor clan ancestors and revered Confucian scholars from past generations, and state rituals such as those

used to greet an envoy from China, those used to signal the start of the agricultural season (sajik), those used to pray for rain, and so. Non-Confucian rituals, unless the government authorized them, were labeled ŭmsa, "illicit rituals" or "licentious rituals."[3]

6) Finally, "Confucianism" is a label applied to an ethical system in which the individual was not just subordinated to the group; the individual was defined in terms of the various roles he or she played in society. The primary ethical values were those that were supposed to prevail in the five relationships (ruler-subject, parent-child, husband-wife, elder brother-younger brother, and friend-friend), as well as the broader virtues of sincerity/integrity and benevolence. In addition, this ethical system required external behavior to conform to the rules of propriety, which demanded that people be treated differently, in accordance with their social status. The primary "sin" in this ethical system was selfishness, a refusal to play one's assigned role in society. Since our emotions often lead us to think of ourselves first, Confucian ethics is also characterized by the distrust of many basic human emotions.

The Confucian ethical system was anthropocentric, in that morality is defined in terms of interactions within the human community rather than interactions between human beings and gods or God. The primary virtues in Confucianism were those virtues that were believed to keep society operating harmoniously. Those virtues, all seen as manifestations of selflessness, include trust/faithfulness, integrity (doing what you are

---

[3] For an example of how the ŭmsa concept was employed, see my "Shamans, Catholics, and Chŏng Yagyong: Tasan's defense of the ritual hegemony of the Confucian state," *Tasanhak* 15,(December, 2009), 139–79. Also see Boudewijn Walraven, "Confucians and Shamans," Cahiers d'Extréme-Asie, 6 (191–92), pp. 21–44.

supposed to do), and propriety (treating others as you should treat them), as well as the essential interpersonal virtues of filial piety, loyalty, and benevolence.

THE RETREAT OF CONFUCIAN METAPHYSICS, POLITICS, SOCIETY, AND CULTURE.

How much of the traditional Confucian way of thinking survives in South Korea today? (I will ignore North Korea in this presentation, since it has gone in a totally different direction since 1945 and, though it is clear that he Confucian legacy is still strong in the DPRK, that legacy operates quite differently north of the DMZ and would require a totally different paper to adequately discuss it.)

First of all, Neo-Confucian metaphysics, the core of Confucianism in the Chosŏn dynasty, is dead in Korea. I know of no respectable philosophers in Korea today who are trying to keep *li/ki* metaphysics alive as a viable philosophy. *Li* and *ki* lack the clear, precise definitions that philosophers prefer for key philosophical terms today. There have been prominent philosophers in Hong Kong (and Boston!) who have worked to maintain philosophical relevance for Confucianism, but they have primarily focused on its ethical foundations.[4] There are no philosophers

---

4 Robert Neville, *Boston Confucianism: Portable Tradition in the Late-Modern World* (Albany: State University of New York Press, 2000; Lauren Pfister, "The Different Faces of Contemporary Religious Confucianism: An Account of the Diverse Approaches of Some Major Twentieth Century Chinese Confucian Scholars," *Journal of Chinese Philosophy* 22. (1995), pp.

doing even that in Korea that I am aware of. Most professors who teach Confucianism in Korean universities are teaching the history of philosophy. They teach Confucianism as an object to be studied, not something to be wrestled with, and applied to, in the modern world. Those few who use Confucian concepts and terminology when they do philosophy graft Confucianism onto a non-Confucian substrata, since philosophy is now conceived in line with the Western notion of philosophy as the search for truth rather than in the traditional sense of a search for the best way to live a moral life. So, if we are looking for someone in modern Korea who is a true Confucian philosopher, we won't find him.[5]

Moreover, one of the core notions in Confucian philosophy even before Neo-Confucianism, the notion that human beings are innately virtuous, has been losing ground in recent decades. According to Gallup Korea, in 1984 59.8% of South Koreans believed that human beings were born virtuous. Only 45.7% affirmed such a proposition in 2004 when Gallup asked Koreans again if they thought human nature was originally good or evil. Over those same two decades, the percentage of those who thought human nature was a mixture of good and evil rose from 14.4% to 31.4%.[6]

5–80.

5 ee the survey in Ch'oe Yŏngsŏng, *Han'guk yuhak sasangsa, vol. V: Kŭn. hyŏndae p'yŏn* [The history of Korean Confucian thought: the modern and contemporary period] (Seoul: Asea munhwasa, 1997).

6 Gallup Korea, *Han'gugin ŭi chonggyo wa chonggyo ŭisik: '84nyŏn, '89nyŏn, '97nyŏn, '04nyŏn chosa kyŏlgwarŭl pigyohan chonggyo yŏn'gusŏ* [The religion and religious attitudes of Koreans: a study of religion based on a comparison of survey results from 1984, 1989, 1997, and 2004] (Seoul: Gallup Korea, 2004), p. 101.

Geomancy, another idea often associated with Confucianism, has also begun to lose popularity. Though Gallup Korea found in 2004 that 55.7% of Koreans said that they believed that children and grandchildren would prosper if their immediate ancestors were buried in a "myŏngdang," a geomatically auspicious spot, an increase over the 48.3% who affirmed that proposition in 1984, at the same time the rate of cremation in Korea increased dramatically between 1970 to 2009 from 10.7% to 65%. Since cremation undermines the alleged effectiveness of geomancy, which assumed that prosperity-enhancing energy moved through the ancestor's bones into the living bodies of their descendants, this rise in the cremation rate is another clear sign that geomancy, and the Confucianism it is associated with, no longer has the important role in beliefs and values it once enjoyed.[7]

Now that we have established that the assumptions behind Confucian philosophy are not as powerful as they once were, what about the social hierarchy? Is it still dominated by Confucian assumptions about who should outrank whom?

Every society has a social hierarchy, and modern Korea is no exception. However, the social hierarchy is no longer defined by the government, nor is it completely defined by Confucian criteria. Education is still important-graduating from the law school at SNU still puts you on the top run of the social ladder, but now you may be joined by medical school grads, business school grads, or engineering school grads, people who would not have ranked high under the old Confucian criteria. So the

---

7 "Cremation Rate Doubles Over Past Decade," The Chosun Ilbo, Sept. 17, 2010 (accessed at http://english.chosun.com/site/data/html_dir/2010/09/17/2010091700 688.html July 3, 2011).

traditional Confucian respect for education remains, but the content of the education that is respected has changed dramatically.

Moreover, the traditional Confucian division of social roles according to gender is fading away. We can see more and more evidence of equal opportunities for women, evident in the growing percentage of women students in the best universities and in the work force. We can also see those changes in public opinion surveys. In 1995, and when the question was asked again in 2005, "eight out of ten respondents agreed with the statement that both the husband and the wife should contribute to household income."[8] Nevertheless, the patriarchy is still strong in Korea, as is clear when we note the lack of women in the Christian pulpits of Korea as well as the gender makeup of the professoriate in both public and private universities.[9] However, upper-class women are no longer confined to their homes, as they were in Confucian Korean.[10]

It is true that there is still a lot of emphasis on the family in Korea, but that can be found in many societies. Many non-Confucian societies, such as in Italy and in Israel, also place a lot of emphasis on the family, so we can't see the strong family orientation of Korea as necessarily a

---

8 Eun Ki-soo, "Family values changing—but still conservative," Kim Kyong-dong, ed *Social Change in Korea* (Seoul: Jimoondang, 2008), p. 149.

9 Namhee Kim, Hea Jun Yoon, Gary N. McLean, "Policy Efforts to increase women faculty in Korea: reactions and changes at universities," *Asia Pacific Education Review* 11. (2010), pp. 285–299.

10 For a nuanced discussion of recent changes in the changes in attitudes toward the proper roles for women in society, see Minja Kim Choe, "Modernization, gender roles, and marriage behavior in South Korea," Chang Yun-Shik and Steven Hugh Lee, *Transformations in Twentieth Century Korea* (New York: Routledge, 2006), pp. 291–309. The pace of change appears to have quickened since that chapter was written.

manifestation of Confucian influence. However, we can see a lingering legacy of Confucianism on how proper family roles are conceived. In 1984, 1989, 1997, and 2004, Gallup Korea asked Koreans three questions which can be interpreted as related to the traditional Confucian expectations for family dynamics. The responses, and how they changed over time, can provide some insight into the role of Confucian beliefs and values in Korea today.

When Gallup asked, "Is it necessary for the adult male in the household to be in charge in order to have an orderly family life?" almost 70% answered "yes" in 1984. That figure declined to 51.6% in 2005. I suspect 51.6% is probably a higher rate of assent than a similar question would elicit in most of North America, but it also shows that Confucian influence is not as strong as it was even 25 years ago.

Gallup also asked, "Should the roles of the males and the females in the family be clearly distinguished?" We see an even sharper decline in response to that question than we did to the previous question. In 1984, almost 73% of Koreans answered that question in the affirmative, but in 2004, only 39.4% did so, while 58.8% said no. Clearly the sharp lines Confucianism drew between male and female responsibilities in the family are now blurring.

We can also see a decline in the traditional Confucianism emphasis on children serving their parents. That decline apparently was well under way even before Gallup began asking questions about filial piety and familial obedience. In 1984, 47.8% of Koreans said that sons and daughters should do what their parents tell them to do rather than do what they themselves want to do. Almost the same percentage 47.2% disagreed. In 2004, however, only a little more than a third of all Koreans (35.9%) said they agreed with that statement, while well over half, 59.6%, said that sons and daughters (I assume they are talking about adult sons and daughters here the Korean term is simply chasik) should be free to do what they think best for themselves.[11]

In the 40 years I have been coming to Korea, I have seen with my own eyes signs of the decline in the traditional Confucian authority for parents over children. In the 1970s, semi-arranged marriages were not at all unusual. Few well-educated young Koreans would dare to marry some-one their parents did not approve of. And, in not a few cases, the parents of the prospective bride and groom would actually meet first to talk about marriage arrangements before the future couple were allowed to get to know each other well. Slowly, however, I began to see groups of both parents and children meeting in tearooms or hotel lobbies to discuss a possible marriage. At first, it appeared that the respective parents did most of the talking while the future bride and groom looked on. Later, I noticed the young people were doing more of the talking while their parents looked on. Now I see young men and women meeting with no parents in sight, and I understand that it is not at all unusual these days for a young man or woman to tell parents whom they plan to marry, rather than asking for the parents to arrange a marriage. Clearly, the traditional Confucian notion that marriage is a family rather than an individual decision is fading away.

This move away from the traditional Confucian respect for parental authority is particularly evident among those born after 1980. One study of adolescents in 17 Asia-Pacific countries found that "younger generations of Koreans are most reluctant in accepting Confucian values...

---

11 These figures can be found in Gallup Korea, *Han'gugin ŭi chonggyo wa chonggyo ŭisik*, 2004, p. 84.

Only 13 percent of the Korean sample respected adults very much... Most of Korea's younger generations do not adhere to Confucian values."[12]

A third area in which we have seen a rapid decline in Confucian influence is government and politics. Obviously, there is no longer a Confucian government in the ROK. There is no king in South Korea, nor are top government officials chosen on the basis of their performance on exams testing their knowledge of Confucian texts. Moreover, Korea no longer is formally subordinate to any other country. Even the term for that subordination, *sadae*, now has negative overtones it did not have before the 20th century. And, though this change took a while, it is now possible to be an active member of an opposition political party without being seen as immoral.

In addition, as the Confucian assumption that human being are innately virtuous has lost ground, its influence over Korean expectations of how their political leaders are likely to behave has also receded. In its place has emerged a recognition that human beings, even leaders of the government, will act to enhance their own self-interest. To offset this tendency, Korea now has a government with checks and balances, something it did not have institutionally during the Chosŏn dynasty.

Moreover, women now can stand on the public stage. Korea still lags behind many countries in the percentage of elected officials who are female, but there are a lot more women officials now than there were during the Chosŏn dynasty, or even just two decades ago. In 1992, only

---

12 Yang Jonghae, "Globalization and value change in Korea, with a special emphasis on the impact of the recent economic crisis and neoliberal reform on the Confucian value system," Chang Yun-Shik, Hyun-Ho Seok, and Donald L. Baker, ed. *Korea Confronts Globalization* (New York: Routledge, 2009), p. 201.

1% of National Assembly members were women. 13% of those elected to the National Assembly in 2004 were women.[13] It is even possible that the next president of the ROK could be a woman, which would put Korea ahead of the United States.

Even though we still sometimes hear Confucian rhetoric from government leaders (more on that later), it would not be accurate to describe the government and politics of South Korea today as a Confucian government. First of all, almost half of the presidents of the ROK, and three out of the last four, have been Christians. None of them have been a self-professed Confucian. Second, we have seen two peaceful transfers of power from one party to another over the 15 years, something unthinkable as recently as 30 years ago. Though during the Chosŏn dynasty factions occasionally dropped out of power for a few years and then regained power later, such shifts in control of the bureaucracy were not as smooth as we saw in 1998 and 2008. In fact, in the Chosŏn dynasty, they usually involved executions, since, in the Confucian worldview, political differences were moral differences. And, of course, the head of state remained in the same family for five centuries when Confucianism reigned over Korea, something that is unthinkable today on this side of the DMZ.

Nevertheless, it would not be correct to say that all Confucian influence on Korea's political culture has been eradicated.[14] A study of South

---

13 Lee On-jook, "More gender equality, but women still held back," *Social Change in Korea*, p. 170.

14 For a statistical analysis of the influence of Confucian beliefs and values on political culture in Korea, see Kwang Yeong Shin and Chulhee Chung, "Confucian Tradition and democracy in South Korea," paper presented at the second Biennial Conference of Korean Studies Association in

Korean political attitudes in the 1990s, when the ROK finally became a true political democracy, revealed "authentic supporters of democratic government comprised only 60 percent of the Korean population."[15] A major reason why Korea still has many people who would choose an efficient authoritarian government over a less efficient democratic one may be that the notion of the autonomous individual, endowed with certain rights on which a government should not infringe, was not part of Korea's Confucian heritage. Instead, Confucianism encouraged people to think of themselves as part of a community, and to put the greater good of that community ahead of their own personal self-interest. As one keen observer argued just a few years ago, "The lack of a solid legal base for the rights of the individual is not simply due to the authoritarian regimes in Korea that have suppressed those rights. The collective ethos is too strong to make room for them[...] Confucianism is still very much alive."[16]

The influence of Confucianism continues to linger in another feature of contemporary Korean life as well: culture. However, the traces of that influence have grown quite faint. Fiction is no longer disdained. Authors of short stories and novels now share the literary limelight with poets. Koreans still like to read history and philosophy (witness the popularity of Do-ol Kim Young-Oak in recent years), although the range of what Koreans consider respectable reading has greatly expanded, as any visit to

---

Australasia, held at Monash University in Melbourne, Australia, in 2001. Available at http://arts.monash.edu.au/korean/ksaa/conference/04chulheechungkwangyeongshin.pdf, Accessed July 8, 2011.

15 Shin, Doh C., *Mass Politics and Culture in Democratizing Korea* (Cambridge: Cambridge University Press, 1999), p. 75.

16 Kim, Uchang, "Confucianism, democracy, and the individual in Korean Modernization," *Transformations in Twentieth Century Korea*, p. 231.

a branch of the Kyobo bookstore chain will confirm. A visit to any art gallery in modern Seoul will confirm that bright colors have replaced the muted colors that were preferred in traditional landscape paintings, and that landscapes are no longer the primary subject of a painter's brush. And the quiet, slow Confucian music of old has been almost completely replaced by Western orchestral music, Christian hymns, and the loud, fast-paced music of K-pop. The most visible evidence of a continuing presence of Confucian culture in contemporary Korea is the ritual music used in a few Confucians rituals that have been preserved as part of Korea's cultural heritage. Otherwise, the culture of contemporary Korea is thoroughly non-Confucian.

SURVIVING SIGNS OF KOREA'S CONFUCIAN PAST

Since there doesn't appear to be much Confucian influence on philosophy, government, social status, and culture in Korea today, we need to ask the question: what exactly is the basis for the claim that opened this paper, that Korea is today the most Confucian country on earth? The answer lies in the pervasiveness in modern South Korea of rhetoric and ritual rooted in Confucianism.

In South Korea today Confucian ethical terms, such as sincerity, filial piety, loyalty, and propriety, continue to play a prominent role in discussions of proper human behavior. Even Christians wield Confucian ethical rhetoric. For example, an evangelical church in Inchŏn, the Inchŏn

Full Gospel Church, has established a Graduate School of Filial Piety.[17] In addition, a prominent Methodist theologian, Yun Sung-Bum (1916–1980), tried in the 1970s to promote a theology that would give a central role to the Confucian concept of sincerity.[18] Moreover, in recent years, institutes have emerged in rural areas to teach the younger generations the traditional Confucian virtues. Once such institute, located near Yŏngju in Kangwŏn province, is called the "Han'guk Sŏnbi munhwa suryŏnwŏn" [the institute for training in the culture of Korean Confucian scholars), and advertises on its web site that it is dedicated to teaching behavioral norms appropriate for human beings (i.e, traditional Confucian virtues and etiquette).[19] Of all the Confucian virtues, it is hyo, filial peity, that gets the most attention today. There is even a Buddhist temple not far from Seoul, Yongju-sa, with a hall on its grounds called the "Institute for teaching filial action" [Hyohaeng kyuyukwŏn] as well as a Museum of Filial Behavior [Hyohaeng Pangmulgwan].[20]

The government, even though it is certainly not a Confucian government, also embraces Confucian moral rhetoric.[21] It is not unusual

---

17 http://www.hyo.ac.kr/Accessed April 17, 2011.

18 Yun Sŏngbŏm, "Han'gukchŏk sinhak: ilmyŏng sŏng ŭi sinhak" [Korean-style theology: a theology focused on the word "sincerity"] Kidokkyo sasang no. 150 (November, 1970), pp. 134–151.

19 http://www.sunbi.info/

20 http://www.yongjoosa.or.kr/Accessed July 3, 2011.

21 For an interesting discussion of government use of Confucian ethical rhetoric to distinguish Korean culture from other cultures, see Hee-jung Kwon, "Making a Confucian country: Cultural discourses and representations of Confucian culture in South Korea," paper presented at the second Biennial Conference of Korean Studies Association in Australasia, held at Monash University in Melbourne, Australia, in 2001.

for government leaders and politicians to accuse those who oppose their policies, including the North Korean government, of being "insincere."[22] Moreover, one of the leading politicians in South Korea's ruling party today led a campaign in the 1970s to revive the "traditional Korean virtues" of loyalty, filial piety, and propriety. It is worth taking a look at what Park Geun Hye (1952–), the daughter of Park Chung Hee, the man who is often given credit for modernizing the Korean economy, had to say three decades ago about those "traditional Korean virtues."

At that time, Park Geun Hye was the head of the "New Spirit Movement," the cultural counterpart to the New Village Movement intended to get Koreans working together to build a modern Korean economy. She traveled around Korea giving speeches about the traditional virtues she believed Koreans needed to preserve and cultivate even as they transformed the material world around them. She described that "New Spirit Movement" as "dedicated to bringing into flower the traditional virtues of chung (loyalty), and hyo (filial piety)."[23] Promoting loyalty is understandable. All governments around the world want those they govern to be loyal to them. But filial piety, in most countries, is not usually considered a prime concern of the government. That fact that the New Spirit Movement gave filial piety as much emphasis as it gave loyalty suggests that Confucian moral rhetoric still resonated with Koreans in the

---

That paper is available at http://arts.monash.edu.au/korean/ksaa/conference/05heejungkwon.pdf. Accessed July 8, 2011.

22 For a typical example, see "NK asked for rice during contact for possible summit," Korean Times March 9, 2011 (accessed July 3, 2011, at http://www.koreatimes.co.kr/www/news/nation/2011/03/1Ja13_82757.html).

23 Park, Keun Hae, *The New Spirit Movement* (Seoul: Naeway Business Journal and Korea Herald, 1979), p. 15.

1970s, and also that the government of that day accepted the traditional Confucian notion that it is the duty of a government to promote the moral character of those it rules over.

It is hard to imagine a major political figure in a society without a Confucian heritage saying, as Park did in the 1970s, "A society where everyone practices hyo is a wholesome society characterized by the overflow of tender human feelings. In other words, hyo is the basis of a vibrant humanity, the first step toward acquiring all the virtues which mark a fully human man."[24] Nor would a major political figure in a non-Confucian society also proclaim the importance of propriety (ye). Yet Park did exactly just that. She said, "I believe that the spirit of chung and hyo can be sublimated and perfected by making Korea once again the nation of eastern proprieties."[25] In order to ensure her audience understood how important she thought the traditional Confucian virtues were, she insisted, "Self-help, diligence, and cooperation have been the key to Korea's rapid rise from rags to riches. We must now concentrate on making spiritual maturity a reality, and this will be achieved through the New Spirit based on chung and hyo."[26] I doubt Park will express those exact sentiments in any political speeches she may make in a possible presidential campaign in the near future. They would appear a little too old-fashioned to the ears of many potential voters, especially young voters. However, I also doubt that she would be embarrassed if someone during that campaign reminded her of those comments. After all, Confucian tradition is still strong enough in Korea that talking about the need for chung, hyo, and ye would not

---

24 Ibid. p. 22.

25 Ibid. p. 28.

26 Ibid. p. 26.

seem all that strange. Moreover, her call three decades ago for a revival of a concern for propriety in Korea was echoed just a few years ago by Hahm Chaibong, then a professor of political science at Yonsei University.[27]

It is when we move beyond ethical rhetoric to the realm of ritual that we see the strongest signs of continuing Confucian tradition in Korea. Obviously, the government of modern Korea does not need to legitimize itself by having the president or members of his cabinet officiate at state-sponsored Confucian rituals. The Altar to Heaven (Wŏn'gudan) erected by King Kojong at the end of the 19th century, and which sits today in front of the Chosŏn hotel in downtown Seoul, may have been restored in recent years, but I haven't heard of President Lee Myung-bak going there to offer ritual homage to heaven. There are still some large Confucian rituals performed in the capital city these days. The Sŏkchŏn ritual on the grounds of the Confucian shrine at Sŏngkyunkwan University, the ritual celebration of Kaech'ŏnjŏl in Sajik Park (where the old altar to the spirits of land and grains remains), and the rituals honoring the spirits of the kings and queens of the Chosŏn dynasty, as well as rituals at various royal tombs outside of Seoul, are held regularly. However, except by the small remnant of older men who still take Confucianism seriously, those rituals are seen primarily as cultural performances, reminding Koreans today of their Confucian past but having no real religious significance today.[28]

Nevertheless, Korea still has many traditional Confucian shrines/

---

27 Hahm Chaibong, "Constitutionalism, Confucian Civic Virtue, and Ritual Propriety," Daniel A. Bell and Hahm Chaibong, ed *Confucianism for the Modern World* (Cambridge, UK: Cambridge University Press, 2003).

28 For more on those rituals, see National Folk Museum, ed, *Han'guk ŭi chesa* [Korea's Sacrificial Rites] (Seoul: National Folklore Museum, 2003).

academies scattered about the countryside. The number of those hyanggyo has remained steady at 232 for several decades.[29] They no longer serve the educational purpose they served during the Chosŏn dynasty. And the people who perform rituals there are fewer in number every year. However, they remain, giving Korea the highest ratio of Confucians shrines to population of any country in the world, more than China, more than Japan, and, I believe, more than Taiwan. When I have visited some of those hyanggyo, I have often found their gates locked. However, I could tell by looking over the wall that they are being maintained. Sometimes I have found some people inside, usually old men talking or playing cards. It was clear to me that the hyanggyo still was a real part of their lives, though the role those hyanggyo played in their lives was much reduced from the role they played in the lives of their ancestors.[30]

We need to turn to the family to find the strongest evidence of the continuing strength of the legacy of Confucianism. Confucian rituals are still very important in Korean family life. Though the traditional rituals for honoring parents and grandparents have been greatly simplified in recent decades, and the number of such rituals performed over a given year has been greatly reduced, most Koreans still appear to feel the need to

---

29 See a list of extant hyanggyo in Han'guk chonggyo sahoe yŏn'guso, ed. *Han'guk chonggyo yŏn'gam* [Yearbook of Religion in Korea] (Seoul: Korea Halimwŏn, 1993), pp. 212–251.

30 On Hyanggyo today, see Kim Hoil, *Han'guk ŭi hyanggyo* [The Confucians shrines of Korea] (Seoul: Taewŏnsa, 2000). For the formal Confucian institutions supporting those hyanggyo, see Km Changt'ae, "Hyŏndae Han'guk yugyo ŭi pyŏndong kwa hyŏnhwang chosa" [An investigation of the current situation of Confucianism in Korea and how it has changed], *Han'guk hyŏndae ŭi yugyo munhwa* [Confucian culture in contemporary Korea] (Seoul: Seoul National University Press, 1999),.

display their filial piety, their love and respect for those who gave them life, with ritual. Moreover, unlike in Japan, where Buddhist ancestor rites are the norm, even the modified ancestor memorial rites in Korea still shows signs of their Confucian origin. In most cases, food is still prepared for the ancestors and a few ritual words are said. As well, the descendants bow to the spirits of their ancestors. It has been estimated that around 90% of Koreans engage in ritual displays of filial piety.[31] However, only about 60% of Koreans try to stay close to the traditional Confucian form of ritual homage to ancestors.[32] The remaining 30%, mostly Christians, refrain from elements of the traditional ritual, showing as bowing before a spirit tablet or offering food to the dead, that they have religious objections to. Nevertheless, the need in Korea to engage in such rituals is so strong that even Christians, who are uncomfortable bowing to spirits, even spirits of departed parents and grandparents, have created their own versions of the traditional Confucian mourning rites.[33]

Therefore it is not an exaggeration to point out that, although almost 30% of South Koreans say they are Christians and another 23% say they are

---

31 Clark Sorensen and Sung-Chul Kim, "Filial Piety in Contemporary Urban Southeast Korea: Practices and Discourses," Charlotte Ikels, ed. *Filial Piety: Practice and Discourse in Contemporary East Asia* (Stanford, California: Stanford University Press, 2004), p. 173.

32 Moon Ok-pyo, "Ancestors Becoming Children of God: Ritual Clashes between Confucian Tradition and Christianity in Contemporary Korea," *Korea Journal* 38:3 (Autumn, 1998), p. 152.

33 Robert E. Buswell, Jr, ed. *Religions of Korea in Practice* (Princeton, New Jersey: Princeton University Press, 2007), pp. 383–82, 434–445; James Grayson, "Ch'udo yebae: A Case Study in the Early Emplantation of Protestant Christianity in Korea', *Journal of Asian Studies*, v. 68 (2009), no. 2, pp. 413–434.

Buddhists, Confucian rhetoric and Confucian ritual both remain central to life in contemporary South Korea.[34] If that is the case, are Confucian moral rhetoric and Confucian family rituals all that Confucianism can offer to modern Koreans? Is there anything else worth keeping from the Confucian tradition that may be relevant in the modern world?

CONCLUSION

I would like to close by suggesting that there still is much that the Confucian way of looking at the world and at society can offer us if we want to construct a more cooperative and harmonious society. First of all, we can draw on the Confucian ethical vocabulary and Confucian rituals that retain meaning today to remind us that human beings are not totally independent and isolated from either the people or the nature that surrounds us. We can revive the Confucian notion of human beings as defined by who and what they interact with, and how they act and interact. We can learn from this Confucian definition of a human being as primarily a social being, defined more by the roles we play in society at large than by our own personal wants and needs, to promote an ethical philosophy that encourages people to put the needs of their community ahead of any private benefit. At the same time, we can adapt Confucian ideas and values to the modern world so that placing the welfare of the community ahead of private benefit does not lead to oppression of women, the uneducated, and other individuals but instead creates an environment

---

[34] National Statistical Office, *2005 Census*, p. 32.

in which all individuals can work together to improve their society, their environment, and their own personal lives. In other words, we can draw on Confucian rhetoric, and some of the philosophical underpinnings of that rhetoric, to foster a sort of "human ecology." By human ecology, I mean recognition that we are not isolated individuals and moreover can be truly human only when we cooperate with our fellow human beings. A stress on our dependence on other human beings for our very existence can combine with an equal stress on our dependence on nature for our existence as human beings, and as a human community, to create a stronger ecological sensitivity. Given the on-going degradation of the environment and the growing interpersonal stress caused by too many people living too close together, such an ecological sensitivity may not only be desirable, it may be essential.

Donald Baker(dbaker@interchange.ubc.ca) *is professor British Columbia University, Canada.*

ECOLOGISM AND CONFUCIAN PRO-LIFE-ISM

By Yoo kwon jong (Yu Kwŏn-jong)

1. INTRODUCTION

The general perception is that the level of environmental destruction faced by mankind has worsened in the twenty-first century. While this may be the result of the emergence of more serious problems, it may also have a lot to do with the expansion and intensification of the awareness of the destruction that has been wrought on the environment. Truth be told, there has been a general increase in the level of awareness of the serious destruction and damage that has been caused to the natural environment. What's more, the observation that the seemingly endless onslaught of natural disasters is closely related to the damage and destruction of nature has also become prevalent within society. The observation of such phenomena has also produced the perception that a vicious feedback cycle has been formed between nature and humans. How much worse will such phenomena become? Can humans survive these phenomena? In this regard, the general level of uncertainty experienced by humans can be perceived as the root cause of the various doomsday scenarios and prophecies involving environmental disasters that have sprung up.

In addition to its warped relationship with the natural environment, humans also face another threat to its survival in the form of its own conflicts. Calamities such as the confrontation between the United States and terrorist groups in the Arabic world, the threat of nuclear weapons, and nuclear plant explosions, are factors that may very well threaten the safety of mankind in the future. The well-being of humanity can only be guaranteed when humankind adopts a truly peaceful lifestyle. As such, the improvement of the relationships between nature and humans, and between humans themselves, represents another important task. The realization that the environmental crisis is actually closely related to human relations has led to the spotlight being directed toward humans and society. The recently emerged fields of social and human ecology can be regarded as the result of these perceptions.[1]

The hands-on activities designed to protect natural ecosystems and normalize the human ecosystem have progressed to become the modern ecologism rooted in ecology. The ecologism of today has become a key theme in various discourses within academic fields such as literature, sociology, and philosophy. Ecologism has also been criticized from various angles. Thus, although ecologism has become a popular theme in the contemporary era, there remains much room for it be modified and supplemented. In particular, the criticism that ecologism, which is based on esoteric and non-empirical factors, has been used in discourses that appeal to emotion rather than reason[2] highlights the necessity, in order for

---

1 Eco-feminism emerged based on similar perceptions toward the relationship between man and woman in order to identify the fundamental problems in the man-centered historical contexts and to correct these problems.

2 Pak Hyŏnjŏng, "Hans Magnus Enzensberge ŭi saengt'aejuŭi pip'an [Hans

it to actually become a realistic alternative, to conduct many discussions and supplement ecologism.

As such, if we accept the goals or original objectives of ecologism, then it becomes necessary to carry out discussions on means to complement and further develop ecologism. The author of the present study has observed the emergence of a trend in Korea towards the positive acceptance of ecologism, and towards its combination with traditional philosophies in order to reinterpret such traditional thoughts as ecological thought or ecological philosophy. Some scholars have advanced the need to develop *ki*-based ecologism based on the traditional Asian notion of *ki/qi* (氣, energy or force) under which humans and nature are regarded as being one.[3] Others have regard Buddhism as the basis for a structure of ecological philosophy that moves beyond ecology, or what can be referred to as Buddhist ecological philosophy.[4] As far as Confucian thought is concerned, some have suggested that the environment-friendly or ecological ideas of Confucian scholars should be labeled as ecologism.[5] This trend should be seen as part of a wider attempt to introduce traditional philosophy to the discourses within the modern humanities.

Magnus Enzensberge's criticism of ecologism]," *Togil munhak* [German Literature] 116 (2010): 140–143.

3 Han Myŏnhŭi, "Tongasia ki-saengt'aejuŭi munhwa wa saengmyŏng chonjung [The Qi of East Asia-ecological culture and respect for life]," http://www.oikozoe.or.kr/bbs/read.cgi?board=data&y_number=26 (accessed May 29, 2011).

4 Kim Chonguk, *Pulgyo saengt'ae ch'ŏlhak* [Buddhist ecological philosophy] Tongguk University Press, 2004.

5 Kim Uktong, *Han'guk ŭi noksaek munhwa* [The green culture of Korea] (Munye Publishing, 2000).

However, there is a need to carefully discuss this trend and phenomenon from the standpoint of critical opinions of ecologism.

Criticism of ecologism can be connected to the criticism of ecological thought as a whole. The following can be regarded as some of the most common criticisms of ecologism: First, ecologism is irrational and unreasonable.[6] Second, there are no grounds from either a natural science or ecological standpoint to support claims of impending environmental doom. Third, ecologism, which has become a political ideology, boasts no real authenticity.[7] These criticisms have emerged as part of the concerns that the rise of ecologism as a political ideology has resulted in its use to obtain economic and political advantages that have no relation with actual ecological problems.

In addition, such criticisms have also paved the way for discussions that have raised fundamental questions regarding ecology or the ecological paradigm, and discussions on how such obstacles can be overcome. In other words, the establishment of ecology and the ecological paradigm that arose from the criticism of modern anthropocentrism also encompassed elements related to the movement beyond the modern philosophy of enlightenment, or the rationalism that stems from this philosophy of enlightenment. Thus, the expression of this will in the form of movement ecologism took the form of antipathy towards anthropocentric and

---

6 Hwang T'aeyŏn, "Kŭndae hamnisŏng inyŏm kwa hwan'gyŏng wigi ŭi hamnijŏk ihae [The ideology of modern rationality and the rational understanding of the environmental crisis]," *Konggan kwa sahoe* [Space and society] 9 (1997): 16–4.

7 Pak Hyŏnjŏng, "Hans Magnus Enzensberge ŭi saengt'aejuŭi pip'an [Hans Magnus Enzensberge's criticism of ecologism]," *Togil munhak* [German Literature] 116 (2010): 144–145.

rational-centered thought.[8] However, this trend leaned heavily towards irrationalism and esotericism. This has been identified as the core problem with ecologism. Even though ecologism may overcome the modern philosophy of enlightenment, it remains undesirable to refuse all the outcomes, be they negative or positive, wrought by modernity.[9] Therefore, many have suggested that ecologism should focus on eliminating the negative aspects of modern rationality and emphasizing the positive ones.

Under such circumstances, what method can be used to facilitate the advent of a recent matter of interest, namely the encounter between Confucianism and ecology or ecologism? The fact that the methods used to link traditional thought with ecology or ecologism in Korea have so far been less than perfect raises the necessity to conduct a more in-depth review of this process from an academic standpoint. To this end, this study conducts a comparison between Confucianism and ecologism, and also seeks to identify the correlation between the two. In addition, the structure of Confucian thought regarding nature and humans is also examined from the standpoint of the fundamental or ultimate goals of Confucianism, a process that is followed up by a review of whether such goals are comparable with those of ecologism. It is hoped that based on such an exercise, the elements of Confucianism which can help ecologism, and vice-versa, the aspects of ecologism that can help Confucianism, can

---

8 Kim Wŏnjung, "Taeji yulli ŭi an'gwa pak: in'gan chungsimjuŭi esŏ saengt'ae chungsimjuŭi ro ŭi chŏnhwan [Inside and outside land ethics: moving from anthropocentrism to eco-centrism]," *Hyŏndae yŏngŏ yŏngmunhak* [Modern English Literature] 54–1 (2010): 10–16.

9 Hwang T'aeyŏn, ibid.

be identified.[10]

2. THE LIMITATIONS OF THE ECOLOGISM DEBATE AND CRITICISM THEREOF

Regardless of the subject being examined, the criteria for criticism should always be established based on specific viewpoints and contexts. In the present study, ecologism is approached from the standpoint of Confucian pro-life-ism. The revision of ecologism from the standpoint of Confucian pro-life-ism has as its goal the identification of the valuable viewpoints and contexts of Confucianism. Confucian thought and tradition can not only be compared with ecologism in the fact that they both teach that human life can be sustainably maintained through a relationship with nature, but also possess the criteria with which to conduct a criticism of ecologism. That being the case, why is Confucianism equated herein with pro-life-ism, a notion that runs contrary to ecologism? Before answering this question, however, this study will focus on whether Confucianism can actually be regarded as pro-life-ism, and, if that is in fact the case, what pro-life-ism and its fundamental elements are.

Pro-life-ism, which is defined as one of the characteristics of Confucianism, is established herein as a response to ecologism. At the same time, it is a notion that emphasizes the characteristics of Confucian

---

10 For more on this kind of discussions, refer to Mary Evelyn Tucker and John Berthrong ed. *Confucianism and Ecology: The Interrelation of Heaven, Earth, and Humans* (Harvard University Center for the Study of World Religions Publications, 1998).

thought which can be used to overcome the limitations of the various forms of ecologism that have taken root in the current era. Confucian pro-life-ism differs from Paul Taylor's biocentrism,[11] which advocates the ethical attitude of respecting nature and individual life forms. This study defines such Confucian characteristics as pro-life-ism.

Fundamentally, Confucianism established the notion that all the life forms in the universe were governed by the principle of heaven and earth.[12] It set up a philosophical structure under which the life of humans and all the beings in the universe were linked together under one system.[13] Confucianism maintained that the extinction of individual life forms should not affect the permanent existence of the species, and as such, human life reached its highest value when it contributed to the perpetuity of the human species.[14] Confucianism stressed that humans, and in particular saints, played an essential role in maintaining the perpetuity of life. In accordance with this idea, Confucianism structured the perpetuity of life forms based on the notion of three elements: heaven, earth and humans (天地人).[15] In this regard, advocates of Confucian pro-life-ism adopted the belief that humans, and in particular saints, played a pivotal

---

11 Kim Chonguk, *Pulgyo saengt'ae ch'ŏlhak* [Buddhist ecological philosophy] (Dongguk University Press, 2004), 102–105.

12 *The Book of Changes* [周易], "天地大德曰生, 生生之謂易," in 繫辭上.

13 For example, Zhang Zai's viewpoint exposed in the *Ximing* [西銘, Western Inscription].

14 Kaji Nobuyuki, trans. Kim T'aejun, *Yugyo ran muŏsin'ga* [What is Confucianism] (Chiyoungsa, 1996), 31–33. Confucianism was regarded as the religion of life.

15 *The Doctrine of the Mean* [中庸], "惟天下至誠爲能盡其性 能盡其性 則能盡人之性 能盡人之性 則能盡物之性 能盡物之性 則可以贊天地之化育 可以贊天地之化育 則可以與天地參矣," in chap. 22.

role in the pursuit of the nurturing and harmony of all living beings.

This perception of Confucianism from the standpoint of the notion of pro-life-ism is employed herein to emphasize the differences with ecologism. The main differences between Confucian pro-life-ism and ecologism can be summarized as follows: First, rather than seeking to analyze or perceive the ecosystem, Confucian pro-life-ism identified the ecosystem's ability to perpetually maintain the life of all beings, including humans, as the ultimate goal. Second, contrary to ecologism which asserts that humans can only become aware of the ecosystem when they remove the modern anthropocentric mentality that promotes their convenience and benefits, Confucian pro-life-ism emphasized the fact that peace within the ecosystem and the succession of life within the universe cannot be achieved without humans being at the center of this process. Third, unlike ecology and ecologism which have focused on changing people's view of the world, Confucian pro-life-ism sought to bring about this goal by changing the very existence of life forms through self-cultivation (修身). The highlighting of these differences should not be construed as belief in the completeness of Confucian thought. Rather, these can be regarded as serving as the criteria with which to examine the problems of ecologism, as well as the complementary aspects between the two.

Various branches of ecologism derived from the ecological viewpoint or ecological thinking,[16] and having a hands-on approach to the actualization of an ecological life, have emerged in the contemporary

16 Wikipedia: The varieties of ecologism include ecologism, ecological romanticism, deep ecology, cultural eco-feminism, social eco-feminism, ecological rationalism, social ecologism, eco-socialism, eco-terrorism, and anti-growth.

era. Nevertheless, the measures implemented by ecologism to actualize the ecological lifestyle have mainly revolved around the stance that it is necessary to bring about fundamental change in the social, economic, and political order. However, with regard to the issue of where the fundamental change in the social, economic, and political order should originate from, the majority of the advocates of ecologism have focused on the need to bring about a change in how people view the world. In this regard, the manner in which ecologists have gone about trying to change people's world view has been criticized in some circles. The ecologists established the hypothesis that the destruction of the ecosystem would eventually result in the extinction of mankind. Critics of this hypothesis have pointed out that as the extinction of mankind due to the destruction of the ecosystem has never been, nor can it be, scientifically proven, such claims are in fact little more than irrational and esoteric prophecies.[17] However, even scientists cannot provide clear answers as to whether such hypotheses will come to pass or not. This point exhibits the lack of rationality and objectivity that plagues ecologism. Furthermore, the acceptance of these non-scientific prophecies runs the risk of reversing the rational academic spirit cultivated by mankind during the modern era. Ironically, the ecological doomsday predicted by advocates of ecologism runs the risk of decreasing their field of study's objective rationality.

Advocates of ecologism focus on changing the existing worldview by implementing various activities and programs. The priority is to develop and persuade the people to accept an enlightened ecological worldview. This includes using methods to change people's perceptions such as

17 Pak Hyŏnjŏng, ibid.

providing a rationally understandable worldview and fundamentally appealing to humans' rational thinking. Such methods can be persuasive as long as they are not combined with ecological doomsday scenarios. For example, an emphasis on the phenomenon of icebergs melting in the North Pole can help raise awareness of the problem of global warming. In Korea, a growing emphasis has been drawn within society over the dark shadow cast by rapid growth, namely the destruction of the natural environment.[18] However, the logic of searching to overcome such problems by identifying anthropocentrism as the main cause of the destruction of the natural environment may be difficult to accept. Above all, viewed from a logical standpoint, doubts can be raised as to whether ecologists' lifestyles or their very existences can truly be fully removed from anthropocentrism, that is non-anthropocentric or physiocentric in essence. In addition, when viewed from the standpoint of fundamental perceptions, ecologism must be included as an anthropocentric thought. As such, calls for the adjustment of the role of humans would be more frank and reasonable than attempts to bring about the removal of anthropocentrism.

Then, how should the role of humans be adjusted? The adoption of an ecological world view can be identified as the first step which ecologism must take in order to achieve concrete effects. Such a transformation can only be successful when people's attitudes towards life are changed and they feel comfortable with the ecological lifestyle. In this regard, the current state of ecologism-related academic discussions can be described

---

18 Examples include the objection to the Lee Myung-bak (Yi Myŏngbak) Government's Four Rivers Project and the lawsuit filed against the construction of the KTX tunnel through Mt. Ch'ŏnsŏng on behalf of a rare breed of salamander found in the Mt. Ch'ŏnsŏng area.

as one in which there has been a lack of discussions of this point and of the organization of detailed implementation programs. In this sense, while discussing changes in objective conditions, ecologism has in reality remained at the stage of cherishing the very simple belief in bringing about change to the main actors. That being the case, isn't it necessary to discuss measures of innovatively changing not only the thinking method of the main actors, but also their lifestyle? Doesn't the success of an ecological strategy ultimately rest on the ability to change the thinking method of the main actors and to change their attitudes and lifestyle? What measures can be implemented to ensure that such changes in attitudes and lifestyles become permanent? Advocates of ecology and ecologism appear to have given little consideration to these questions. This can be construed as the main reason why this study introduces a logical extension, in the form of a Confucian vantage point, namely pro-life-ism, as a viable alternative.

Such formulation of issues is also connected to the shortcomings of ecologism or ecology that can be observed from the standpoint of Confucianism. Hans Magnus Enzensberge defines ecological problems as an imbalance and lack of functionality between all the species found in the organic cycle linking together nature and human society."[19] At the current point, these problems will not be resolved even if anthropocentrism is removed. The ecological reality should be explained based on precise factor analysis and periodic variables.[20] Human's are the ones who must play the core role in correcting the imbalance and lack of functionality

---

19 Pak Hyŏnjŏng, "Hans Magnus Enzensberge ŭi saengt'aejuŭi pip'an [Hans Magnus Enzensberge's criticism of ecologism]," *Togil munhak* [German Literature] 116: 158.

20 Ibid.

affecting this organic cycle structure. Although other life forms are also involved in this process, humans must play the decisive role. To this end, there is a need to change humans' attitudes toward life or to change human beings as a whole. Changing human beings means to change their essence through Confucianism-based self cultivation or ritual learning. More to the point, this can be understood as fundamentally changing the systemic cycle of the patterns of humans' awareness and physical actions through self-cultivation.

3. THE ORIENTATION OFCONFUCIAN PRO-LIFE-ISM

Can Confucianism actually become a useful thought or truth in this new era? Can it contribute to the opening of a new sphere in ecologism, or to the expansion of ecological culture, as postulated in this study? The discussion of the correlation between ecologism and Confucian thought holds implications not only in terms of the task of identifying whether ecological elements can be found in Confucian thought. Rather, it also holds great significance with regards to the development of positive elements of ecologism which can contribute to tasks such as the improvement of the relationship between the natural environment and humans, and between human groups within human society. Furthermore, this will pave the way for Confucianism to contribute to the civilization of the future; however, this can only come to pass when Confucian ecologism-related thought is reorganized to reflect the contemporary context. This can be construed as the reason why, despite the differences in the systems and positions of the two theories, this study searches for the ecological elements found in Confucian thought, defines these ecological elements as Confucian pro-life-ism rather than Confucian ecologism, and explores the complementary nature of the Confucian and ecological theories.

Few studies have attempted to reinterpret Confucianism from the standpoint of ecology or ecologism. Existing studies have been limited to attempts to identify the elements of Confucianism that are in keeping with the framework of ecologism, and especially that link Confucian thought to ecologism.[21] The present study found few papers in Korea which considered the correlation between Confucian thought and ecology or ecologism. Kim Uktong's work can be regarded as the only one that partially sought to relate and compare Korean Confucian scholars' thoughts with ecologism.[22] Dealing not only with the Confucian thought but also Shamanism and Tonghak (Eastern Learning), Kim Uktong's study focused on analyzing the types of ecological thought found in Korean tradition. As part of his review of the similarities between ecologism and Confucian thought, Kim labeled Yi Kyubo's thought as 'human ecology' and that of Sirhak scholars as Silsa kusi (實事求是, Seeking Evidence)–based ecologism. Kim's opinions were based on the perception that Confucianism originated from a nature-friendly world view. However, this attempt fails to alleviate the doubts as to whether Confucianism can really be defined as ecology or ecologism. Despite the similarities, the original positions and goals of Confucian scholars were

---

21 This phenomenon has not been limited to Confucianism. The same method has been employed in conjunction with all traditional Korean philosophies.

22 Kim Uktong, *Han'guk ŭi noksaek munhwa* [The green culture of Korea] (Munye Publishing, 2000), 163–280.

not identical to those of ecology or ecologism. In other words, Kim's paper seeks to fit the framework of ecologism into Confucianism, or to derive only the similarities between the two. Thus, this becomes little more than an attempt to forcibly unify two different forms of logic.

At this juncture, it is essential that we first clarify the fact that Confucianism boasts a theoretical structure that consists of goals and a worldview that differ from those of modern ecologism. That being the case, the effects of theoretical convergence can be ascertained by comparing ecologism with Confucianism. In other words, there is a need, in order to heighten the theoretical completeness and concrete effects of modern ecologism, to engage in the process of discussing the spheres or theoretical elements of Confucianism that can apply to ecologism. Several methods can be employed to attain this goal. First, although the goals and world view of Confucianism are fundamentally different from those of ecologism, one can nevertheless search for the aspects that can be regarded as ecological elements, or promote a mutual dialogue between the two fields. This method can be regarded as the one that has been employed in existing studies. The second method revolves around comparing the goals of ecologism and Confucianism in order to identify measures through which the characteristics of Confucianism that differ from ecologism can be reconciled with the latter. This stands in stark contrast with efforts to simply compare Confucian methods with ecologically-readjusted Confucianism that is rooted in the framework of ecologism. Rather than focusing on revealing the elements of Confucianism that are in accord with ecologism, this second method focuses on the search within the tradition of Confucianism for measures to complement modern ecologism.

As it has already been discussed above, the former method will be omitted herein. Studies that have employed the second method have to date headed in two directions. The first, which has had much to do with the fact that ecologism needs to activate its imaginative force based on the comprehensive metaphor of the interrelationship between humans and nature, has been that of using the Confucian world view to strengthen the ecological imagination.[23] This attempt to strengthen the imaginative force can be regarded as plausible because of the fact that Confucianism not only established a paradigm under which all beings in the world were connected in a more fundamental manner than ecology, but also setup its goals based on more comprehensive and greater subjects than has been the case with those of natural or human ecology. The other direction has been that of studying the hands-on methods employed in Confucianism and then grafting them onto ecologism.

One important aspect should be considered with regards to the strengthening of imaginative force. Here, imaginative force refers to eventually inducing concrete actions rather than mere thinking. Inducing concrete actions means to bestow a fundamental relationship and order to the links between life forms and humans and between humans themselves, and then making them live under such relationships and order. Therefore, the strengthening of imaginative force is meaningful only when it is connected to the strengthening of the power of execution. As such, when viewed from an academic standpoint, any attempt to compare Confucianism with ecology, or even to apply Confucianism to ecology, in order to strengthen the imaginative force must be based on a thorough

---

23 For more on this, please refer to Han Myŏnhŭi's Qi-centered environmental theory (Han Myŏnhŭi, *Han'guk ŭi saengt'aejuŭi munhwa wa sasang: Kim Uktong ŭi* Han'guk ŭi noksaek munhwa [The ecological culture and thought of Korea: Kim Uktong's *The Green Culture of Korea*] (Munye Publishing, 2000), 267.

review of even the methods used to accumulate the direct experiences of life which are derived from the Confucian metaphor. Even if it leaves aside the actual hands-on methods employed and the detailed process to bring this about, a theoretical study should at the very least include this element. Only then can imaginative force help to strengthen hands-on activities and change the life of beings.

It is important to conduct research on how a Confucian pro-life-ism based hands-on methodology can be applied to ecology or ecologism. The hands-on methodology can be divided into two elements. The first is a method of self-cultivation that creates new beings by cultivating individuals' minds and bodies. The other is the establishment of rites and ceremonies (儀禮) and etiquette (禮義) which can be used to coordinate and unify the everyday behavioral patterns of the members of a group with the Confucian world view. Existing studies have placed great importance on self-cultivation methods.[24] While self-cultivation is also regarded as being of great importance in the present study, rites and ceremonies (儀禮), elements which ecologism is so far devoid of, are herein considered alongside self-cultivation. Self-cultivation (修身) methods, as well as rites and ceremonies (儀禮), were not established in conjunction with ecological goals and notions. Some individuals have pointed out that its transformation into a political ideology has resulted in modern ecologism losing its genuineness. Furthermore, it has also been used as a strategic ideology by the advanced countries to maintain the gap with the de

---

24 Michael C. Kalton, "Extending the Neo-Confucian Tradition: Questions and Reconcept-ualization for the Twenty-First Century," in *Confucianism and Ecology: The Interrelation of Heaven, Earth, and Humans*, ed. Mary Evelyn Tucker and John Berthrong (Harvard University Center for the Study of World Religions Publications, 1998), 96–99.

veloping and underdeveloped countries. As a result, modern ecologism does not look pure. To this end, ecologism's ability to ensure its genuineness is predicated on its acceptance of the self-cultivation (修身) and rites and ceremonies (儀禮) traditionally used as a method to preserve the genuineness of Confucianism and Confucian scholars. The goals pursued by ecologism cannot be resolved simply by changing the worldview or by strengthening imaginative force. Rather, such goals can only be achieved when the customs, habits, individual attitudes and group lifestyle have been altered.

In addition, some have placed great importance on efforts to reestablish the positive legacy of modern rationality in the contemporary era. However, a discussion that takes into consideration Korea's traditional, cultural and spiritual contexts should be held as to how the modern rationality of the West should be accepted and developed in Korea. Such consideration can be considered to consist of the careful establishment of the fundamental position which Korea should take with regards to accepting the various kinds of ecologism and life ethics-related arguments in the West, and the conduct of a process that involves the filtering and linking of such debates. The application of ethical methods that are rooted in a different context of thinking and culture than the traditional thought of Korea can be regarded as futile. Moreover, the inherent strangeness of such an exercise may result in complicating its implementation or its acceptance in an academic manner. Therefore, it is essential to criticize and link them from the standpoint of Korean tradition. At this juncture, it becomes necessary to consider the Confucian tradition as the criteria upon which the fundamental position of Korea should be established. In particular, Confucianism, in its capacity as the entity which has organized the human experience in a manner designed to ensure the perpetuity of life, has played the role of fundamental metaphor for contemporary Koreans.

There is no way to tell whether ecologism will be the ultimate solution to environmental or human problems in the future. As previously mentioned, if ecologism eventually fails, then the inherent problem in the ecologism paradigm may very well emerge as the cause of this failure. This inherent problem can be defined as the basic position of ecology and ecologism that the mere cognition of the ecosystem will result in hands-on activities. However, Confucianism, and in particular the Neo-Confucianism of the Chosŏn era, did not accept this basic position. Thus, Confucianism can be seen as having observed the relationship of all the elements that lay between human perceptions and actions, or the order of activities within humans, in a much more precise manner than ecologism or ecology, and as having accumulated more experience. Ecology and ecologism inherited the long tradition of Western philosophy, which itself originated from the ancient Greek Philosophy, 'cognition leads to practice.' Both seek to motivate concrete action by strengthening the imaginative force of Western philosophy, establishing and extending such perceptions during the process of implementing ecological movements. However, neither implements an academic approach to the process or methodology of embedding ecological activities in the independent lifestyle and everyday life of humankind.

On the other hand, cognition and practice are in Confucianism connected to each other in a different type of order. From its vantage point, it is cognition that can be strengthened or become true through practice. Thus, the ability to strengthen cognition is predicated on changing the state of the individual mind and body, or the actual life structure, prior to changing the world view. These are the fundamental differences between Confucianism and ecologism. Viewed from this standpoint, Confucianism can be used to complement ecologism.

4. THE COMPLEMENTARITY OF ECOLOGISM AND PRO-LIFE-ISM

Confucianism and Ecology was the first study which comprehensively reviewed the relationship between ecologism and Confucianism and showed the latent potential of this field.[25] This book featured papers presented during an academic conference held in the United States. Although the book contains various standpoints and contents as a result of the fact that many authors took part in the compilation process, it is a valuable book which deals with the connection between Confucianism and ecology.

Presented as part of a review of the relationship between Confucianism and ecology, the papers included in this book reflect the theme of the conference, which revolved around subjects which had the same code as ecology or could be understood through ecology. However, these papers did not simply review the elements of Confucianism that meshed with ecology. Based on the premise that the essential orientation of Confucianism is not very different from that of modern ecology, the papers found in this book discussed the contents which ecology could take away from Confucianism. One of the key points is that although

---

25 Mary Evelyn Tucker and John Berthrong ed. *Confucianism and Ecology: The Interrelation of Heaven, Earth, and Humans* (Harvard University Center for the Study of World Religions Publications, 1998).

ecology should remove the anthropocentrism that has developed as a result of modern enlightenment, the focus should be on changing rather than overcoming or eliminating the spiritual values and lifestyle represented by modernity so as to bring them into line with the orientation of ecological thinking.[26] In other words, although ecology criticizes modern civilization, this criticism should be limited to the negative outcomes of modern civilization. Instead, modern civilization's positive efforts to heighten the sustainability of humans and the earth should be emphasized. Here, the focus should be on the transformation and development of modern values and lifestyles rather than the elimination thereof. In this regard, special attention should be paid to the discussions on the prospects of Confucianism contributing to the process of this transformation and development. Confucianism's ability to contribute to this process is predicated on the following: first, Confucianism uses a method of promoting harmony with nature that centers on humankind; second, the Confucian notion of self-cultivation (修身) is regarded as an important hands-on methodology. It is on these points that this study will now focus.

Let us begin by discussing the position of promoting human-centered harmony with nature. In his work *Beyond the Enlightenment Mentality*, Tu Weiming defined this position as that of anthropocosmism. This concept is compared to ecologism's definition of modern thought and civilization as anthropocentrism in which the main position of ecology is regarded as non-anthropocentrism. Ecology and ecologism regard the evils of modern

---

26 Tu Weiming, "Beyond the Enlightenment Mentality," in *Confucianism and Ecology: The Interrelation of Heaven, Earth, and Humans*, Mary Evelyn Tucker and John Berthrong ed. (Harvard University Center for the Study of World Religions Publications, 1998), 3–9.

civilization as having originated from anthropocentric tendencies, and view this in a negative manner. However, Tu Weiming suggested that, in accordance with the philosophical structure of *The Doctrine of the Mean* (中庸), the achievement of harmony with nature could only be achieved if humans were positioned at the center. His concept was derived from the notion of the three elements of heaven, earth and humans (天地人) found in traditional Confucianism.

As such, Tu Weiming's line of reasoning revolves around the search for a method through which to establish the harmonious coexistence structure between nature and humans pursued by ecology that highlights the intellectual tradition of mankind from primitive thought to modern civilization and the contemporary era. Based on the position that Confucianism and ecology have fundamentally different starting points and conceptual structures, Tu sought to find the point at which these two theories intersect. Maintaining that the tradition of Confucianism was not clear in terms of relating meaning to ecology, Tu adopted the position that it was necessary to carry out the task of clearly identifying the correlations between the two theories.[27] Compared to Korean scholars who hastily derived ecological elements from Confucian thought, Shamanism, and Tonghak (Eastern Learning) and defined them as the ecology of Confucianism or Shamanism, or who searched for the relationship and similarities between Buddhism and ecology, which was then defined as Buddhist ecophilosophy, Tu's attitude can be regarded as being very prudent and rational.

In addition, Tu also stressed the fact that the spiritual legacy of

---

[27] Ibid.

modernity contains many virtues which should be maintained and developed in the contemporary era, as well as in the future. For example, rationality, freedom, equality, human rights, and distributive justice[28] are regarded as virtues which even ecological thinking designed to move beyond the modern intellect should accept and further develop. Such values have resulted in humans being positioned at the center of human thought and judgment in the modern era. These values also played a great role in the improvement and reform of the conditions of human life from the modern era onwards. That being the case, should this be taken to mean that modern people who accept ecology, which possesses an ecologically reorganized world view and ecological attitude towards life, should eliminate all of these values from their lives? If we define ecologism as the removal of anthropocentrism, then does this mean that we must also get rid of all these values and the modern lifestyle? Ecology and ecologism do not have any appropriate answers to these questions. Thus, although ecology and ecologism identify humankind as the main practical actor, they cannot grant him an appropriate status within their world view. Further, although humans are the main actors in practical activities, ecology and ecologism must endlessly deny the central status of humanity, and push the latter, which is regarded as one part of nature, to the margins.

All actions must inevitably be carried out by humans. Even though ecologism refuses anthropocentrism, the role of humans remains very important for the simple reason that such refusal is in fact implemented by humans themselves. As ecologism seeks to create beings that are different

[28] Ibid., 19.

from modern humans, it therefore inevitably grants an important role to humans when it comes to the protection of nature. For ecologism to actually be successful, it must bring about a change in human's thinking and practices, and further, change human's very lifestyle. Attempts to bring about such changes have taken the form of the actualization of eco-community life.[29] This cannot be brought about without the existence of humans and the roles assigned to them. Nevertheless, the notion of non-anthropocentrism found in ecologism is from a conceptual standpoint set up in such a manner that inevitably pits it against modern anthropocentrism. This results in cases of conspicuous hostility toward anthropocentric culture and civilization.

However, this can also take the form of an inherent self-contradiction. In order to move toward concrete and persuasive practices, this rigid framework of perception must be removed. A good example of this can be found in the standpoint of the Norwegian scholar Arne Naess who has been regarded as the founder of deep ecology. Arne Naess' t-type community can be regarded as one that experiences and emphasizes the great self (大我) by combining humankind with nature.[30] The notion of

---

29 Yang Haerim, "Saengt'ae minjujuŭiwa saengt'ae kongdongch'ejŏk sayu [Eco-democracy and the concept of eco-community]," *Hwan'gyŏng ch'ŏrhak* (Han'guk hwan'gyŏng ch'ŏrakhoe) 10 (2010).; Cho Chŏngok, "Isangjŏk saengt'ae chuŭijŏk chayŏn'gwan e taehan ch'ŏlhakchŏk in'ganhakchŏk hwan'gyŏng yullijŏk koch'al: togil sangt'ae kongdongch'e ŭi ye [A philosophical, human, and environmental ethical consideration of the ideal ecological view of nature]," *Ch'ŏrhak kwa hyŏnsanghak yon'gu* (Han'guk hyŏnsanghakhoe) 25 (2005).

30 Mun Sunhong, "*Pullip wi ŭi sasang: kŭnbon saengt'aehak ŭi ch'angsija Arne Naess* [The philosophy of the blade of grass: Arne Naess, the creator of deep ecology]," http://newhamgil.cafe24.com/xe/?document_srl=1677(accessed

the great self (大我) and petty self (小我), which was shared and developed in the Confucian and Daoist Schools in Asia, is a logical framework that makes it possible to unify all life forms, and further the universe, around humans. In other words, this notion is based on creating order and harmony between all life forms in a manner that revolves around humans. The development of ecologism is predicated on a reconsideration of methods that do not accept humans as the main actor, or that adhere to a non-anthropocentric standpoint in order to avoid falling into the trap of anthropocentrism, and this despite the fact that the actual practices needed to ensure coexistence within the ecosystem should also come from humans. This can be regarded as shining the light on the blind spot evident in the dichotomous thought structure of the Western world, and on the rigid epistemological limitations that can only logically gain persuasive power when this element is overcome.[31]

Second, let us discuss how the Confucian theory of self-cultivation (修身) should be applied to ecologism. This can be regarded as the method of moving from the petty self (小我) to the great self (大我). At the same time, it lies at the center of the method of harmonizing and maintaining the flow of life within a universe in which humans are positioned at the center. This position is one that has already been argued by Michael Kalton. Kalton regarded the theory of self-cultivation (修身) as a means to control and reflect on the internal desire of human beings and reviewed the possibility thereof. In particular, Kalton interpreted the notion of principle (理) found in Neo-Confucianism as a type of evolutionary

May 29, 2011).

31 Gregory Bateson, trans. Pak Chidong *Chŏngsin kwa chayŏn* [Mind and nature: a necessary unity] (Kkach'i, 1990), 112–151.

theory within which principle (理) reflects the system used to maintain the life of all the beings within the universe and heightens the correlations and complexity of the life forms.[32] Let us go into further detail on this topic in the following section.

5. CONFUCIAN PRO-LIFE-ISM AND WIGI CHIHAK (爲己之學, LEARNING FOR ONESELF)

Confucianism is a philosophy that incorporates various countenances. Therefore, although Confucianism was originally rooted in interests and goals that are different from ecologism, it can nevertheless be compared with ecologism, and a discussion of its complementarity can be held. Furthermore, Confucianism possesses the conceptual mechanisms needed to heighten or even exceed the correlation that exists with ecologism. One example is principle (理). While principle (理) is originally one, it exists in various beings. This can be interpreted as a notion that encompasses the biocentric egalitarianism pursued by ecologists, especially deep ecologists.[33] However, no Confucian scholars believed that the goals of Confucianism could be achieved solely through cognition of principle (理). Therefore, the belief that the ecological world view can lead to normal and sincere practice can, when approached from the standpoint of Confucianism, be criticized. While cognition can be regarded as a

---

[32] Mary Evelyn Tucker and John Berthrong ed. ibid., 85.

[33] Ibid.

starting point, this must also be accompanied by an experiential process that involves practice. In other words, to achieve clearer and more precise cognition one must develop experiential perceptions through practice. This can be regarded as the Confucian method of true understanding (眞知). Confucianism separates true understanding (眞知) from knowledge based on hearing and seeing (聞見知), and maintains that true knowledge cannot be achieved without a combination of knowledge and practice. This can be identified as the reason why the Confucian theory of self-cultivation (修身) that seeks to promote true understanding (眞知) can contribute to ecologism.

However, Kalton's discussion of the Confucian theory of self-cultivation (修身) is limited to self-introspection at the epistemological level. This can be regarded as the result of the failure of Confucianism to consider the conceptual or methodological ecosystem related to the organization of the theory of self-cultivation (修身). The Confucian theory of self-cultivation (修身) was closely related to the methodology of the study of the mind (心學) that prevailed during the era of Neo-Confucianism. In this regard, there is no denying that Confucianism is closely related to the methods through which introspection (内省) is brought about. Nevertheless, the development of the conditions for introspection (内省) is not an easy task. While one of the criteria for introspection (内省) is principle (理), which in turn is secured from the internal mind, ritual and ceremonial regulations also constitute important criteria. As it is in keeping with the objective norms known as rites (禮), the notion of principle (理) should be perceived not only from the standpoint of the internal mind of a person, but should also be actualized in one's life within the external world. Thus, based on a concerted structure that involved both principle (理) and rites (禮) Confucianism viewed thinking and practice, or motivation and result, as being in accord with one another. Confucianism also viewed the process of changing from a lower to a higher state of correspondence between principle and rites as being made possible by self-cultivation (修身). In other words, self-cultivation (修身) is regarded as a methodology to organize the internal mind and external world into a system where the mind and body is harmonized with principle (理) and rites (禮).

Furthermore, are principle (理) and rites (禮) a simple cultural device which can be temporarily regulated by humans? Or are they a device through which, based on the consideration of the general evolution and changes within nature, the role of humans can be appropriately granted and regulated? These questions cannot be easily answered. Be that as it may, such a cultural device must be based on abundant experiences and knowhow accumulated over a long period of time, much as is the case with the principles and rites accumulated in ancient China and subsequently diffused to Asian countries. However, at the current point in time in which interest has been focused on the problems within the ecosystem, rites (禮) become an especially important tool through which to establish the norms needed to coordinate and optimize the relationship between nature and humans and to achieve social integration. If by ecological problems we mean the imbalance and lack of functionality between all the species under the organic cycle system that combines nature and human society as Hans Magnus Enzensberge has pointed out, then it becomes very important to establish a ritual device, for example, Confucian rites (禮), which can be used to reform individual and group life, including everyday life, towards a nature-friendly environment, or which can reorganize the patterns of individual and group behavior. The circulatory system linking together nature, humans, and society should move beyond its current characteristics of environmental destruction and conflict-laden relations and towards the actualization of the virtues of reconciliation and coexistence based on the establishment of ritual devices and ritual practices.[34]

However, one can also identify other reasons why the introduction of a ritual device such as Confucian rites (禮) should be considered. Rites (禮) can be regarded as a device that respects the law of nature and produces an individuality that pursues the state of mean (中庸) and central harmony (中和) rather than one which produces an individuality in which humans' conquest or control of nature is perceived as being natural. This is connected to The Doctrine of the Mean (中庸), which states that it is possible to harmonize and develop all beings in the universe centering on humankind by achieving central harmony (中和). Furthermore, the principle of pursuing the harmony and development of all beings through the achievement of the central harmony (中和) of human nature is fundamentally embedded in rites (禮). Thus, rites (禮) can clearly be perceived as a normative principle through which to simultaneously appropriately control[35] and satisfy human desire. Moreover, this normative principle can be used to properly cultivate humankind,[36] and to establish an awareness of frugality as a more virtuous deed than extravagance. Finally, rites represent the essence of the heavenly principle (天理) and the

---

34 For more on ritual devices and ritual practices, please refer to Hitoshi Imamura and Shinsuke Imamura, 儀禮のオントロギ-人間社會を再生産するもの [Rites and ceremonies used to reproduce the ontology of human society] (Tokyo: Kodansha, 2007), 31–36.

35 The Book of Rites [禮記], The term minfang [民坊] found in the section of the same name refers to the normative device used to control human desire.

36 *Xun Zi* [荀子], The chapter entitled "Theory of the Proprieties [禮論] states that rites [禮] are the norms through which humans achieve cultivation.

ceremony and rule (儀則) of human affairs.

In addition, rather than simply preventing the destruction of nature, rites (禮) constitute a device that can alter the organization and reproduction of nature in a nature-loving and life-protecting manner. This can be likened to the claim made by Gregory Bateson that it is impossible to expect that a crime can be eradicated simply by punishing the criminal act.[37] A crime can refer to a specific action labeled as a 'crime,' or to parts of this action. It is an error of basic logic to regard that all crime can be eradicated from this world by continuously punishing criminal behavior or parts of such criminal behavior. A crime refers to the method in which a certain behavior is formed. As such, the reorganization of the method through which criminal behavior is formed becomes the way to eradicate and prevent crime.[38] Similarly, ecologism must focus on whether it should limit itself to ending behavior that destroy ecosystems, or try to reform the method through which such behavior is formed. It goes without saying that the second option represents a more desirable one. To this end, Confucianism may represent not only an important foundation through which to successfully entrench this method, but also a prototypical methodology. Put differently, the actualization of ecologism in Korea can be brought about by actively highlighting the use of Confucianism as a self-modification system which can modify the lifestyle (including both thinking and practice) of modern nature-destructive society. Of course, this should be predicated on the bringing of Confucianism into line with life in the contemporary era.

---

37 Gregory Bateson, trans. Pak Chidong, *Chŏngsin kwa chayŏn* [Mind and nature: a necessary unity] (Kkach'i, 1990), 152.

38 Ibid.

That being the case, the method of self-cultivation (修身) based on principle (理) and rites (禮), or the so-called Neo-Confucian notion of *wigi chihak* (爲己之學, learning for oneself) should be regarded as a method to establish balance and harmony as the center of humans' efforts to establish a mutual prosperity structure with other life forms. Although the tradition of *wigi chihak* (爲己之學, learning for oneself) originated from the Confucianism of the pre-Qin era, it was strongly emphasized under Neo-Confucianism, and in particular within the Cheng-Zhu School (程朱學). This took the form within Chosŏn of a learning structure called Sage Learning (聖學) that emphasized cultivating the mind and body in a balanced and harmonious manner based on internal introspection and rites (禮). True understanding (眞知) and actual practice (實踐), as well as the fathoming of principle (窮理) and strenuous effort (力行), were also emphasized as being essential in order to achieve *wigi chihak* (爲己之學, learning for oneself). This methodology is aimed at forming the everyday behavioral pattern of humans, and ultimately, at leading the change in beings, and also includes the sound organization and entrenchment of the functions of internal emotions such as feelings, prudence and will that emerge within the internal mind of humans, as well as the general types of human behaviors that constitute the external expression of these emotions. Here, the notion of *wigi chihak* (爲己之學, learning for oneself) can be regarded as being best suited to form this methodology. The reinterpretation of the method of *wigi chihak* (爲己之學, learning for oneself) in a contemporary manner and its combination with adjusted rites (禮) and principles (理) will make possible humans' achievement of harmony based on the three elements of heaven, earth, and human.

Furthermore, *wigi chihak* (爲己之學, learning for oneself) constitutes an important methodology with which to achieve the goals of Confucianism, which regards life as being important and promotes the perpetuity of life. As evidenced by the ethics regarding the mutual prosperity of all life forms in the universe found in the Western Inscription (西銘) section of Yi Hwang's Ten *Diagrams of Sage-Learning* (聖學十圖), the development of the notion of Confucianism as pro-life-ism and its ability to complement ecologism is predicated on the cultivation of humankind as the main actor in establishing a structure of harmony and mutual prosperity. Although this differs from ecologism, which adopted non-anthropocentrism, advocates of ecologism should actively consider and incorporate this line of reasoning.

In addition, the inherent problem of ecologism identified at the beginning of this study, namely its doomsday epistemology, is in fact related to the lack of flexibility found in the epistemological traditions of the West. On a more fundamental level, it is the result of the rigid perception of the phenomenon of life and systems. Considered from the standpoint of evolutionary theory, there is no concrete proof that the doomsday epistemology emphasized by ecologists will hit the earth's life system or that it can even be regarded as a simple logical hypothesis. Rather, it becomes essential to pay attention to the fact that the earth has its own self-modification system[39] to preserve life forms. Viewed from the dynamic standpoint of Confucianism, more attention should be paid to the view of change with continuity (變通) best explained by the concepts of circulation (循環) and *kungch'ikpyŏn pyŏnch'ikt'ong* (窮則變 變則通, when out of means, seek change. Then opportunities will come). This implies that the life structure of the earth possesses a complicated and refined

39 Gregory Bateson, ibid, 130.

self-modification and restoration capability that is well beyond the imagination of ecologists, and exposes an attitude which is contrary to the groundless and extreme doomsday hypothesis advanced by the ecologists.

6. CONCLUSION

This study sought to develop a complementary relationship between ecologism and Confucian pro-life-ism. There are various ecological thinking methods, and the direction in terms of the application of such methods has yet to be concretized. In Korea, discussions on connecting ecologism with traditional thought have been activated in the field of literature, ethics and philosophy. However, no discussions related to Confucianism have yet to be actively carried out. Discussions on Confucianism and ecologism have not been actively carried out at the global level. The book entitled *Confucianism and Ecology* is considered herein as being of academic value. This book includes in-depth discussions on applying Confucian notions to ecology and ecologism. To this end, the present study was prepared based on this book. Furthermore, this study attempts to relate the aspects of Confucianism which can contribute to contemporary society to the ecologist movement.

The present study selected ecologism rather than ecology as the subject to be compared to Confucianism. This is because while the latter constitutes a natural scientific theory, ecologism seeks to heighten the imaginative power and practices of humans. Ecologism has yet to be fully introduced in Korea, with only a few books and studies having been published. Furthermore, no clear analysis of the ecological practice movement has to date been conducted. This clearly shows that Korean society features different contexts than those found in Western society. That being the case, this study attempted to criticize and overcome the logical holes and practical weaknesses of the general trend of ecologism towards non-anthropocentrism or biocentrism based on the framework of Confucian pro-life-ism. In addition, this study also sought to find a method to combine the notion of *wigi chihak* (爲己之學, learning for oneself), which was further deepened as part of the Confucian tradition of Chosŏn, as well as the methodology of the Study of Rites (禮學), with ecologism. This study can be used to extend and deepen the complementary relationship between ecologism and Confucian tradition through further detailed and broadened considerations.

Translated by Michael Bujold and Young-ki You

Yu Kwŏn-jong (ykj111@cau.ac.kr) *is a professor in the Department of Philosophy at Chung-Ang University, Korea.*

THE CURRENT STATE OF THE ECOLOGICAL DISCOURSE WITHIN KOREAN CONFUCIANISM AND ITS FUTURE OUTLOOK

By Kim Sea-jeong

I. INTRODUCTION

Is the Four Major Rivers Project currently being implemented in Korea designed to bring about ecological restoration as the government has asserted? Or will it wind up destroying the ecology as environmental organizations and ecological specialists have clamored? If the latter turns out to be true, then not only the people and beings currently residing on the Korean peninsula, but also future generations, will find themselves facing a tremendous ecological disaster. Once seriously damaged, the natural ecosystem established over several thousands of years cannot be easily restored. Although this fact should be a serious cause for apprehension as far as the present project is concerned, the government, seemingly oblivious to the concerns of the public, has blissfully overseen the destruction of the ecosystem on a national scale in the name of green growth. The Korean nation has boasted of being nature-friendly, having respect for life, and loving peace since the days of Tan'gun. However, one cannot help but to question whether such traditions actually exist when looking at the Four Major Rivers Project.

Of course, such ecological crises occasioned by the destruction of ecosystems are not only our problem. The rapid development of science and technology and global industrialization has meant that, on the surface, mankind has over the past few centuries enjoyed a level of material well-being that has been unrivalled since the beginning of history. However, a closer look reveals that such advancements have been accompanied by serious environmental problems. These include the disposal of nuclear waste, air pollution, water pollution, the need to limit fossil fuel use, deforestation, an explosive increase in the population, acid rain, the destruction of the ozone layer, and global warming. The destruction of ecosystems has been based on the 'mechanical view of the world' and the 'anthropocentric' orientation behind Western modernity. The mechanical view of the world defines nature, that is, all beings other than man, as an extension of spiritless objects that are unable to think, and perceives organisms as automated machines.[1] By objectifying nature and not recognizing natural objects right to life, as well boasting an anti-bioethical outlook under which no ethical awareness of the destruction of nature and life forms exists, the mechanical view of the world made possible a technology-oriented attitude that was used to justify the technological manipulation of life forms.[2] In addition, the traditions of Judaism and Christianity in the West maintained that while humans endowed with reason, souls, and virtue could have their own values and rights, the

---

1 Kim Chaehŭi, *Sin'gwahak sanch'aek* [Promenade through new science] (Kamyŏngsa, 1995), 20–29/74–79.

2 Kim Kukt'ae, *Kwahak kisul munmyŏng ŭi panhwan'gyŏngsŏng* [The anti-environmental nature of scientific and technological civilization], vol. 17, *Kwahak sasang* (Bŏmyangsa, 1996), 158–159.

instrumental value of natural beings lay in their ability to foster human prosperity. The 'anthropocentrism' and 'instrumental view of nature' in the West[3] granted the rational justification for man's conquest and rule over nature.[4] The mechanical view of the world, anthropocentrism, global industrialization, and the significant development of science & technology removed nature's vitality, and degraded it to the status of a mere implement to fulfill human desires and interests through a mutual engagement that has resulted in the thorough conquest, destruction, and exploitation of nature, all of which has led to an ecological crisis at the global level. The crisis faced by ecosystems ultimately threatened the survival of the human race that had to coexist with nature. As such, mankind now finds itself having paid a great price, in the form of ecological disasters, for its material well-being.[5]

It was amidst such a crisis awareness that the animal rights and environmental movements began to spring up in the West during the 1960s. With such movements serving as a backdrop, environmental philosophies and ethics started to form in the West.[6] Various theories were also developed. These ranged from individualistic environmental ethics

---

3 See Michael E. Zimmerman eds., *Environmental Philosophy—From Animal Rights to Radical Ecology* (New Jersey: Prentice Hall, 1998), 34–36/80–84.

4 Pak Imun, *Munmyŏng ŭi wigi wa munhwa ŭi chŏnhwan* [The crisis of civilization and cultural transition] (Minŭmsa, 1996), 76–80.

5 Kim Sea-jeong, "Hwangyŏng yulli e taehan tongyang ch'ŏrhakchŏk chŏpkŭn: yuga ch'ŏrhak ŭl chungsim ŭro [The Asian philosophical approach to environmental ethics: with a special focus on Confucian philosophy]," *Pŏmhan ch'ŏlhak* (Bumhan Philosophy Association) 29 (2003): 58.

6 Michael E. Zimmerman eds., *Environmental Philosophy—From Animal Rights to Radical Ecology,* 1–2.

such as 'anthropocentric environmental ethics', animal liberation, animal rights, and biocentrism, to ecology-centered environmental ethics such as deep ecology, social ecology, and ecological feminism.[7] In addition, the ecological crisis has created new interests in Asian philosophies such as Confucianism, Buddhism, and Taoism that are laden with ecological characteristics as well as organic elements. To this end, studies have been carried out in Korea since the late 1990s that have sought to reinterpret the traditional philosophies of Asia from modern viewpoints such as environmental ethics, ecological philosophy, and bioethics, and to search for alternatives which can be used to resolve the problems associated with the current ecological crisis.[8] Ecological discourses related to Korean Confucianism have also been conducted in conjunction with this trend. Unlike environmental and ecological discourses in the West, which have been around for forty-fifty years, the study of the ecological discourse within Korean Confucianism only has a short history of some ten years. The results of such studies have also been limited to the initial and proclamation levels. There is a need to resolve many tasks in order for the ecological discourse within Korean Confucianism to cement its status

---

7 Kim Sea-jeong, "Yuga saengt'ae tamnon ŭl t'onghae pon yuga saengt'ae yulli The ecological ethics of Confucianism as viewed through ecological discourses in Confucianism]," T*ongsŏ ch'ŏlhak yŏn'gu* (Korean Society For Philosophy East-West) 50 (December 2008): 81–84.

8 As part of this trend, I have dealt with Confucian philosophy in the following papers, "Hwangyŏng yulli e taehan tongyang ch'ŏrhakchŏk chŏpkŭn: yuga ch'ŏrhak ŭl chungsim ŭro [The Asian philosophical approach to environmental ethics: with a special focus on Confucian philosophy]" and "Yuga saengt'ae tamnon ŭl t'onghae pon yuga saengt'ae yulli [The ecological ethics of Confucianism as viewed through ecological discourses in Confucianism]."

as an actual alternative which can be used to resolve the ecological crisis. As such, the time has come to move beyond the proclamation of mere assertions that Korean Confucianism includes an abundance of organic elements and ecological characteristics. In this regard, this study examines the current state of the ecological discourse within Korean Confucianism by analyzing and criticizing studies that have been conducted on this topic over the past ten years. Once this has been carried out, a discussion of the future tasks that must be achieved in order to ultimately position Korean Confucianism as a practical and detailed alternative that can be used to resolve the crisis afflicting ecosystems today will be undertaken.

II. THE CURRENT STATE OF THE ECOLOGICAL DISCOURSE WITHIN KOREAN CONFUCIANISM

Only a few studies have dealt with Korean Confucianism from the perspectives of environmental philosophy, environmental ethics, ecological philosophy, and ecology (hereafter referred to as 'ecological perspectives' for convenience) over the past ten years. In terms of the materials that deal with Korean Confucianism from an ecological perspective, the present research found three books, nine papers related to Neo-Confucianism, and eight papers related to Sirhak (Practical Learning).

A. BOOKS

Kim Uktong. *Han'guk ŭi noksaek munhwa* [The Green Culture of Korea]. Munye Publishing, 2000.

Han Myŏnhŭi. *Tongasia munmyŏng kwa han'guk ŭi saengt'aejuŭi* [East Asian Civil-ization and Korean Ecologism]. Philosophy and Reality Publishing, 2009.

Pak Hŭibyŏng. *Han'guk ŭi saengt'ae sasang* [Ecological Philosophy of Korea]. Tolbegae, 1999.

B. PAPERS RELATED TO KOREAN NEO-CONFUCIANISM

Kim Sangjin. "*Kosan kugokka* ŭi sŏngnihakchŏk saengt'ae insik [The Neo-Confucianism based ecological perceptions found in the *Kosan kugokka*]." *Sijohak nonch'ong* (Han'guk sijo hakhoe) 20 (2004): 51–73.

Chang Sŭnggu. "T'oegye sasang ŭi saengt'ae ch'ŏrhakchŏk chomyŏng [Highlighting Yi Hwang's ecological philosophy]." *T'oegye hakpo* (The T'oegye Studies Institute) (2001): 227–249.

Chŏng Yŏnjŏng. "Sin Hŭm ŭi sisegye e mich'in *Chuyŏk* saengt'aegwan ŭi yŏnghyang [The influences of the ecological views found in the *Book of Changes* on Sin Hŭm's poetry]." *Onji nonch'ong* (Onji hakhoe) 27 (2011): 231–261.

Lee Dong-hee (Yi Tonghŭi). "Sŏngnihak ŭi hwangyŏng ch'ŏrhakchŏk sisa [Environmental philosophical implications of Neo-Confucianism]." *Tongyang ch'ŏrhak* (The Society for Asian Philosophy in Korea) 13 (September 2000): 27–52.

Ro Young-chan (No Yŏngch'an). "Yulgok ujuron ŭi saengt'aeronjŏk amsi tŭl [The ecological allusions contained in Yi I's theory of the cosmos]." *Yuhak sasang kwa saengt'aehak* [Confucianism and Ecology], Mary Evelyn Tucker and John Berthrong, ed., trans. Oh Chŏngsŏn. (Yemun sŏwon, 2010), 249–268.

U Ŭngsun. "Chang Yu ŭi sayu pangsik e taehan han ihae—saengt'aehakchŏk insik ŭi mosaek [Understanding Chang Yu's way of thinking—searching for ecological perceptions]." *Han'guk hanmunhak yŏn'gu* [Journal of Korean Literature in Hanmun] (Society of Korean Literature in Hanmun) 33 (2004): 67–92.

Yi Chongho. "T'oegye Yi Hwang ŭi yugich'e ujuron kwa saengt'ae sasang [Yi Hwang's theory of the organic universe and ecological thought]." *Han'guk hanmunhak yŏn'gu* [Journal of Korean Literature in Hanmun] (Society of Korean Literature in Hanmun) (2004): 33–65.

Yi Kiyong. "Yulgok ŭi chayŏn ihae wa ch'ŏnin kyoyŏ–Han'gukchŏk chayŏn'gwan ŭi sae p'aerŏdaim mosaek ŭl wihan siron [Yi I's perception of nature and the relationship between heaven and man–Search for a new paradigm in terms of the Korean-style view of nature]." *Journal of Asian Philosophy* (The Society for

Asian Philosophy in Korea) 13 (2000): 91–127.

Yu Sŏngsŏn. "Yulgok simnon e kŭn'gŏhan hwan'gyŏng yulli ŭi mosaek [Search for environmental ethics based on Yi I's theory of the mind]." *Yulgok sasang yŏn'gu* (Association of Yulgok Study) 4 (2001): 73–100.

C. PAPERS RELATED TO KOREAN SIRHAK (PRACTICAL LEARNING)

Kim Chiyŏng. "Hong Taeyong ŭi *Ŭisan mundap* ŭl t'onghae salp'yŏ pon Han'guk saengt'ae sasang ŭi kanŭngsŏng [Korean ecological thought as viewed through Hong Taeyong's *Ŭisan mundap*]." *Ŏmun yŏn'gu* 33–2 (Summer 2005): 431–449.

Kim T'aeo. "Hyegang sasang ŭi saengt'aejuŭijŏk kyoyuk wŏlli [The ecological education principle contained in Hyegang's thought]." *Philosophy Education* (The Philosophy Education Society of Korea) 35 (2008): 261–284.

______. "Hyegang ŭi taedongnon kwa sot'ongnon kŭrigo kyoyuk saengt'aehak [Hyegang's theories of great harmony and communication and educational ecology]." *Philosophy Education* (The Philosophy Education Society of Korea) 41 (2010): 243–268.

Ch'a Sŏnghwan. "Chŏng Yagyong kyŏnghak sasang i saengt'ae hwan'gyŏng wigi ŭi sidae e chunŭn sisajŏm [The implications of Chŏng Yagyong's thought regarding the Confucian Classics in terms of the ecological crisis]." *Tamnon* (The Korean Association of Socio-Historical Studies) 201 (2010): 5–31.

Ch'oe Yŏngjin. "Inmulsŏng tongiron ŭi saengt'aehakchŏk haesŏk [An ecological interpretation of the theory of the Sameness-Difference of *Human* and Material Nature]." *Journal of Confucian Thought* (The Korean Society of Confucianism) 10 (1998): 57–68.

Ch'oe Yŏngjin and Yi Haenghun. "Ch'oe Han'gi unhwaron ŭi saengt'aehakchŏk haesŏk [An ecological interpretation of Ch'oe Han'gi's theory of functional activity]." *Taedong munhwa yŏn'gu* (Taedong Institute for Korean Studies) 45 (2004): 119–139.

Pak Sumil. "21 segi munmyŏng kwa Pak Chiwŏn ŭi saengt'ae chŏngsin [The civilization of the twenty-first century and Pak Chiwŏn's ecological spirit]." *Journal of East Asian Cultures* (Institute for East Asian Cultures, Hanyang University) 47 (May 2010): 215–241.

______. "Kyoyuk ŭi kwanjŏm esŏ pon Pak Chiwŏn ŭi saengt'aejŏk sigak kwa kŭ ŭimi [Pak Chiwŏn's ecological perceptions as viewed from the educational standpoint and the implications thereof]." *Onji nonch'ong* (Onji hakhoe) 25 (2010): 261–288.

1. INTRODUCTION TO THE BOOKS

Let us now summarize the above-mentioned three books. Pak Hŭibyŏng's Han'guk ŭi saengt'ae sasang (Ecological Philosophy of Korea) (1999) was the first book in the field of literature to approach Korean traditional philosophy from an ecological standpoint. This book can be evaluated as the origin of ecological discourse in the field of Hanmun (classical Chinese writing) literature. Pak identified three ecological perspectives as being embedded in Korean traditional philosophy.[9] First, all beings in the universe were regarded as being fundamentally equal. Second, man and civilization were introspectively approached from the standpoint of objects (物, *mul*). Third, a strong focus was placed on the unification of the way (*dao*) of nature and human life. This book contains a total of eleven papers, namely three papers on the Taoist scholar Yi Kyubo, two papers each on the Neo-Confucian scholars Sŏ Kyŏngdŏk and Sin Hŭm,[10] and two papers apiece on the Sirhak scholars Hong Taeyong and Pak Chiwŏn.[11]

---

9 Pak Hŭibyŏng, *Han'guk ŭi saengt'ae sasang* [Ecological philosophy of Korea] (Tolbegae, 1999), 15–36.

10 "Sŏ Kyŏngdŏk ŭi chayŏn ch'ŏrhak [Sŏ Kyŏngdŏk's philosophy of nature]," "Sŏ Kyŏngdŏk ŭi ch'ŏllisi [Sŏ Kyŏngdŏk's philosophical poems]," "Sin Hŭm ŭi hangmun kwa sasang [Sin Hŭm's learning and thought]," "Sin Hŭm ŭi chayŏn sihak [Sin Hŭm's poems about nature]."

11 "Hong Taeyong ŭi saengt'aejŏk segyegwan [Hong Taeyong's ecological view of the world]," "Hong Taeyong sasang e issŏsŏ mul a ŭi sangdaesŏng

The characteristics and significance of this book can be summarized as follows. First, the key significance of this book lies in the fact that it introduced the ecological discourse in the field of literature. In particular, it greatly influenced ecological studies in the field of Sirhak. For instance, Kim T'ae-o introduced the three ecological views found in Korean traditional thought suggested by Pak Hŭibyŏng, and studied Ch'oe Han'gi's ecological characteristics in his paper, "Hyegang sasang ŭi saengt'aejuŭijŏk kyoyuk wŏlli (The ecological education principle contained in Hyegang's thought)" (2008). Furthermore, Pak Hŭibyŏng's "Pak Chiwŏn ŭi myŏngsim e taehan saengt'ae munhakchŏk chŏpkŭn (The eco-literary approach of Pak Chiwŏn toward the profound mind)" was further concretized as 'ecology of the profound mind' in Pak Sumil's paper, "21 segi munmyŏng kwa Pak Chiwŏn ŭi saengt'ae chŏngsin (The civilization of the 21st century and Pak Chiwŏn's ecological spirit)" (2010).[12] In addition, Kim Chiyŏng's "Hong Taeyong ŭi *Ŭisan mundap* ŭl t'onghae salp'yŏ pon hanguk saengt'ae sasangŭi kanŭngsŏng (Korean ecological thought as viewed through Hong Taeyong's *Ŭisan mundap*)",[13]

---

kwa tongilsŏng [The role of the relativity and sameness of objects and the self in Hong Taeyong's thought]," "Pak Chiwŏn sasang e issŏsŏ ŏnŏ wa myŏngsim [The role of language and the profound mind in Pak Chiwŏn's thought]," "Pak Chiwŏn ŭi sanmun sihak [Pak Chiwŏn's prose poems]."

12 Pak Sumil, "21 segi munmyŏng kwa Pak Chiwŏn ŭi saengt'ae chŏngsin [The civilization of the 21st century and Pak Chiwŏn's ecological spirit]," *Journal of East Asian Cultures* (Institute for East Asian Cultures, Hanyang University) 47 (May 2010).

13 Kim Chiyŏng, "Hong Taeyong ŭi *Ŭisan mundap* ŭl t'onghae salp'yŏ pon Han'guk saengt'ae sasang ŭi kanŭngsŏng [Korean ecological thought as viewed through Hong Taeyong's *Ŭisan mundap*]," *Ŏmun yŏn'gu* 33-2 (Summer 2005).

is not very different from Pak Hŭibyŏng's analysis of Hong Taeyong's ecological view of the world found in his work, *Ŭisan mundap* (醫山問答). Second, although the title of this book is *Han'guk ŭi saengt'ae sasang* (Ecological Philosophy of Korea), this book does not conduct a comprehensive introduction of Korean thinkers, but rather is limited to a smattering of individuals. It does not deal with the individuals who can be regarded as the major figures within Korean Confucianism, and who authored the majority of the studies related to the ecological discourse, namely Yi Hwang, Yi I, and Ch'oe Han'gi. As such, this book merely highlights the ecological elements and characteristics of Korean Confucianism as a whole. This denouement can be regarded as a result of the fact that this book was a collection of existing presentations and papers rather than a planned work on Korean ecological thought in general. Third, as they were written from an introductory standpoint, the majority of the papers in this book, with the notable exception of three or four of them, suffer from a lack of concreteness and depth. Furthermore, as the author majored in Korean literature, his analysis of the relevant works is one that is rooted in a literary standpoint. As such, this work is characterized by a limited discussion of philosophical thought and philosophical analysis.

The second book is Kim Uktong's *Han'guk ŭi noksaek munhwa* (The Green Culture of Korea) (2000). Kim Uktong, who is a scholar of English Literature, deals with traditional Korean thought from the standpoint of ecological literature. Among the many papers included in this book, only one, "*Sirhak sasang kwa noksaek sasang* (Sirhak thought and green thought)" is related to Korean Confucianism. Kim argues that one of the things which set Sirhak (Practical Learning) apart from traditional Confucianism was the amount of attention they paid to nature and the environment. Kim maintains that green thought is evident in the work of Sirhak scholars and that many of them exhibited an interest in ecologism. Furthermore, Kim stresses that contrary to modern capitalism, economic reform as viewed by Sirhak scholars was a process that involved 'using nature in an ecological manner akin to the notion of 'sustainable development and growth' of today.[14] Based on this premise, the book goes on to introduce the ecological elements and characteristics found in the philosophy of Sirhak scholars from the *Kyŏngse ch'iyong hakp'a* (經世致用學派, School of Administration and Practical Usage), *Iyong husaeng hakp'a* (利用厚生學派, School of Profitable Usage and Benefiting the People), and *Silsa kusi hakp'a* (實事求是學派, School of Seeking Evidence).

Kim Uktong's book is progressive in that it addresses not only the Sirhak scholars from the *Iyong husaeng hakp'a*, but also scholars such as Yu Hyŏngwŏn and Yi Ik from the *Kyŏngse ch'iyong hakp'a*, as well as scholars such as Chŏng Yagyong from the *Silsa kusi hakp'a*. This can be regarded as being in stark contrast with Pak Hŭibyŏng, who only dealt with three Sirhak scholars who belonged to the *Iyong husaeng hakp'a*. Although this work deals with various Sirhak schools, the author does not discuss the similarities and differences between the three schools, as well as their organic connections, except to mention that the scholars from the *Iyong husaeng hakp'a* exhibited the most greenness in terms of their ecologism.[15] Furthermore, the book for the most part is concerned with the ecological elements found in the works of individual Sirhak scholars, and is very limited in terms of seeking to conduct a comparison, or to identify organic

---

14 Kim Uktong, *Han'guk ŭi noksaek munhwa* [The green culture of Korea] (Munye Publishing, 2000), 219.

15 Kim Uktong, *Han'guk ŭi noksaek munhwa* [The green culture of Korea] (Munye Publishing, 2000), 221.

connections, between such Sirhak scholars.

Let us now take a look at Han Myŏnhŭi's T*ongasia munmyŏng kwa Han'guk ŭi saengt'aejuŭi* (East Asian Civilization and Korean Ecologism) (2008). Only one of the book's six chapters deals with Korean Confucianism, namely Chapter 3: Korean traditional thought and the view of nature, ecological implications.[16] In addition, the content pertaining to Korean Confucianism contained in this book is further diluted as a result of the fact that this chapter addresses not only Korean Confucianism, but other Korean traditional schools of thought such as Buddhism, Taoism, and Tonghak. Han Myŏnhŭi divides the main ecological issues addressed by such schools of thought into 1)the connectivity of nature, 2)the non-instrumental value of nature, 3)ecological limitedness of society, and 4) the ideological concretization program. Han regards philosophies that incorporated issues 1) and 2) as falling under the category of 'passive ecologism.' Meanwhile, a philosophy that incorporated all four issues is defined as one that is engaged in 'active ecologism.' Han separates Korean Confucianism into Neo-Confucianism and Sirhak (Practical Learning). The author delves into which of these issues Neo-Confucianism and Sirhak incorporated, what category Neo-Confucianism and Sirhak fall under, and the ecological implications and limitations of these two

---

16 Chapter 3. *Han'guk ŭi chŏnt'ong sasang kwa chayŏn'gwan, saengt'aejŏk hamŭi* [Korean traditional thought and the view of nature, ecological implications]; 2. *Han'guk Yubulsŏn ŭi sasang kwa chayŏn'gwan* [Korean Confucian, Buddhist, and Zen thought and their respective perceptions of nature]: 109–131; 3. *Han'guk ŭi Sirhak, Tonghak, kŭrigo chayŏn'gwan* [Korea's Sirhak and Tonghak and their perception of nature]: 131–141; 4. *Han'guk chŏnt'ong sasang ŭi saengt'aejŏk hamŭi* [The ecological implications of Korean traditional thought]: 142–150.

philosophies.[17]

Han Myŏnhŭi's book can be regarded as featuring the following implications and limitations. In terms of the work's positive implications, it is important to note that in his capacity as a scholar who majored in Western philosophy, and in particular environmental philosophy, Han has helped to widen the scope of studies by conducting an ecological discourse from the standpoint of comparative philosophy. This runs contrary to the majority of those involved in ecological discourses within the field of Asian philosophy, who have either majored in Asian philosophy or literature. Second, the majority of the papers related to the ecological discourse within Korean Confucianism have been limited to the mere revelation of the organic or ecological elements embedded in Korean Confucianism. In this regard, Han's work should be lauded for having introduced a new methodology and for having suggested the limitations of an ecological approach to Korean Confucianism. Moreover, it should also be commended for having suggested measures to overcome such limitations based on more in-depth discussions. On the other hand, the analysis of Korean Neo-Confucianism and Sirhak is too simple and generalized. Furthermore, Korean Neo-Confucian and Sirhak scholars exhibited different characteristics and trends across different periods. Nevertheless, Han's determination of whether the above four issues were incorporated into Korean Neo-Confucianism and Sirhak is based on a generalization of the ecological studies conducted by a handful of scholars; this comes as part of his attempt to radically separate the groups

---

17 Han Myŏnhŭi, T*ongasia munmyŏng kwa Han'guk ŭi saengt'aejuŭi* [East Asian civilization and Korean ecologism] (Philosophy and Reality Publishing, 2009), 101–150.

into those that promoted passive and active ecologism, an approach that is open to criticism.[18]

Although saddled with the above-mentioned limitations and problems, these three books are nevertheless of great academic value and significance when it comes to the development of the ecological discourse as it pertains to Korean traditional thought. While Pak Hŭibyŏng and Kim Uktong can be said to have started the ecological discourse in the field of literature, Han Myŏnhŭi should be seen as having suggested a new direction for the ecological discourse within the field of philosophy. However, all three of these books can be regarded as introductory works that do not deal with the ecological thought found in Korean Confucianism in a profound manner. The publication of books that include an account of the ecological thought found in Korean Confucianism in general must therefore be seen as a task to address in the future.

2. INTRODUCTION TO THE PAPERS

Approximately nine papers that deal with Korean Neo-Confucianism from an ecological standpoint have so far been published. While one paper is concerned with Neo-Confucianism in general (Lee Dong-hee [Yi Tonghŭi], "Sŏngnihak ŭi hwan'gyŏng ch'ŏrhakchŏk sisa (Environmental philosophical implications of Neo-Confucianism)"), two deal with Yi Hwang (Chang Sŭnggu, "T'oegye sasang ŭi saengt'ae ch'ŏrhakchŏk chomyŏng (Highlighting Yi Hwang's ecological philosophy)" and Yi

18 A detailed discussion of this matter will be undertaken in Chapters III and IV.

Chongho, "*T'oegye* Yi Hwang ŭi yugich'e ujuron kwa saengt'ae sasang (Yi Hwang's theory of the organic universe and ecological thought)"). Meanwhile, four papers have as their subject Yi I (Yi Kiyong, "Yulgok ŭi chayŏn ihae wa ch'ŏnin kyoyŏ—Han'gukchŏk chayŏn'gwan ŭi sae p'aeradaim mosaek ŭl wihan siron (Yi I's perception of nature and the relationship between heaven and man—Search for a new paradigm in terms of the Korean-style view of nature)"; Yu Sŏngsŏn, "Yulgok simnon e kŭn'gŏhan hwan'gyŏng yulli ŭi mosaek (Search for environmental ethics based on Yi I's theory of the mind)"; Roh Yŏngch'an, "Yulgok ujuron ŭi saengt'aeronjŏk amsi tŭl (The ecological allusions contained in Yi I's theory of the cosmos)"; Kim Sangjin, "Kosan kugokka ŭi sŏngnihakchŏk saengt'ae insik (The Neo-Confucianism based ecological perceptions found in the *Kosan kugokka*)"). In addition, while one paper deals with Chang Yu (U Ŭngsun, "Chang Yu ŭi sayu pangsik e taehan han ihae—saengt'aehakchŏk insik ŭi mosaek (Understanding Chang Yu's way of thinking—searching for ecological perceptions)"), another is concerned with Sin Hŭm (Chŏng Yŏnjŏng, "Sin Hŭm ŭi sisegye e mich'in chuyŏk saengt'aegwan ŭi yŏnghyang (The influences of the ecological views found in the Book of Changes on Sin Hŭm's poetry)"). The superficial characteristics pertaining to the ecological discourse within Korean Neo-Confucianism found in these papers can be summarized as follows.

First, the majority of these papers were focused on a few scholars. While there were many Neo-Confucian scholars, these papers focused exclusively on Yi Hwang, Yi I, Chang Yu and Sin Hŭm.[19] Moreover, when we consider that there was only one paper written about Chang Yu and another about Sin Hŭm, we can rightfully conclude that these studies were for the most part concerned with Yi Hwang and Yi I. In addition, there was only one paper written about the ki philosopher Sŏ Kyŏngdŏk, an individual who could easily be considered a main subject of interest when it comes to the organic characteristics and ecological elements of Neo-Confucianism.[20]

Second, leaving aside the papers related to literature, little attention has been paid to the ecological approach in Neo-Confucianism from the standpoint of philosophy. While the literary approach was employed in papers dealing with Yi Hwang (Yi Chongho's paper), Yi I (Kim Sangjin's paper), Chang Yu and Sin Hŭm, those that approached the topic from the standpoint of philosophy consisted of Yi Tonghŭi's general survey of Neo-Confucianism, Chang Sŭnggu's paper on Yi Hwang, and papers by Yi Kiyong, Yu Sŏngsŏn and Roh Yŏngch'an that dealt with the philosophy of Yi I. To this end, while Yu Sŏngsŏn's paper, "Yulgok simnon e kŭn'gŏhan hwan'gyŏng yulli ŭi mosaek (Searching for environmental ethics based on Yi I's theory of the mind)" includes environmental ethics in its title,

---

19 Even if we add the two papers, "Sŏ Kyŏngdŏk ŭi chayŏn ch'ŏrhak [Sŏ Kyŏngdŏk's philosophy of nature]" and "Sŏ Kyŏngdŏk ŭi ch'ŏlli si [Sŏ Kyŏngdŏk's poems of philosophy]" found in Pak Hŭibyŏng's book to this total, this only amounts to five scholars who were in effect covered by such studies.

20 The two papers about Sŏ Kyŏngdŏk included in Pak Hŭibyŏng's book, *Han'guk ŭi saengt'ae sasang* [Ecological philosophy of Korea] were respectively a general introduction to Sŏ Kyŏngdŏk's ki philosophy and poems. One would be hard-pressed to state that these papers dealt with his work from an ecological standpoint.

it only introduces Yi I's mind theory in a general manner without really delving into environmental ethics or an ecological approach and analysis. As such, if we exclude Yu's paper, then that leaves us with only four papers in the field of philosophy.

Third, compared to the field of literature, the range of figures dealt with in the field of philosophy is rather narrow. More to the point, while studies have been conducted on five scholars, namely Yi Hwang, Yi I, Chang Yu, Sin Hŭm, and Sŏ Kyŏngdŏk, in the field of literature, only Yi Hwang and Yi I have been examined in the field of philosophy.

There are approximately eight papers that highlight the Sirhak from the ecological standpoint. In this regard, while two papers are about Pak Chiwŏn (Pak Sumil, "21 segi munmyŏng kwa Pak Chiwŏn ŭi saengt'ae chŏngsin (The civilization of the twenty-first century and Pak Chiwŏn's ecological spirit)" and "Kyoyuk ŭi kwanjŏm esŏ pon Pak Chiwŏn ŭi saengt'aejŏk sigak kwa kŭ ŭimi (Pak Chiwŏn's ecological perceptions as viewed from the educational standpoint and the implications thereof)"), another two papers are concerned with Hong Taeyong (Ch'oe Yŏngjin, "*Inmulsŏng tongiron* ŭi saengt'aehakchŏk haesŏk (An ecological interpretation of the theory of the Sameness-Difference of *Human* and Material Nature)" and Kim Chiyŏng, "Hong Taeyong ŭi *Ŭisan mundap* ŭl t'onghae salp'yŏ pon Han'guk saengt'ae sasang ŭi kanŭngsŏng (Korean ecological thought as viewed through Hong Taeyong's *Ŭisan mundap*)." Moreover, there is also one paper about Chŏng Yagyong (Ch'a Sŏnghwan, "Chŏng Yagyong kyŏnghak sasang i saengt'ae hwan'gyŏng wigi ŭi sidae e chunŭn sisajŏm (The implications of Chŏng Yagyong's thought regarding the Confucian Classics in terms of the ecological crisis"), and three papers about Ch'oe Han'gi (Ch'oe Yŏngjin, "Ch'oe Han'gi unhwaron ŭi saengt'aehakchŏk haesŏk (An ecological interpretation of Ch'oe

Han'gi's theory of functional activity)"; Kim T'ae-o, "Hyegang sasang ŭi saengt'ae-juŭijŏk kyoyuk wŏlli (The ecological education principle contained in Hyegang's thought)"; Kim T'ae-o, "Hyegang ŭi taedongnon kwa sot'ongnon kŭrigo kyoyuk saengt'aehak (Hyegang's theories of great harmony and communication and educational ecology)"). While two papers were prepared by a scholar in the field of philosophy (Ch'oe Yŏngjin), one was produced by a specialist in the field of literature (Kim Chiyŏng), four by individuals involved in the field of education (Pak Sumil, Kim T'ae-o), and one in the field of sociology (Ch'a Sŏnghwan). The major characteristics of these papers related to Sirhak can be summarized as follows.

First, broad studies were carried out on the major representative Sirhak scholars such as Pak Chiwŏn, Hong Taeyong, Chŏng Yagyong, and Ch'oe Han'gi, all of whom belonged to the Pukhak (Northern Learning) School.

Second, these papers were limited to the study of individual scholars. While Yi Tonghŭi dealt with the ecological characteristics found in Korean Neo-Confucianism in general, no papers addressed the issue of the ecological elements and characteristics exhibited in Sirhak thought per se.

Third, various vantage points were used in conjunction with these papers. For example, while Ch'oe Yŏngjin focused on philosophy, Kim Chiyŏng's *approach was based on the* literature field, Pak Sumil and Kim T'aeo's the field of education, and Ch'a Sŏnghwan's the sociology field. This can be regarded as the result of the fact that while Sirhak focused on the theories of *Kyŏngse ch'iyong* (經世致用, Administration and Practical Usage) and *Iyong husaeng* (利用厚生, Profitable Usage and Benefiting the People), Neo-Confucianism was concerned with the *yi-ki theory* (理氣論,

basic principles and the atmospheric force of nature), mind-nature theory (心性論), and the theory of self-cultivation (修養論).

Fourth, there was a general lack of research conducted in the field of philosophy. While Yi Tonghŭi, Chang Sŭnggu, Yi Kiyong and Roh Yŏngch'an produced papers that were related to Neo-Confucianism from a philosophical standpoint, only Ch'oe Yŏngjin, who wrote papers about Hong Taeyong and Ch'oe Han'gi, produced papers about Sirhak from the standpoint of philosophy. Moreover, while some studies about Neo-Confucianism from the standpoint of philosophy were conducted in an in-depth manner, the above-mentioned papers on Hong Taeyong and Ch'oe Han'gi were introductory works at best.

These problems regarding ecological approaches to a field of Korean Confucianism that includes Neo-Confucianism and Sirhak can be regarded as a result of the short history of the study of the ecological discourses within Korean traditional thought, and the general lack of specialists and interest. In this regard, the significance of the ecological discourse within Korean Confucianism will be assessed in sections III and IV based on the results of the above-mentioned studies.

III. THE ECOLOGICAL CHARACTERISTICS AND LIMITATIONS OF KOREAN NEO-CONFUCIANISM

In this section, an analysis of the ecological characteristics and problems of Korean Neo-Confucianism will be carried out based on an examination and criticism of the research that has highlighted Korean

Neo-Confucianism from the ecological standpoint. After having conducted a general introductory analysis of Korean Neo-Confucianism, the present study will then analyze the works on Yi Hwang (1501–1570) and Yi I (1536–1584).

1. THE ECOLOGICAL CHARACTERISTICS OF KOREAN NEO-CONFUCIANISM IN GENERAL

In his book (Chapter 3 *Han'guk ŭi chŏnt'ong sasang kwa chayŏn'gwan, saengt'aejŏk hamŭi* [Korean traditional thought and the view of nature, ecological implications]), Han Myŏnhŭi sought to identify the general ecological characteristics exhibited in Korean Neo-Confucianism. Han divided the main ecological issues addressed within Neo-Confucianism into 1)connectivity of nature, 2)the non-instrumental value of nature, 3)the ecological limitedness of society, 4)the ideological concretization program. Han regarded a philosophy that incorporated issues 1)the connectivity of nature and 2)the non-instrumental value of nature as falling under the category of 'passive ecologism.' Meanwhile, he defined a philosophy that incorporated all four of these themes as falling under the category of 'active ecologism.'[21] Korean Neo-Confucianism, with individuals such as Yi Hwang, Yi I and Sŏ Kyŏngdŏk at the center of this movement, accepted the notion of the 'organic connectivity of nature' under which man and nature were regarded as being organically connected based on the notion of the oneness of heaven, earth, and

---

[21] Han Myŏnhŭi, T*ongasia munmyŏng kwa Han'guk ŭi saengt'aejuŭi* [East Asian civilization and Korean ecologism] (Philosophy and Reality Publishing, 2009), 49–52.

humanity (天地人合一). As Korean Neo-Confucianism regarded nature and mankind as having come into being from the way (道), the Great Ultimate (太極) as the law of nature, and nature as the origin of life, Han also argued that it also encompassed the notion of the 'non-instrumental value of nature'. As such, Neo-Confucianism is regarded in his study as falling under the category of 'passive ecologism.' However, he maintained, the incorporation of an 'ideological concretization program' in Neo-Confucianism could have resulted in a form of ecologism that is far from desirable at the practical level. In addition, Neo-Confucianism boasts a rational (理性)—superior thinking structure that places an excessive amount of emphasis on principle (理, *yi*). As it is very authoritative, Neo-Confucianism possesses a history of accepting class-oriented stratification. As this class discrimination had room to develop into discrimination against nature, it became difficult for Neo-Confucianism to incorporate the 'ecological limitedness of society.' For these reasons, Han maintained that it was difficult to place Neo-Confucianism in the active ecologism category.[22]

Han's assertion that Neo-Confucianism encompassed 'the connectivity of nature and the 'non-instrumental value of nature' is not very different from those found in previous works on Neo-Confucianism. Furthermore, the reason why Neo-Confucianism did not have any practical program to socially concretize an ecologism-based ideology can be construed as being because the destruction caused to the ecosystems at the time was yet not very serious. However, there is room for debate as far as Han's assertion that it was difficult to see that Neo-Confucianism

---

[22] Ibid., 143–144.

clearly accepted the 'ecological limitedness of society' is concerned. As principle (理, *yi*) was a universal notion that applied to both man and nature, it could very well be seen as the basis for equality between man and nature, and the foundation for the granting of intrinsic value to nature. Furthermore, it does not stand to reason that Neo-Confucianism inevitably favored discrimination against nature because it accepted class-oriented stratification. While the basis of 'ecological limitedness of society' is the acceptance that there are limits to the material growth of a society,[23] Neo-Confucianism at the time was based on an agrarian society in which man was subordinated to nature. Furthermore, given the basic belief in the unity of man and heaven (天人合一), assertions that material growth could be infinitely implemented would have been hard to support. In this regard, it would be more appropriate to perceive the 'ecological limitedness of society' as being embedded in Neo-Confucian scholars' continuous calls for the removal of human desire and the extinguishment of human desire and greed.

In his paper, Yi Tonghŭi asserted that Neo-Confucianism boasted a third view of nature that differed from the anthropocentrism and naturism of the West. The third view of nature, which is a convergence of the humanism of Confucianism and the unique organic view of nature found in Neo-Confucianism, can be referred to as 'humanistic ecology' or 'organistic humanism.' This third view of nature is identified as a very dynamic and dialectic viewpoint under which the two viewpoints of environmental ethics are harmonized.[24] In the case of Korean Neo-

---

23 Ibid., 50.

24 Yi Tonghŭi, "Sŏngnihak ŭi hwan'gyŏng ch'ŏrhakchŏk sisa [Environmental philosophical implications of Neo-Confucianism]," *Tongyang ch'ŏlhak*

Confucianism, Yi Hwang's theory of principle (主理論, *churiron*), which is an ethical position, can be regarded as having anthropocentric tendencies. On the other hand, Yi I's theory of vital energy (主氣論, *chugiron*), which is based on the integration of man and nature, can be regarded as having physiocentric or naturecentered tendencies, or to be more specific non-anthropocentric tendencies. However, as the difference between these viewpoints was viewed as minor, Yi Tonghŭi stressed the fact that Neo-Confucianism represented the common base of both Yi Hwang and Yi I, and asserted that Korean Neo-Confucianism boasted what he refers to as 'humanistic ecology (nature-friendly anthropocentrism). Moreover, he argued that this humanistic ecology was very relevant to the current discussions on environmental philosophy in the contemporary era.[25]

This establishment of a new view of nature that revolves around the definition of Korean Neo-Confucianism as 'humanistic ecology' can be regarded as a meaningful attempt to revive traditional thought. However, the attempt made in this paper to ultimately unify the philosophical diversity of Korean Neo-Confucianism, which is at an earlier point in the study divided into the theory of principle, theory of vital energy, theory of only-yi or rationalism (唯理論, *yuriron*), and the theory of only-ki (唯氣論, *yugiron*), by binding these thoughts under the banner of 'humanistic ecology' can be regarded as being problematic. The diverse schools of thought in the West, such as technocentrism, ethical anthropocentrism, ecologism, and romanticism, not only conflicted with one another, but also developed as a result of their mutual criticism and moderation of each

---

(The Society for Asian Philosophy in Korea) 13 (September 2000): 35.

25 Ibid., 49.

other. Furthermore, Yi's assertion that humanistic naturalism (which is not physio-centrism because it is based on human superiorism) and nature-friendly humanism (which is not anthropocentrism because it is based on nature-friendly tendencies) can be regarded as a new view of nature to be found within Neo-Confucianism[26] creates the impression that Neo-Confucianism developed in a dialectic manner that involved embracing both anthropocentrism and physio-centrism. However, as such a position runs the risk of becoming one that is 'neither this nor that,' more profound discussions on this matter are required.

2. YI HWANG'S THEORY OF ONE PRINCIPLE (一理): OBJECT AND HUMAN ONENESS (物我一體) AND THE MIND OF HEAVEN AND EARTH (天地之心)

In his paper, Chang Sŭnggu identified Yi Hwang's perception of nature as one that was rooted in the Daoistic view of nature. In addition to highlighting Yi Hwang's thought from the standpoint of ecological philosophy, Chang also attempted to reestablish Yi Hwang's perception of respect (敬). For Yi Hwang, nature was a world of truth and life from which vivid life forms emerged, a world of purity devoid of all human desires, a world of aesthetics within which the beauty of the four seasons unfolded, and, in its capacity as the indefinite source, the origin of all beings. As previously mentioned, Chang defined Yi Hwang's view of nature as being rooted in the 'Daoistic view of nature.'[27] When highlighted

---

26 Ibid., 35.

27 Chang Sŭnggu, "T'oegye sasang ŭi saengt'ae ch'ŏrhakchŏk chomyŏng [Highlighting Yi Hwang's ecological philosophy]," *T'oegye hakpo* (The

from the standpoint of ecological philosophy, it is difficult to regard Yi Hwang's thought, which was based on the unity of heaven and man, as having originated from anthropocentrism. It is also difficult to regard it as having been rooted in biocentrism or ecologism. Rather, Chang argues that Yi Hwang's thought included elements of both. Moreover, he maintains that while Yi Hwang's theory of principle may have emphasized the universality of the whole more than the uniqueness of individuals, Yi Hwang maintained a neutral position in which he refused the dichotomy between individualism and holism. Lastly, Chang stresses that while Yi Hwang recognized the intrinsic value of all beings based on the concept of *iil punsu* (理一分殊, Principle is one but its manifestations are diverse), he did not perceive all beings in nature as being of the same value as man.[28] Yi Hwang's 'ethics of respect (敬)' emphasized the need to respect all beings without prejudice, and to behave in a manner that was based on the rational determination of the need to achieve harmony with nature. Yi Hwang thought that peace within the ecosystem could be maintained by heightening control over oneself based on the ethics of respect (敬) and the development of one's true nature.[29] Chang Sŭnggu concludes that although Yi Hwang's thought respected the existence of ecosystems and all beings, it was in the end relatively more realistic because it did not dash into excessive idealism or extremism like advocates of deep ecology.[30]

Written from the standpoint of literature, Yi Chongho's study revolves around the premise that Yi Hwang's profound emotional

T'oegye Studies Institute) (2001): 236.

28 Ibid., 237–241.

29 Ibid., 246.

30 Ibid., 249.

understanding of humanity can be combined with ecological thought to create the aesthetics of coexistence (共生) and mutual betterment (相生). Yi approached the structure and characteristics of Yi Hwang's organic view of the universe from the standpoint of the notion of *manmul ilch'e* (萬物一體, all things are of one body) contained in the "Sŏmyŏngdo (西銘圖: Diagram of the Western Inscription)." For Yi Chongho, Yi Hwang's organic view of the universe boasts the following characteristics. First, for Yi Hwang, the world was based on the notion of the oneness of objects and man (物我一體) under which all beings and man are connected to one another through the one principle (一理). This can be referred to as the 'organic view of the universe'. Second, man is depicted as the most intelligent being within this organic universe where all things are regarded as one substance, and as the mind of heaven and earth. The placement of man at the center of the universe is closely connected to the emphasis on the obligation to maintain the superiority of man toward others while simultaneously exercising benevolence towards the latter. Third, the endangerment of the relationship between *manmul ilch'e*, objects and the self) can be regarded as the result of the supremacy of the individual mind or the selfishness of the self. In order to overcome the estrangement between objects and the self, the selfishness of the self must be removed and the impartial mind of the non-self expanded.[31] Yi Chongho also introduced concrete examples of the ecological thought evident in Yi Hwang's life and work such as his poem exhibiting his affection for plums,

---

31 Yi Chongho, "T'oegye Yi Hwang ŭi yugich'e ujuron kwa saengt'ae sasang [Yi Hwang's theory of the organic universe and ecological thought]," *Han'guk hanmunhak yŏn'gu* [Journal of Korean Literature in Hanmun] (Society of Korean Literature in Hanmun) (2004): 41–51.

and his emphasis on the spirit of forgiveness (恕), the exercise of sympathy (惻隱), the aesthetics of coexistence (共生) and mutual betterment (相生) as the means to practice benevolence (仁), notion of equality, economy in expenditure and love for men (節用愛人), as well as the *silsa kusi* (實事求是, Seeking Evidence)—based and pro-ecological thought evident in his studies on rites (禮學).[32] Lastly, Yi Chongho regarded Yi Hwang's thought as being consistent with a philosophy of existence based on Confucius' concept of benevolence and Mencius' notion of non-endurance (不忍). Yi Hwang asserted that although both man and nature were alive, man should be the only one to die if such a fate is inevitable. This is because if nature dies, then the 'benevolence' that constitutes the very seed of existence will also disappear. Furthermore, all beings could be revived through the regeneration of benevolence. Yi Chongho concluded that this not only represents the key to elucidating Yi Hwang's ecological thought, but could also serve as the basis for the establishment of a uniquely Korean ecological philosophy.[33]

Such an attempt to identify elements and implications which can be used to establish a new ecological philosophy and thought in Yi Hwang's thought is indeed a fresh undertaking. However, the granting of excessive importance to Yi Hwang's thought may lead to the emergence of other problems. A perusal of Chang Sŭnggu's paper might lead one to believe that all the ecological problems society faces today could be resolved through the application of Yi Hwang's thought. For example, the assertion that Yi Hwang's thought was more rooted in reality than deep ecology

---

32 Ibid., 52–59.

33 Ibid., 62.

makes it look as if Yi Hwang's thought has already emerged as a direct and realistic alternative through which to actually resolve the current ecological crisis. Can it really be maintained that Yi Hwang's thought is more practical than deep ecology? Although deep ecology has excessive features, it has suggested detailed alternatives that are based on an astute diagnosis of the ecological crisis afflicting modern society. However, the same does not hold true where Yi Hwang's thought is concerned. Yi Hwang did not suggest any alternatives to analyze the ecological crisis based on a realistic problem awareness, or to resolve such problems. Only we who are living through the contemporary era can apply Yi Hwang's thought to the reality as pertains to the problems that have caused this ecological crisis. Furthermore, while the assertion that Yi Hwang's thought possessed both elements of anthropocentrism and ecologism and maintained a neutral position between individualism and holism, would seem to cover both aspects, it can be attacked from both of these sides when applied to actual problems.

Yi Chongho's paper can be assessed as having helped to develop the ecological thought embedded in Yi Hwang's study from both the standpoint of literature and philosophy. Moreover, by shedding light on the practical aspect of Yi Hwang's ecological thought evident in his own life, Yi Chongho also introduced the possibility that the ecological discourse within Korean Confucianism could move beyond the 'knowledge' level and into that of concrete 'action.' However, Yi Chongho's paper is also plagued by a fundamental problem. Yi Hwang's emphasis on anthropocentrism and human subjectivity evident in his statement that man, as the most intelligent of all beings, represented the mind of heaven and earth, as well as his proclamation of the oneness of objects and self (物我一體) based on the one principle (一理), can be regarded as a clear departure from the tenets of deep ecology. On the other hand, his claim that nature had to be chosen over man in a situation where one had to inevitably choose between the two is definitely reminiscent of the tenets of deep ecology. The duality of Yi Hwang's thought could help to position it as a new alternative with which to overcome the problems caused by anthropocentrism and ecologism. However, it also runs the risk of being nothing more than an idle ideological argument that is unable to resolve any problems related to the ecological crisis. Furthermore, when focused on preserving the earth, based on the notion of the oneness of the earth and man, the argument can lead to regarding the sacrifice of man in order to preserve the earth as being inevitable under a mentality that degrades the status of man. To this end, it is necessary to pay attention to Han Myŏnhŭi's assertion that ecologism is inherently limited by the fact that its propensity to sacrifice man and culture for the earth as a whole exposes it to claims of eco-fascism.[34] There is a need to conduct more in-depth discussions as to how Yi Hwang's ecological thought can be differentiated from the anthropocentrism and ecologism of the West, and how Yi Hwang's thought can overcome the limitations inherent in such philosophies.

3. YI I'S THEORY OF THE COSMOS AND ECOLOGICAL PERCEPTIONS

Three papers related to Yi I were published in the field of philosophy. In his study, Yi Kiyong suggested that Yi I's philosophy of nature and man

34 Han Myŏnhŭi, Mirae sedae wa saengt'ae yulli [Future generations and ecological ethics] (Philosophy and Reality Publishing, 2007), 240.

was based on the relationship between heaven and man (天人交與, *ch'ŏnin kyou*), and that while the relationship between man and nature was mutually complementary, the main actor in this relationship was man.[35] However, other than simply stating the difference between the two, Yi Kiyong makes no mention of how Yi I's view of nature differs from that of the modern West. Furthermore, Yi Kiyong does not engage in any detailed discussions on how Yi I's theory of *ch'ŏnin kyou* could be used to replace and overcome the problems inherent in the modern western perception of nature. Yu Sŏngsŏn's paper does not include any contents related to environmental and ecological discourse other than his suggestion in the conclusion that, "Yi I's awareness of ethics rooted in his theory of the mind can provide an effective motivation for the establishment of environmental ethics for the twenty-first century."[36] On the contrary, Ro Young-chan analyzes the ecological characteristics contained in Yi I's cosmological theory in a profound manner.[37] In his study, Ro advances the argument that the development of an ecological theory that can

---

35 Yi Kiyong, "Yulgok ŭi chayŏn ihae wa ch'ŏnin kyoyŏ—Han'gukchŏk chayŏn'gwan ŭi sae p'aeradaim mosaek ŭl wihan siron [Yi I's perception of nature and the relationship between heaven and man—Search for a new paradigm in terms of the Korean-style view of nature]," *Journal of Asian Philosophy* (The Society for Asian Philosophy in Korea) 13 (2000): 98–125.

36 Yu Sŏngsŏn, "Yulgok simnon e kŭn'gŏhan hwan'gyŏng yulli ŭi mosaek [Searching for environ-mental ethics bases on Yi I's theory of the mind]," *Yulgok sasang yŏn'gu* (Association of Yulgok Study) 4 (2001): 98.

37 Ro Young-chan, "Yulgok ujuron ŭi saengt'aeronjŏk amsi tŭl [The ecological elusions found in Yi I's theory of the cosmos]," in *Yuhak sasang kwa saengt'aehak* [Confucianism and ecology], ed. Mary Evelyn Tucker and John Berthrong, trans. O Chŏngsŏn (Yemun sŏwon, 2010), 249–268.

truthfully preserve the earth is predicated on the abandonment of the anthropocentric or earth-oriented perception in favor of a cosmological one.[38] Ro concludes that Yi Hwang interpreted the *yi* (理, principle) and *ki* (氣, vital energy) in an anthropological manner and developed an anthropological-based cosmology that was based on a dichotomous perception of yi and ki. On the other hand, by defining yi and ki as fundamentally and naturally neutral cosmological notions that do not have any intrinsic ethical characteristics, Yi I essentially interpreted *yi* and *ki* in a cosmological manner.[39] Based on his analysis of the *Yŏksuch'aek* (易數策), Ro concluded that Yi I perceived the 'universe' as 1)a vital, active, and changing entity rather than as a fixed physical object or mechanical entity, 2)as a hermeneutical rather than simple physical entity, 3)and as an open system rooted in specific principles and regularity. In addition, Yi I viewed the universe as a mystery which could not be recreated as a rational or conceptual framework, and asserted that man regarded the universe as majestic and stood in awe of the mystery that is the cosmos. Rather than a relationship between subjectivity and objectivity, Yi I perceived the relation between man and the universe as one between two subjectivities.[40] Yi I advocated a universal theory of the cosmos that was not dependent on human values. To this end, Ro advanced the idea that this could become the basis for the development of a theory of cosmological ecology. Ro also

---

38 Ibid., 251.

39 Ro Young-chan, "Yulgok ujuron ŭi saengt'aeronjŏk amsi tŭl [The ecological elusions found in Yi I's theory of the cosmos]," in *Yuhak sasang kwa saengt'aehak* [Confucianism and ecology], ed. Mary Evelyn Tucker and John Berthrong, trans. O Chŏngsŏn (Yemun sŏwon, 2010), 255.

40 Ibid., 261–262.

called for the development of a theory of cosmological ecology in which man opens up to the universe based on a mutual acceptance of nature and the cosmos that is achieved by not only seeing and listening to the mystery and pain of the cosmos, but also learning from the latter.[41]

Kim Sangjin can be regarded as the only scholar in the field of literature who focused on Yi I's poem, *Kusan kugokka* (高山九曲潭)[42] from the standpoint of ecological literature, and analyzed the characteristics and implications evident in this poem in terms of ecological literature. The emphasis on harmony between heaven, man and nature found in the *Kusan kugokka* makes this work consistent with the basic principles of ecologism. In this regard, Kim Sangjin identified the following three ecological perceptions evident in Yi I's poem. The first was his cognizance of nature as the basic sphere in which human life resided. Yi I's concept of choosing a place for residence (卜居) and living place (精舍) hints at an ecological perception in which nature is regarded as the basis (house) of human life.[43] The second was his awareness of the beauty of the changing seasons. This was evident in the ideological expression *it'ong kiguk* (理通氣局, existence of the universal *yi* within the changeable and limited *ki*) akin to the ecological spirit rooted in the principles of coprosperity, connectivity and circularity. This rotation of the four seasons encompassed not only the preservation of the law of the ecosystem, but also the will

---

41 Ibid., 267–268.

42 "*Kusan kugokka* [高山九曲潭]," in vol. 10, *Yulgokhak yŏn'gu ch'ongsŏ* [Collection of essays on the studies of Yulgok] (Yulgok Society, 2007), 459–484.

43 Kim Sangjin, "*Kosan kugokka* ŭi sŏngnihakchŏk saengt'ae insik [The Neo-Confucianism based ecological perceptions found in the *Kosan kugokka*]," *Sijohak nonch'ong* (Han'guk Sijo Hakhoe) 20 (2004): 58–59.

to maintain this law.[44] The third ecological perception can be identified as an awareness of the cosmos as a place where man and nature exist in harmony.

More to the point, one finds in this particular poem clear indication of the belief that heaven and man, I and others, as well as man and nature, have been harmonized with one another and have achieved harmony within the framework of nature. Kim Sangjin stressed the fact that the clear description in the *Kusan kugokka* of nature as an unspoiled ecosystem raises the possibility of it not only being read as an ecological poem, but also serving as an impetus for the revival of ecological literature in the contemporary era.[45]

Ro Young-chan can be regarded as having saliently highlighted the ecological characteristics and implications of Yi I's thought by contrasting his thought with that of Yi Hwang. However, Ro's study does not introduce any detailed measures or alternatives as to how the realistic problem known as the ecological crisis can be resolved. Ro's simple statement that the notions of *igi chimyo* (理氣之妙, the perfect relationship between principle (*yi*) and energy (*ki*)), *it'ong kiguk*, and *kiballisŭng* (氣發理乘, ki (*force*) leads and yi (principle) follows) constitute the philosophical basis of Yi I's perceptions of ecology leaves much to be desired. The following problems can be identified with regards to Ro's assertions regarding Yi I's ecological approach. Yi I's assertion that man represents the 'mind of heaven and earth'[46] because only man has

44 Ibid., 63–64.

45 Ibid., 71.

46 Yulgok chŏnsŏ [栗谷全書], "人者, 天地之心也, 人之心正, 則天地之心亦正, 人之氣順, 則天地之氣亦順矣," in vol. 14, 雜著 1, 天道策.

been granted the rightful *ki* of yin and yang (陰陽) can be regarded as proof that he accepted the differentiation between man and all beings. Furthermore, the assertions that the four beginnings (四端) and seven emotions (七情) originated from the *kiballisŭng*, and that the adoption of a meditation method based on the change of physical substance (矯氣質) can help restore the noble spirit (浩然之氣) by correcting changeable force (human mind)[47] opens up the claims that Yi I perceived principle (*yi*) and force (*ki*) as being value-neutral cosmological notions that did not possess any moralistic characteristics to debate. Although Yi I showed more naturalistic tendencies than Yi Hwang, whose focus was more on the moral, Yi I also regarded man and ethics as being of great importance. In this regard, if we regard Yi I as having employed principle (*yi*) and force (*ki*) based solely on value-neutral cosmological notions, then we have no other choice but to errantly conclude that he was in fact an ecologist rather than a Confucianist.

---

47 Yi Kiyong, "Yulgok ŭi chayŏn ihaewa ch'ŏnin kyoyŏ—Han'gukchŏk chayŏn'gwan ŭi sae p'aeradaim mosaek ŭl wihan siron [Yi I's perception of nature and the relationship between heaven and man—search for a new paradigm for the Korean-style view of nature]," *Journal of Asian Philosophy* (The Society for Asian Philosophy in Korea) 13 (2000): 111–118.

IV. THE ECOLOGICAL CHARACTERISTICS AND LIMITATIONS OF KOREAN SIRHAK

No papers have to date been produced that have approached Korean Sirhak (Practical Learning) as a whole from an ecological standpoint, or discussed its ecological characteristics in a profound manner. In his study entitled, "Sirhak sasang kwa noksaek munhwa (Sirhak thought and green culture)" Kim Uktong raises the possibility that along with the concepts of liberty, science, and reality suggested by Ch'ŏn Kwanwu, ecologism could also be pointed out as another characteristic of Sirhak (Practical Learning). Kim asserted that Sirhak scholars showed a level of interest in nature that went beyond simple economic reforms. More to the point, the economic reforms called for by the Sirhak scholars were fundamentally different from the tenets of modern capitalism that seeks to maximize profits. In this regard, the Sirhak scholars intended to develop and use nature in an effective and nature-friendly manner. They also regarded man and nature not as dichotomous beings, but rather as one organic entity. Kim stresses the point that the economic logic of Sirhak is reminiscent of the modern notion of 'sustainable development and growth.'[48] The term 'sustainable development,' which first emerged in the UN report entitled "Our Common Future" published in 1987, is defined as development that meets the needs of the present without compromising the ability of future generations to meet their own needs.[49] Anthropocentric environmental

---

[48] Kim Uktong, *Han'guk ŭi noksaek munhwa* [The green culture of Korea] (Munye Publishing, 2000), 219.

[49] Wikipedia, http://enc.daum.net/dic100/contents.do?query1=10XXX959

ethics are derived from how man's ethical ob-ligations toward the natural world impact interactions with other humans. The need to respect the rights of man can be regarded as the reason why we create specific limitations and restrictions when we discuss the environment, and the manner in which we should treat all the beings who reside on the earth other than man. In addition, there is also a need to protect and enhance the well-being of mankind, including that of people from the third-world and future generations.[50] That being the case, Sirhak, which as mentioned before evokes the notion of 'sustainable development and growth,' can be accepted as being closer to anthropocentric environmental ethics than ecocentrism. However, Kim Uktong's analysis of individual Sirhak scholars from the standpoint of ecological elements inherently contrasts with his assertion that Sirhak thought was akin to 'sustainable development and growth.' There is a clear need to determine whether Sirhak thought was more in keeping with anthropocentric environmental ethics or ecocentrism. The absence of any further discussions on Korean Sirhak as a whole in a detailed and profound manner makes it essential to discuss the ecological characteristics of Korean Sirhak. This task is carried out herein by analyzing and criticizing the work that has so far been conducted on the ecological discourses of Bukhak (Northern Learning) scholars such as Hong Taeyong (1731–1783), Pak Chiwŏn (1737–1805), Chŏng Yagyong (1762–1836) and Ch'oe Han'gi (1803–1877), individuals who have been the main topic of interest in the study of Sirhak scholars.

---

19 (accessed April 27, 2011).Publishing, 2000), 219.

50 Hwang Kyŏngsik, *Kaebang sahoe ŭi sahoe yulli* [Social ethics of an open society] (Philosophy and Reality Publishing, 1997), 380–381.

1. EQUALITY BETWEEN MAN AND OBJECTS (人物均) AND ECOLOGICAL EGALITARIANISM

Although Han Myŏnhŭi purportedly discusses the Sirhak School as a whole in Chapter 3 of his book, "Ecological implications of Korean traditional thought and views of nature," the actual focus is in fact limited to Hong Taeyong and Pak Chega. As such, Han's essay can be regarded as a discussion of the Pukhak (Northern Learning) School. Han's evaluation of Sirhak is based on the previously mentioned four main ecological themes. First, in the case of Hong Taeyong, Han assessed that his assertion that man and nature enjoyed equal rights in the eyes of the heavens could be construed as evidence that Sirhak fell under the category of a passive ecologism in which the connectivity of nature and the non-instrumental value of nature are embedded. Furthermore, Hong Taeyong's emphasis on the egalitarian view of society, abolition of the discrimination between legitimate and illegitimate, abolition of the discrimination between the four classes of society (scholars, farmers, artisans and tradesmen), and his introduction of policy measures designed to correct the land system that served as the basis of public life can also be perceived as evidence that Korean Sirhak to some extent accepted the 'ideological concretization program'. However, such conclusions are clouded by the presence of the notion of *Iyong husaeng* (利用厚生, Profitable Usage and Benefiting the People) emphasized by Pak Chega. Stressing the fact that money and goods were like a well, in that they had to be continuously utilized once they started to be used or they would dry out, Pak Chega placed great importance on consumption as a means to activate production. To this end, Sirhak runs the risk of moving towards the heightened use of nature if guidelines with which to appropriately control this tendency towards *Iyong husaeng* are not implemented. As such, Sirhak cannot accept the 'ecological limitedness of society' under a state in which no clear guidelines to curb the *Iyong husaeng*'s natural proclivity towards nature have been established.[51]

While Han sets out to discuss Korean Sirhak as a whole, he in fact limits himself to the study of the thought of Hong Taeyong and Pak Chega. Although Han encompasses the thought of these individuals in the overarching category called Sirhak, the Sirhak School in fact boasted a variety of schools of thought. While the Sirhak School was separated into proponents of the notion of *Iyong husaeng hakp'a* (利用厚生學派, School of Profitable Usage and Benefiting the People), *Kyŏngse ch'iyong hakp'a* (經世致用學派 School of Administration and Practical Usage), and *Silsa kusi hakp'a* (實事求是學派, School of Seeking Evidence), the analysis of the four main ecological themes must in reality be undertaken at the individual Sirhak scholar level. For example, the blanket claim that all Sirhak scholars who advocated the notion of *Iyong husaeng* unconditionally failed to incorporate the concept of the 'ecological limitation of society' is rendered baseless by the fact that Pak Chega did in fact incorporate such a concept into his thought.

---

51 Han Myŏnhŭi, *Tongasia munmyŏng kwa Han'guk ŭi saengt'aejuŭi* [East Asian civilization and Korean ecologism] (Philosophy and Reality Publishing, 2009), 147–148.

1) The ecological characteristics of Pak Chiwŏn

In his study, Pak Sumil divided the ecological spirit of Pak Chiwŏn into the following elements: 1)ecology of living creatures, 2)relational ecology, and 3)ecology of the profound mind. First, Pak Chiwŏn's view of the world was one that was rooted in the criticism of the futile pursuit of justification found in Neo-Confucianism and calls for the focus to be placed on useful concepts anchored in reality. For example, Pak supported the notion of *Iyong husaeng* under which use nature was to be used and society reformed in an effective manner that enhanced the well-being of the people. To this end, rather than destroying and exploiting nature, Pak Sumil stresses the fact that Pak Chiwŏn advocated using nature in a more ecological manner that was based on respect of nature. The practicality inherent in Pak Chiwŏn's worldview was a notion that was based not simply on the usefulness of materials and capital, but also on the aesthetic values of man. Pak Sumil maintains that Pak Chiwŏn's ecological thought was one in which he viewed nature from the realistic standpoint of others, and accepted the true nature of objects found in nature.[52] Based on this understanding, Pak divided the ecology of Pak Chiwŏn into the following three elements. The first is what he referred to as the ecology of living creatures. Pak Chiwŏn perceived nature as a being that is intricately connected to man, not as one that is separated from the latter. Nature is viewed as a living organism (life form) that spontaneously

---

52 Pak Sumil, "21 segi munmyŏngkwa Pak Chiwŏn ŭi saengt'ae chŏngsin [The civilization of the twenty-first century and Pak Chiwŏn's ecological spirit]," *Journal of East Asian Cultures* (Institute for East Asian Cultures, Hanyang University) 47 (May 2010): 220–221.

emanates, develops, and changes. Pak equated the ebbs and flows of nature with human activities. Thus, we can see that Pak Chiwŏn's ecological thought was rooted in reality and civilization.[53] The second was the so-called relational ecology. Relational ecology revolves around the careful observation of the relationship between man and nature in a manner that does not perceive these entities in a superficial manner and that also rejects dichotomous approaches. Once this comes to pass, one can discover a new truth that could not be seen with existing values. Furthermore, one should not engage in any discrimination or prejudice because the truth could be differently perceived depending on the situation. Pak also emphasized the need to move beyond the stratification of values and move towards the equality of all beings.[54] Under this notion of the equality of all beings, humans and tigers fall under the same category of animals from the standpoint of the heavens regarded as being a higher level than man. All beings, regardless of whether they are ants or humans, live together and occupy their own unique positions under the heavens.[55] Thus, 'relational ecology' can as such be evaluated as Pak Chiwŏn's strategy to dismantle centrism and place the periphery on an equal standing with the center.[56]

---

53 Ibid., 227.

54 Ibid., 227–230.

55 In his work *Hojil* (虎叱, a political fable of the Qing dynasty) Pak Chiwŏn states, "You often mention about heaven when discussing principle and nature (性). However, from the standpoint of heaven, tigers and humans are both regarded as animals. Viewed from the standpoint of the magnanimous heavens and earth that have given life to all beings, tigers and grasshoppers, silkworms and bees, ants and humans all live together. They should not quarrel or be estranged from one another."

56 Pak Sumil, *21 segi munmyŏng kwa Pak Chiwŏn ŭi saengt'ae chŏngsin* [The civilization of the 21st century and Pak Chiwŏn's ecological spirit], 233.

The third is the ecology of the profound mind. The profound mind (冥心) is a practical concept that can be defined as a responsive attitude to reality. The actual meaning of profound mind can be defined as: 1)viewing the world in an objective manner without falling into the trap of prejudice, 2)refusing the self, and 3)doing away with all vanity by emptying the ego. To Pak Chiwŏn, the profound mind was a practical concept that moved beyond idealism and towards a responsive attitude towards reality. The profound mind brings about an ecological awakening by compelling us to reflect on and reconsider notions that we had heretofore perceived as being clear, and requiring us to put into practice this newly awakened thought in a manner that moves well beyond mere idealism.[57]

In his work, Pak Sumil presents an organized assessment of the ecological spirit embedded in Pak Chiwŏn's thought. Pak Chiwŏn criticized the errant prejudice encompassed in 'self-centrism' and 'anthropocentrism,' and called for the removal of fallacies through a process of self-abnegation rooted in the profound mind and the move towards the actualization of the equality of all beings. This runs contrary to the tenets of Neo-Confucianism under which man is defined as the heart of heaven and earth (天地之心). Pak Chiwŏn's ecological spirit implies an overcoming of the anthropocentric prejudice of today in which human beings endowed with reason and souls are regarded as possessing intrinsic values. Such assertions, namely that the stratification of values should be destroyed as we do away with discrimination and prejudice and move toward the equality of beings, are similar to those found in the ecological

57 Ibid., 234–236.

egalitarianism rooted in ecocentrism.[58] However, regardless of Pak Sumil's explanation, it cannot be denied that the concept of *Iyong husaeng* that revolves around the efficient utilization of nature is one in which 'nature' is perceived as an implement to make life better for man. As this contrasts with the inherent thought behind the equality of beings, more in-depth discussions and assessments of this issue are required.

2) Hong Taeyong's ecological thought

Ch'oe Yŏngjin's study, "*Inmulsŏng tongiron* ŭi saengt'aehakchŏk haesŏk (Ecological interpretation of the theory of the Sameness-Difference of Human and Material Nature)", introduced Hong Taeyong's theory of the oneness of man-nature-animals (人物性同論) as part of his wider analysis of the *inmulsŏng tongiron* (人物性同異論, debates on whether the original nature of man and animal (or objects) is the same). Ch'oe's study includes the open-ended declaration that Hong Taeyong's theory of the oneness of man-nature-animals can serve as an important theoretical basis upon which to implement the current task of overcoming anthropocentrism. In this regard, this study cannot really be regarded as having analyzed the *inmulsŏng tongiron* from an ecological point of view.[59]

---

58 Naess defined the deep ecology movement as advocating an ecological egalitarianism under which all beings have "equal rights to live and bloom" based on a relational, total-field image. (Arne Naess, "The Shallow and Deep, Long-Range Ecology Movement: A Summary," Inquiry 16 (1973): 96–96.)

59 Ch'oe Yŏngjin, "Inmulsŏng tongiron ŭi saengt'aehakchŏk haesŏk [Ecological interpretation of the theory of the sameness-difference of human and material nature]," *Journal of Confucian Thought* (The Korean Society of

Based on his analysis of the *Ŭisan mundap*, Kim Chiyŏng divided Hong Taeyong's ecological thought into the 'mind of animals or objects (物)', 'the transformation of the earth into our fundamental base,' and 'the restoration of the earth's *ki* (地氣) in his study entitled, "Hong Taeyong ŭi *Ŭisan mundap* ŭl t'onghae salp'yŏ pon Han'guk saengt'ae sasang ŭi kanŭngsŏng (Korean ecological thought as viewed through Hong Taeyong's *Ŭisan mundap*)". Although published in 2005, Kim's very basic study never reaches the level of sophistication found in Pak Hŭibyŏng's 1999 study, "Hong Taeyong sasang e issŏsŏ mul-a ŭi sangdaesŏng kwa tongilsŏng (The relativity and similarity of nature and oneself in Hong Taeyong's thought)," a study that was based on the author's own analysis of the *Ŭisan mundap*.[60] To this end, Pak Hŭibyŏng's study can be regarded as the premiere work on Hong Taeyong.

Pak Hŭibyŏng argues that not only were Hong Taeyong's epistemology and ontology laden with ecological aspects, but his ecological leanings were also evident in his general perceptions of the relationship between objects, between nature and human, and between nations.[61] Based on his analysis of Hong's writing, *Ŭisan mundap* which is regarded as saliently highlighting Hong Taeyong's position regarding the relationship between

Confucianism) 10 (1998): 57–68.

60 Kim Chiyŏng, "Hong Taeyong ŭi *Ŭisan mundap* ŭl t'onghae salp'yŏ pon Han'guk saengt'ae sasang ŭi kanŭngsŏng [Korean ecological as viewed through Hong Taeyong's *Ŭisan mundap*]," *Ŏmun yŏn'gu* 33–2 (Summer 2005): 431–449.

61 Pak Hŭibyŏng, "Hong Taeyong sasang e issŏsŏ mul-a ŭi sangdaesŏng kwa tongilsŏng [The relativity and similarity between nature and the self found in Hong Taeyong's thought]," *Han'guk ŭi saengt'ae sasang* [Ecological philosophy of Korea] (Tolbegae, 1999), 278.

the self and nature (物我), Pak separated Hong Taeyong's ecological thought into four elements. The first is an introspection on anthropocentrism that is rooted in equality between man and objects (人物均). In his novel, Hong Taeyong's character of Sirong responds to the Confucian scholar Hŏja's statement that man was the most precious of all the life forms under heaven and earth by advocating the equality of man and objects. More to the point, he argued that while from the standpoint of man himself man was regarded as a more precious being than the other life forms, the other life-forms were regarded, when viewed from the standpoint of the heavens, as being as precious as man.[62] In its capacity as the origin of all the beings, heaven was regarded as the *t'aehŏ* (太虛, Great Emptiness). Viewed from the standpoint of *t'aehŏ*, all beings, despite their phenomenal differences, are equal. Pak claims that by perceiving nature and the self (物我) from the standpoint of the *t'aehŏ*, Hong Taeyong in effect established the theoretical basis with which to reflect on and eventually overcome anthropocentrism.[63] Second, Hong viewed the earth (地) as an organic living being. Hong Taeyong asserted that the earth was a living creature (活物), and perceived the earth as an enormous sphere within which the life activities of man and nature alike were carried out. Moreover, the earth itself was a living organic being, and all beings on earth were organically related to each other. Hong Taeyong's ecological insight

---

62 *Tamhŏnjip* [湛軒集], 4, *Ŭisan mundap* [醫山問答], Chapters 18–19. "天地之生, 惟人爲貴.[...] 以人視物, 人貴而物賤, 以物視人, 物貴而人賤, 自天而視之, 人與物均也.[...] 今爾曷不以天視物, 而猶以人視物也?"

63 Pak Hŭibyŏng, "Hong Taeyong sasang e issŏsŏ mul-a ŭi sangdaesŏng kwa tongilsŏng [The relativity and similarity between nature and the self found in Hong Taeyong's thought]," *Han'guk ŭi saengt'ae sasang* [Ecological philosophy of Korea] (Tolbegae, 1999), 280–281.

regarding the close organic relationship between man and nature became the basis for his theory of the oneness of man-nature-animals.[64] The third element is a rejection of self-centrism and an emphasis on equal relations between beings. Hong Taeyong rejected self-centrism and accepted the existence of horizontal relational networks between beings. The oneness of nature and the self thus becomes the epistemological and ontological basis for a world where it is possible to achieve harmony, coexistence, and mutual prosperity between all beings without any center. Hong Taeyong's *yŏgoe ch'unch'uron* (域外春秋論, theory of the independent history of each nation) can be regarded as part of his cognizance of a world where relational networks are established between the main actors within a structure devoid of an exclusivist center. Under Western modernity, nature, much like the various other nations, is perceived as the other, and treated as an implement to be used and controlled. However, Hong Taeyong perceived nature as a main actor that alongside man promotes the harmony and coexistence between nature and mankind and between the different nations. This can be viewed as Hong Taeyong's profound ecological thought, and as a vantage point that is clearly differentiated from the tenets of Western nationalism.[65] The fourth element that can be identified is a critical attitude toward civilization. Hong Taeyong viewed human desire and the development of civilization as having led to the emergence or worsening of the exploitation of nature, man's conquest of other men, ownership, war, extravagance, waste, empty formalities and vanity, and deceit. As civilization develops, the distinction between the

---

64 Ibid., 283.

65 Ibid., 284–290.

self and nature worsens, and man moves further away from supreme harmony. This can be regarded as having originated from the fact that the characteristics of civilization were perceived from the position of nature or heaven rather than from that of man.[66]

Pak's study clearly exposes the characteristics of Hong Taeyong's ecological thought in a profound and organized manner. Hong Taeyong exhibited a clearly different position from Neo-Confucianists when it came to the perception of nature and the relationship between nature and man. Although Yi Hwang and Yi I promoted the organic view of nature (cosmos), both scholars identified man as the most outstanding being of all. More to the point, man's status as the 'mind of heaven and earth' was regarded as the basis for the acceptance of the hierarchal differences between man and all other beings. However, Hong Taeyong criticized anthropocentrism on the grounds that man and nature should be regarded as equal from the standpoint of equality between man and objects. He also maintained a critical position with regards to human civilization, which he regarded as having caused the distinction between the self and nature and as having forced man to grow further away from the supreme harmony. Furthermore, although he claimed equality between man and objects, Hong Taeyong did not directly assert the oneness of objects (nature) and man; meanwhile, Yi Hwang and Yi I both supported, based on the notion of one principle (理一), the oneness of objects (nature) and man. Although Hong Taeyong promoted the need to perceive nature from the standpoint of heaven, he did not assert that man could or should participate in the development of all beings between heaven and

---

66 Ibid., 292.

earth. Viewed from this vantage point, Hong Taeyong's philosophy can be said to have been more akin to ecocentrism than anthropocentrism. Hong Taeyong's thought is consistent in part with deep ecology, which promotes the notion of 'ecological egalitarianism' under which all beings have an equal right to live and bloom.[67] Furthermore, the critical attitude toward civilization under which nature is perceived as having been further exploited and the distinction between the self and nature worsened as a result of the development of human desires and civilization can be linked to Arne Naess' assertion, "Man does not have any right to deplete the wealth and diversity of nature; we should maintain smaller human populations and decrease man's encroachment of nature".[68] However, Hong Taeyong's excessive egalitarianism and criticism of civilization may also lead to the same problems as those associated with deep ecology. Deep ecology identifies man and nature as equal members of the life community, and attaches the same value to man and all beings in nature. However, by doing this, deep ecology runs the risk of degrading the value and status of human beings, which can be seen as the utmost result of global evolution, in favor of nature, while degrading man to the status of accessory to nature. In the extreme case, it opens itself up to the criticism that it represents an example of an ecofascism under which man is regarded as being expendable in the name of actualizing the true value of the natural ecosystem.[69] As such, there is a need to discuss this issue

---

67 Arne Naess, "The Shallow and Deep, Long-Range Ecology Movement: a Summary," *Inquiry* 16 (1973): 95–96.

68 Michael E. Zimmerman eds., *Environmental Philosophy—From Animal Rights to Radical Ecology*, 196–197.

69 Kim Sea-jeong, "Saengt'aegye wigi wa yuga saengt'ae ch'ŏrhak ŭi paljŏn

within the wider ecological discourse on the thought of Hong Taeyong, a scholar whose leanings were closer to deep ecology than those of any other scholar.

2. CAN CHŎNG YAGYONG BE REGARDED AS AN ECOLOGIST?

Ch'a Sŏnghwan's paper, "Chŏng Yagyong kyŏnghak sasang i saengt'ae hwan'gyŏng wigi ŭi sidae e chunŭn sisajŏm (The implications of Chŏng Yagyong's thought regarding the Confucian Classics in terms of the ecological crisis)" can be regarded as the only study that approaches Chŏng Yagyong's thought from an ecological standpoint. Ch'a shed new light on Chŏng Yagyong's thought from the standpoint of 'ecological environmental politics', a position that is closely related to sociology. The characteristics of Chŏng Yagyong's ecological and environmental thought, that is, as seen by Ch'a Sŏnghwan, can be summarized as follows. First, the universe surrounding man forms the house in which the former lives. Viewed from the standpoint of human nature, only man can rule the

---

panghyang [The crisis of ecosystems and the direction of the development of ecological philosophy within Confucianism]," *Ch'ŏrhak yŏn'gu* (Korean Philosophical Society) 85 (2003): 94–95. For example, Tom Regan asserted, "Advocates of synoptic anti-anthropocentrism who find themselves in a situation where they must kill man or a rare wild flower will inevitably see the killing of man as being justified in order to protect the rare wild flower which contributes to the integration, stability, and beauty of the land community." (No Hŭijŏng, "Hwan'gyŏng yullihak esŏ ŭi kaech'eron kwa ch'ongch'eron ŭi t'onghap" (Ph.D. diss., Korea National University of Education, 2002), 114.)

world.[70] For example, Chŏng Yagyong asserted, "Animals and plants are part of an order in that they all exist to elevate man, to keep man warm, to raise man, and to serve man. What else can rule the world except man? Heaven regards this world as a house within which man is expected to pursue virtue. The sun, moon, stars, trees and grass, and animals are all entities which support this house."[71] Second, the life forms which make up the ecosystem enjoy different natures (性). There are three different natures. While trees and grass boast life but lack knowledge, animals enjoy life and knowledge. Meanwhile, the nature of man is characterized by life, knowledge, exquisiteness, and an orientation towards good. Third, man con-tributes to reaching the acme of central harmony by organically connecting the natural realm to the entire cosmos, thereby achieving a functional balance and bringing about the harmonized prosperity of all beings. However, in accordance with the standard of morality (愼獨, *sindok*, moral behavior even when one is alone), the virtue of central harmony can only be possessed by virtuous man. Fourth, the nature of man can be achieved through the complete actualization of the nature of objects, a role which allows man to be positioned as the ruler of this world.[72]

---

70 Ch'a Sŏnghwan, "Chŏng Yagyong kyŏnghak sasang i saengt'ae hwan'gyŏng wigi ŭi sidae e chunŭn sisajŏm [The implications of Chŏng Yagyong's thought regarding the Confucian Classics in terms of the ecological crisis]," *Tamnon* (The Korean Association of Socio-Historical Studies) 201, (2010): 7–8.

71 Chŏng Yagyong, *Kukyŏk yŏyudang chŏnsŏ: Nonŏ kogŭmju* (Kyŏngjip III), trans. Institute of Honam Studies (Chunnam University Press, 1989), 134–135.

72 Ch'a Sŏnghwan, *Chŏng Yagyong kyŏnghak sasang i saengt'ae hwan'gyŏng wigi ŭi sidae e chunŭn sisajŏm* [The implications of Chŏng Yagyong's thought

Ch'a Sŏnghwan asserted that the characteristics of Chŏng Yagyong's ecological and environmental thought were rooted in Chŏng's perception that the universal ecological environment, which he believed existed to serve man, could not automatically function without the intervention of the latter. Such intervention was limited to special measures on the part of saints such as the establishment of institutions to actualize the nature of objects that make up the ecological environment. In order to make the universal ecological environment that constituted a house for man function, a form of ecological environmental politics known as the ideal state of central harmony (致中和) had to be established by virtuous men endowed with a sacred mind who served the heavenly ruler (上帝).[73]

Based on these assertions, Ch'a Sŏnghwan introduced new modern images of saints, virtuous men, and ordinary people, all of which he regarded as important elements of universal ecological environmental politics. For example, the saint can be interpreted as a 'cultural intellectual' who develops the ecological ethics needed to actualize the true nature of the objects that make up the universal ecological environment that serves as the house of man. Meanwhile, the virtuous man can be likened to a new political bureaucrat who is able to move beyond merely serving the interests of the human world and continuously maintain balance and harmony with nature. Lastly, the 'public' referred to by Chŏng Yagyong is one that can accept the imposition of regulatory regulations by the cultural intellectuals as part of their environmental vision and environmental politics, with these regulations perceived as being inevitable for the

regarding the Confucian Classics in terms of the ecological crisis], 9–21.

73 Ibid., 23.

survival and prosperity of the entire human race, and this even if they may conflict with their actual interests.[74]

Ch'a Sŏnghwan's study reestablishes the characteristics of Chŏng Yagyong's ecological and environmental thought from the standpoint of 'ecological environment politics,' and searches for political measures that could be used to resolve the current ecological crisis. His study stands out from other papers, which focused exclusively on the identification of ecological elements and the significance thereof, in that Ch'a introduces detailed measures with which to resolve the current crisis. However, despite its significance, his ecological approach to Chŏng Yagyong inevitably suffers from the following fundamental problems. In fact, when compared with other Confucian scholars, Chŏng Yagyong's thought can be regarded as having been endowed with relatively few ecological elements, and as having leaned more towards anthropocentrism than ecologism. For example, unlike other Confucian scholars, Chŏng Yagyong did not support an 'organic view of the universe' that was based on the notions of *mul-a ilch'e* (物我一體, oneness of objects and man) and *manmul ilch'e* (萬物一體, all things are of one body), which in turn originated from the concepts of *iil punsu* (理一分殊, Principle is one but its manifestations are diverse) and *ilgi yut'ong* (一氣流通, man and nature are connected to one another based on one *ki*). He also did not claim equality between man and objects or ecological egalitarianism like the scholars of the Pukhak (Northern Learning) School. Rather, Chŏng Yagyong asserted that the universe was the 'house of man' whose fruits man was meant to benefit from, that man was the only creature that could rule the world, and that

74 Ibid., 25–28.

the nature of man was the highest of the three natures he identified. Such assertions can become the basis for human chauvinistic behavior in which, much like the anthropocentric and instrumental views of nature found in the modern West, man is perceived as being superior to any other creatures within nature. Contrary to anthropocentrism, Chŏng Yagyong maintained that man had an important responsibility and mission vis-à-vis nature. To this end, he asserted that man could only actualize his true nature by actualizing the true nature of objects. However, this mission was perceived as being the task of saints and virtuous men alone; moreover, Chŏng's inability to suggest any detailed measures to save nature and all beings results in such assertions being of little more than declarative significance. Chŏng Yagyong's thought exhibits the periodic limitations, in that such efforts were regarded as being dependent on the capacity of saints and virtuous men rather than the public. These problems are also evident in the type of universal ecological environment politics clamored for by Ch'a Sŏnghwan. A situation in which cultural intellectuals and political bureaucrats become the main actors in the establishment of ecological ethics and institutions rather than the public inevitably results in the public having to passively follow the former. Such a situation leads to the creation of another hierarchal order, and can as such be regarded as running contrary to the tenets of ecologism.

2. CH'OE HAN'GI'S GREAT HARMONY AND A COMMUNICATION-BASED ORGANIC SOCIETY

There are three studies related to Ch'oe Han'gi. In his philosophy-based study, "Ch'oe Han'gi unhwaron ŭi saengt'aehakchŏk haesŏk (Ecological interpretation of Ch'oe Han'gi's theory of functional activity)," Ch'oe Yŏngjin identified the characteristics of Ch'oe Han'gi's view of nature found in his theory of circulation and change (運化論), and delved into the possibility of using it as an alternative solution for the current ecological crisis. Ch'oe Yŏngjin analyzed the structure and characteristics of Ch'oe Han'gi's theory of circulation and change, which he divided into three aspects: The true nature of *ki*, triple structure of circulation and change (運化), and the oneness of man and nature. Ch'oe Yŏngjin asserts that the seeds for the development of an alternative philosophy with which to overcome the ecological crisis lies in these elements. Ch'oe Han'gi's theory of circulation and change, which promotes the oneness of man and nature, differs from the Neo-Confucianism based view of nature in that it is rooted in the tangible ki. It also differs from the mechanical view of nature found in the Western world in that while it regards the objective entities of nature as being important, it does not neglect the possibility of nature as an ethical prototype.[75]

On the other hand, in his two studies, "Hyegang sasang ŭi saengt' aejuŭijŏk kyoyuk wŏlli (The ecological education principle contained in Hyegang's thought)" and "Hyegang ŭi taedongnon kwa sot'ongnon kŭrigo kyoyuk saeng-t'aehak (Hyegang's theories of great harmony and communication and educational ecology)," Kim T'ae-o highlighted Ch'oe Han'gi's thought from the standpoint of education, and in particular educational ecology. Kim identified three aspects as the characteristics

---

75 Ch'oe Yŏngjin and Yi Haenghun, "Ch'oe Han'gi unhwaron ŭi saengt'aehakchŏk haesŏk [Ecological interpretation of Ch'oe Han'gi's theory of functional activity]," *Taedong munhwa yŏn'gu* (Taedong Institute for Korean Studies) 45 (2004): 119–136.

of Ch'oe Han'gi's perception of ecology contained in his study of ki. The first is the presence of a oneness (一統)—based disciplinary structure. Ch'oe Han'gi's study of *ki* (氣學) was based on a perception of the heavens, earth, and nature as well as society and individuals from the standpoint of the organic circulation of ki. Ch'oe's study of *ki* (氣學) was rooted in a philosophical structure that emphasized the unified principle of three movements: circulation and change of great *ki* (大氣運化), circulation and change in people (統民運化), and circulation and change in individuals (一身運化). The second was the division of nature (自然) from what should be (當爲). Ch'oe Han'gi maintained an organic standpoint when it came to the continuity that exists between the ways of nature and man, "The way of man originates from the way of heaven, and the ability to surmise (推測, to form a notion from scant evidence) originates from the flow of movements (流行)."[76] However, the presence of ontological and epistemological gaps between nature and man result in, based on the way of heaven (nature) being identified as the standard for the way of man (what should be), continuity having to be pursued from the standpoint of the principle of the oneness of the ability to surmise and the flow of movements.[77] The third is the dialectic between organicism and mechanism. The relationship between man and nature is perceived as being both organic and mechanical at the same time. Mechanism is based on the belief that man is not the only being that possesses a transcendental nature or rational cognitive capability. All beings in the heavens and on earth have been bestowed original natures by *ki*. Ch'oe Han'gi even

---

76 *Ch'uch'ŭngnok* [推測錄], "人道出於天道, 推測出於流行," 2, 天人有分.

77 *Ch'uch'ŭngnok* [推測錄], 2, 『自然當然』, "自然者, 天地流行之理. 當然者, 人心推測之理也. 學者, 以自然爲標準, 以當然爲工夫."

compared the ki of the mind, which he labeled as the cognitive capability as well as the body of man, to a mechanic. Ch'oe Han'gi's notion of mechanism should be viewed as being of great ecological value in that it effectively seeks to limit the arrogance of man toward nature.[78]

Furthermore, Kim T'aeo identified two elements as the key to the ecological education principle contained in Ch'oe Han'gi's thought: the theory of great harmony (大同論) and the theory of communication (疏通論). When viewed from the ecological standpoint, the theory of great harmony can be regarded as having three overarching characteristics: The first is that of great love. More to the point, Ch'oe Han'gi asserted that philanthropic love toward man and nature should be regarded as true love.[79] Here, the philanthropic spirit under which one loves both man and nature should be perceived as the key to Ch'oe Han'gi's understanding of the notion of great harmony. The second is the notion of the continuous transformation of *ki* through circulation (運化承順). The circulation of the ki of heaven and man results in the basic orientation of man and nature being that of mutual communication and harmony. Ch'oe Han'gi defined the movement of air, or natural sphere, and the movement of the body (individuals) and people (society), or human sphere, as the great harmony of circulation (大同運化). The great harmony of circulation in turn refers to the continuous transformation of *ki* through circulation (運化承順) under which the human way follows the heavenly way, and subjective ethics are

---

78 Kim T'aeo, "Hyegang ŭi taedongnon kwa sot'ongnon kŭrigo kyoyuk saengt'aehak [Hyegang's theories of great harmony and communication and educational ecology]," *Philosophy Education* (The Philosophy Education Society of Korea) 41 (2010): 246–253.

79 *Injŏng* [人政], 25, 愛有大小.

consistent with objective nature. The third is the belief that great harmony is based on the notion of the fundamental orientation towards peace. Ch'oe Han'gi maintained that the *ki* of circulation originally emerged to achieve peace between the self and others, and that this peacefulness was a normal attribute of any relationship.[80] Three overarching characteristics were also identified in conjunction with the theory of communication: The first is the penetration of the supernatural ki. Communication can as such be defined as the supernatural *ki*'s ability to penetrate man and nature. Man and all beings in the universe are equal in that they are all vital or instrumental beings endowed with the supernatural *ki*. The second is related to post self-centrality. Narrow-minded subjectivity can be regarded as a barrier that stops mutual communication between the self and objects. The ability to smoothly communicate with others is as such intricately related to the removal of the narrow self-centric mindset. The third is the flexibility of change. The ability to engage in smooth and profound communication is predicated on the presence of the flexibility needed to deal with various situations. Ch'oe Han'gi regarded the penetration of the supernatural *ki* as the essence of communication. By appropriately controlling one's state in a manner that removed self-centrality, Ch'oe intended to pave the way for true com-munication. Ch'oe Han'gi's theory of communication can be evaluated as having provided an approach with which to restore the ecological relationship between

---

80 Kim T'aeo, "Hyegang ŭi taedongnon kwa sot'ongnon kŭrigo kyoyuk saengt'aehak [Hyegang's theories of great harmony and communication and educational ecology]," *Philosophy Education* (The Philosophy Education Society of Korea) 41 (2010): 246–253.

humans and between man and nature.[81] While from the standpoint of educational ecology, the way of great harmony can be identified as the search for love and peace, the way of communication can be likened to the quest for modesty and self-introspection. While under the former, Korean education should make efforts to focus on the love of others and a larger and wider love of life, Kim T'ae-o maintains that the latter compels Korean education to view the wisdom of self-introspection and modesty from the standpoint of mutual communication between nature and man, society and man, and between humans themselves.[82]

Kim T'ae-o not only actively delved into the ecological characteristics of Ch'oe Han'gi's thought, but also searched for measures to establish educational ecology that could be applied to the modern era. In this regard, it can be evaluated as being of greater academic value than the other studies on this topic. Ch'oe Han'gi's thought, which was discussed in the above-mentioned three studies, shares many similarities with ecocentrism. First, the assertion found in the preface to *Kihak* (氣學) that, "There is only *ki* in the universe, no other complete beings exist," the oneness structure and the principle of three circulations, as well as the circulation of the great *ki*, can be regarded as the basis for the provision of 'intrinsic values' to all beings within the universe rather than only select ones. Moreover, the assertions that man and nature, both of which exist between heaven and earth, are composed of the same mechanical elements (器), and that man and all beings have been equally granted a true nature,[83] can be perceived as providing the basis for 'ecological

81 Ibid., 253–261.

82 Ibid., 264–265.

83 *Ch'uch'ŭngnok* [推測錄], 3, 「推情測性」/6, 「推物測事」

egalitarianism.' Lastly, the theory of great harmony based on the great love of philanthropy, continuous transformation of circulation (運化承順), and peace-orientation, as well as the theory of communication based on the penetration of the supernatural *ki*, post self-centrality, and the flexibility of change, can be viewed as being similar to the notion of 'self-realization' advanced by Arne Naess and the 'life community' advocated by Thomas Berry.[84] Nevertheless, Ch'oe Han'gi's thought should not be regarded as being akin to ecocentrism. Although Ch'oe Han'gi's study of ki to some extent includes traditional organic characteristics, he in reality exhibited a stronger affinity for modern scientific technology than other Confucian scholars. His work also encompassed a mechanical thinking structure under which all beings within the universe were regarded as being composed of mechanical elements, including the organs found in the human body.[85] In Ch'oe Han'gi's study of *ki*, anthropocentrism and physiocentrism, mechanical and organic theories, as well as modern and

---

84 Arne Naess pointed out that the resolution of the current ecological crisis is predicated on the maximization of self-realization through the expansion of the self or ego towards nature as a whole, including animals and plants. For his part, Thomas Berry believes that overcoming the ecological crisis requires a move from 'anthropocentric norms' to 'biocentric norms'. This move towards biocentric norm includes the realization that the life community made up of all living species is actually a bigger entity with greater value, and that the main interests of man would be best served by accepting the need to enhance the preservation of this wider life community. (Kim Sea-jeong, "Saengt'aegye wigi wa yuga saengt'ae ch'ŏrhak ŭi paljŏn panghyang [The crisis of ecosystems and the direction of the development of ecological philosophy within Confucianism]," Ch'ŏlhak yŏn'gu (Korean Philosophical Society) 85 (2003): 94.

85 Ch'uch'ŭngok [推測錄], 6, "天是器也, 地亦器也, 人亦器也."; Sin'git'ong (神氣通)/2, "人身形體, 是一機械也."

traditional elements, were all viewed as constantly transforming as a result of their interactions and mutual influence on one another. This duality in terms of Ch'oe Han'gi's study of *ki*, which exhibited elements of organic and mechanical theories, opens him up to the criticism that his theory is nothing more than obscure syncretism which is neither true to modern scientific technology nor to the traditional, flexible, organic view of the world.[86] In this regard, it becomes necessary to clearly verify the duality of Ch'oe Han'gi's study of *ki*, and to resolve the problems occasioned by this duality. In addition, Kim T'aeo's assertion[87] that Ch'oe Han'gi's notion of mechanics, under which even the *ki* of the mind (心氣), a concept that refers to man's cognitive capability, was compared to mechanics, is of great ecological value in that it limited human arrogance toward nature is open to debate. The period in which Ch'oe Han'gi lived was not one in which the abuses occasioned by anthropocentrism had yet become evident. As such, Ch'oe Han'gi's perception of man as a mechanism equal to all other beings may result in a refusal of the positive significance of the ontological value or uniqueness of man. The mere fact that man is different from other beings does not automatically translate into the former's destruction of nature. This can be regarded as being rooted in anthropocentrism, which was itself based on the rationalism of Western modernity. Rather, the Asian perception of man as the mind of all beings in the heavens and on earth, and of man as a being endowed with the

---

86 Ch'oe Chindŏk, "Hyegang kihak ŭi ijungsŏn ge taehan pip'anjŏk sŏngch'al [Critical introspection of the duality of Hyegang's study of ki]," *Hyegang Ch'oe Han'gi* (Ch'ŏnggye, 2000): 140–141.

87 Kim T'aeo, *Hyegang sasang ŭi saengt'aejuŭijŏk kyoyuk wŏlli* [The ecological education principle contained in Hyegang's thought], 271.

highest level of *ki*, identified man as a being to whom the responsibility and mission of subjectively participating in the achievement of harmony amongst all beings in the universe has been bestowed. As such, rather than evaluating it in an unconditionally positive manner, there is a need to critically approach Ch'oe Han'gi's comparison of the human's mind of ki to a mechanism.

V. CONCLUSION

This study analyzed the study of the 'ecological discourse within Korean Confucianism' which has been carried out since the late 1990s. The history of the study of the ecological discourse within Korean Confucianism is much shorter than that of the environmental and ecological discourses in the Western world, which, stimulated by the environmental movement of the 1960s, started in earnest in the 1970s. Even if we account for the fact that this particular field of study only started to be active recently, the results of the study of the ecological discourse within Korean Confucianism so far can only be regarded as having been insignificant. Only twenty research papers have been produced over the past ten years. Moreover, when we exclude the studies that are of an introductory or declarative nature, only ten papers related to the ecological discourse within Korean Confucianism have so far been published. Thus, this field of study has remained at an introductory level. However, this does not mean that the ecological discourse within Korean Confucianism is devoid of implications, or that it has no future. The problems that have caused the ecological crisis cannot be resolved in one day. These problems cannot be resolved by a single theory or measure. To this end, the ecological discourse within Korean Confucianism may emerge in the future as an alternative discourse with which to resolve the problems associated with the ecological crisis. However, many tasks need to be addressed before the ecological discourse within Korean Confucianism can move from the realm of the possible to the realistic. In this regard, this study summarizes the ecological characteristics and problems exposed by the analysis of the ecological discourse within Korean Confucianism and also takes a look at the future tasks that will need to be resolved.

First, let us take a look at the ecological discourse within Korean Neo-Confucianism. Scholars such as Yi Hwang and Yi I were at the forefront of the ecological discourse within Korean Neo-Confucianism. The ecological character-istics and problems exposed by the ecological discourses within Korean Neo-Confucianism can be summarized as follows. First, the ecological characteristics of the Korean Neo-Confucianism that revolved around Yi Hwang and Yi I can be identified as an 'organic view of the universe,' in which the self and external objects are regarded as one body based on the principle of oneness. Second, Korean Neo-Confucianism includes both elements of anthropocentrism and ecocentrism. Third, while Yi Hwang exhibited anthropocentric tendencies, Yi I boasted ecocentric ones. Fourth, although Korean Neo-Confucianism includes abundant ecological characteristics, it differs from ecocentrism in that it defines man as the most intelligent being and as the symbol of the mind of heaven and earth. Emphasizing these aspects makes it possible to establish alternatives with which to overcome the problems stemming from ecocentrism as well as the abuses occasioned by anthropocentrism. On the other hand, it is important to remember that failure to establish an organized and realistic theory and measures that reflect realistic conditions may result in allowing the anthropocentric and ecocentric elements of Korean Neo-Confucianism to block the creation of anything other than an obscure theory which cannot play any role in the resolution of concrete problems.

Next, let us look at the ecological discourse within Sirhak (Practical Learning). As even individuals from the same Pukhak (Northern Learning) School such as Pak Chiwŏn, Hong Taeyong, Chŏng Yagyong, and Ch'oe Han'gi exhibited their own tendencies, it becomes difficult to include all Sirhak scholars in one group. Be that as it may, the ecological characteristics of the Pukhak (Northern Learning) School represented by Pak Chiwŏn and Hong Taeyong can be summarized as follows: First, they regarded nature as a living creature (活物) and as an organic being. They also believed that an organic relationship existed between man and nature. Second, they criticized the notion of the superiority of man by asserting that when viewed from the standpoint of heaven, man and nature were equal. Third, contrary to Neo-Confucian scholars, they did not identify man as the symbol of the mind of heaven and earth. Their claims of the equality between man and objects are in many ways reminiscent of the notion of ecological egalitarianism found in ecocentrism. However, the notion of *Iyong husaeng* that revolves around the efficient utilization of objects inherently conflicts with the concept of the equality of beings in that it regards nature as an implement with which to improve human life. Furthermore, an overemphasis on the equality of man and objects runs the risk of descending into ecofascism.

Contrary to other Sirhak scholars, Chŏng Yagyong's thought featured more anthropocentric elements than ecological ones. Rather than emphasizing the notion of the self and external objects as one body or the equality of man and objects, Chŏng's beliefs were more akin to anthropocentrism. For instance, he believed that nature and the universe constituted the house in which man existed, only man could rule the world, and that man boasted the most advanced nature. However, Chŏng Yagyong's awareness of man's responsibility to nature is evidenced by his claims that man could only actualize his true nature by actualizing the true nature of all beings. Nevertheless, such human responsibilities were perceived as being an onus that was carried only by saints and virtuous men. As such, it may be unreasonable to seek to identify ecological characteristics in Chŏng Yagyong's thought. That being said, one of the related tasks which should be undertaken is that of finding ways to harmonize the anthropocentric elements in his thought with ecocentrism. Furthermore, it is essential that practical measures that make it possible for the common people to not only actively participate in this process, but also assume the reins thereof, be drawn up. Meanwhile, unlike Chŏng Yagyong, Ch'oe Han'gi's thought can be perceived as having been laden with organic and ecological elements. First, Ch'oe possessed an organic view of the universe that was based on the notion of the circulation of the one *ki*. Second, Ch'oe's assertions that man and nature were composed of *ki*, and that all entities that existed between the heavens and earth were granted their unique natures, may become the basis for ecological egalitarianism. Third, the theory of great harmony through philanthropy, continuous transformation of circulation, and peace-orientation, as well as the theory of communication based on the penetration of the supernatural *ki*, post self-centrality, and the flexibility of change, can be regarded as being akin to the notions of 'self-realization' and 'life community' found in ecocentrism. However, Ch'oe Han'gi's study of ki suffers from the duality of boasting both organic and mechanical characteristics. In this regard, there is a need to address the problems caused by this duality.

As such, even though Korean Confucianism includes an abundance of ecological elements and characteristics, Neo-Confucianism and Sirhak (Practical Learning) differed in terms of the details, and such differences were also visible on an individual scholar basis. Furthermore, one also finds instances in which organic and mechanical theories coexisted within a scholar's anthropocentric approach. These aspects may work as positive factors that will help to enrich the ecological discourse within Korean Confucianism. However, the following tasks must be resolved in order for such a denouement to come to pass.

First, there is a need to extend the scope of research subjects. Although organic and ecological elements can be found in the thought of many Confucian scholars, only nine scholars, including Yi Hwang, have been dealt with as part of the study of the ecological discourse within Korean Confucianism. The ecological characteristics of Korean Confucianism can only truly be comprehensively highlighted when studies have been conducted on various scholars and theories, and the basis for the establishment of the Korean-style ecological theory needed within contemporary society has been prepared.

Second, it is essential that specialists be educated as part of efforts to establish an ecological philosophy and ethics that is based on Korean Confucianism. To date, only seven of the studies on ecological discourse within Korean Confucianism have been produced by experts in the field of philosophy. Including Lee Dong-hee, there are only six researchers in this field. In other words, each researcher has produced approximately one paper. Truth be told, practically no specialists in the field of 'Korean Confucianism and ecology' have been produced. In this regard, having failed to position itself as an actual and realistic alternative to the resolution of the ecological crisis as well as to conduct studies related to the ecological characteristics of Korean Confucianism in an in-depth manner, the ecological discourse has to date constituted nothing more than a temporary discourse. The ecological discourse within Korean Confucianism can only move beyond being an empty echo and entrench itself as a realistic alternative when numerous specialists capable of addressing these tasks in a concentrated and consistent manner are produced.

Third, there is a need, based on the results of the studies conducted at the initial stage of the search for the ecological significance and implications of Korean Confucianism, to move to the second stage of the reorganization and recreation the ecological implications of Korean Confucianism. To this end, there is a need to develop an understanding of the environmental and ecological philosophy/ethics of the Western world, as well as to perceive the general problems related to the ecological crisis within contemporary society. It is essential to move beyond the matter of focusing on the past or present and create a new ecological philosophy that integrates past and present as well as east and west.

Fourth, it is necessary to clearly identify the ecological characteristics of Korean Confucianism that differentiate it from the tenets of the ecological discourse in the Western world. The assertion that Korean Confucianism features many of the ecological characteristics found in the Western world can be regarded as little more than a starting point. For Korean Confucianism to become an important part of the attempts to resolve the ecological crisis, the unique characteristics of Korean Confucianism must be highlighted in order to help resolve the problems which the ecological discourse in the Western world have encountered; furthermore, concrete alternatives should be established through the advent of a creative encounter between the ecological discourses of the East and West.

Fifth, it is necessary to suggest realistic measures through which to resolve the ecological crisis, and to implement them in an active manner. While advocates of Buddhism have implemented concrete practical measures pertaining to the ecological crisis, Korean Confucianism has yet to prepare realistic and detailed alternatives that could help to resolve this crisis. Furthermore, the willingness to implement such measures, or even to design tools through which to gain feedback, has been sorely lacking. Confucianism cannot ignore the fact that the *Kyŏngse ch'iyong* (經世致用, Administration and Practical Usage) school of thought advocates the study of self-discipline (修己), governing others (治人), being self (成己), being things (成物), enlightening the lucid virtue (明明德), and approaching the people (親民). Korean Confucianism's ability to survive under the current ecological crisis is predicated on the active search for concrete measures, and further, the development of opportunities to implement such measures.

Kim Sea-jeong (kimshd@cnu.ac.kr) is *a Professor of Philosophy at Chungnam National University, Korea.*

Translated by Michael Bujold and Young-ki You

THE ORIGIN AND PRESERVATION OF RELIC FORESTS AND CONFUCIANISM IN KOREA

By Kim Jongwon, Lee Junga, Lim Jeongcheol and Hwang Sookyoung

1. INTRODUCTION

There are various types of relic forests including traditional rural forests (Jang Dongsoo and Kim Hakbeom 1993, 19–31; Kim Jongwon and Lim Jeongcheol 2007, 133–188), historical forests and ancient forests in Korea. These relic forests are characterized by the fact that they are very original and unique cultural forests corresponding to the indigenous local cultures. Traditional rural forests exist within the area of influence of village communities, having historical and cultural significance, and for this reason they are forests that play a special role in clan communities or village communities. Historical forests have been preserved since they have historical significance, which is confirmed by extant historical records. Ancient forests also have a long forest age.

The authors of this article judge that the original form of these relic forests was well maintained qualitatively and quantitatively until the end of the nineteenth century before the introduction of modern science to Korea, due to the practice of Chosŏn Korea's Confucian values. In fact, Korea's relic forests rapidly started to degenerate and decline at the beginning of the twentieth century after the annexation and occupation of Korea by the Japanese. Because of frequent human interference due to the forests' low-altitude locations, their qualitative degradation and structural disturbance have continued until now. The Japanese colonial era (1910–1945), the Korean War (1950–1953), and the projects for the improvement of living environments carried out as part of the Saemaŭl Movement (in the 1970s) can all be said to be historical events that have had a severely negative impact on the relic forests. The intensive human interference with these relic forests has been proven by examining their species composition (Kim Jongwon 1993, 83).

Meanwhile, since the 1990s, many relic forests have been designated as targets of protection through legal designations as 'Natural Monuments' or 'Forest Genetic Resources Reserve', etc. and have been administered by the state or local governments (Choi Jaiung and Kim Dongyeob 2000, 51–65; Korea Forest Service 2006, 47). Moreover, at the state and local levels, by means of various methodological strategies, many academic studies on the preservation, restoration and recreation of these forests have been carried out (Jang Dongsoo and Kim Hakbeom 1993, 19–31; Jang Dongsoo, Lee Kumok and Kim Hakbeom 1993, 77–89; Kim Hakbeom 1992, 239–257). Nevertheless, these efforts have been found to have resulted in a series of management strategies that have negatively affected the integrity of the entire structure of the forests due to the removal of undergrowth trees (Kang Hyunkyung et al. 2004, 63–74) or the introduction of foreign species or invasive alien species to the sites of relic forests.

Ultimately, the surviving relic forests have in fact been quantitatively reduced despite the recent active measures taken in the fields of policy making, academic studies and management (Kim Jongwon and Lim

Jeongcheol 2006, 81–114). For instance, about 70% of the historical forests in the Kyŏngju area have already disappeared (Hwang Sookyoung 2011, 9–11), and even the existing historical forests continue to be seriously damaged by distorted forest-management strategies.

The authors of this article judge that the reason for this result is that the authorities involved in managing relic forests fundamentally misunderstand their true nature. In other words, with the designation of the relic forests as targets of protection, the preceding studies carried out for their theoretical support were mainly limited to an interpretation of these forests as historical monuments and lacked a naturalistic understanding of them. Regarding the origin of the relic forests, it seems that the humanistic view that perceives them as "forests artificially formed by certain classical scholars or communities" (Kim Hakbeom, Jang Dongsoo, and Lee Seungje 2003, 90–93; Park Jaechul et al. 2004, 27–32) is an erroneous one that has given rise to a distorted forest-management strategy, while an academic understanding of the relic forests based on natural science has not been developed.

Since a forest is an aggregate of plant species that repeats the processes of birth, death and regeneration as time passes and a superorganism with life (interrelation among species) and ecology (interrelation among biological communities), it definitely has an origin. Thus, this tells us that essential and fundamental interpretations and discussions on the artificial origin and natural origin of the forests, at least for the recognition of the value of relic forests, must be undertaken.

This study selected five representative relic forests considering the size of the forests and the integrity of their phytosociological species composition and tries to prove the origins of the forests eco-sociologically. Especially, it attempts to discuss the interrelationship between relic forests and Korea's Confucian values that were dominant until the end of the nineteenth century. Ultimately, this study examines the Confucian mentality behind the relic forests and tries to propose preservation strategies for their effective maintenance.

2. MATERIALS AND METHODS

This paper examined five representative relic forests as shown in Table 1.

Table 1. Relic Forest Types and Examples

Types		Remarks	Examples
Traditional rural forests		Forests influenced by indigenous communities, having historical and cultural significances.	Mansongjŏng, Sŏngbaksup, Karosup, Sangnim
Historical forests		Forests preserved due to their historical significance, and their histories confirmed by records.	Kyerim
Ancient forests		Old-growth forests.	Karosup, Sangnim, Kyerim
Cultural forests	*pibo* (裨補) forests	Forests blocking parts of the open view from a Korean traditional geomantic standpoint and surrounding the space to alleviate its positive *qi* (氣).	Mansongjŏng
	yŏpsŭng (厭勝) forests	Forests enhancing *qi* by blocking evil spirits from the outside.	Sŏngbaksup
	pangp'ung (防風) forests	Windbreak forests that block and buffer prevailing winds.	Mansongjŏng, Karosup
	poŏn (保堰) forests	Forests established for flood prevention work.	Sangnim
	religious forests	Forests connected with religious beliefs and/or hero-worshipping myths.	Kyerim

Mansongjŏng (萬松亭) covers Hahoe Village, P'ungch'ŏn-myŏn,

Andong-si, Kyŏngsangbuk-to, and is a traditional, *pibo* (裨補) and windbreak (防風) forest. It is known that in the middle of the Chosŏn Dynasty, Kyŏmam (謙庵) Ryu Unyong (柳云龍, 1530–1601) planted 10,000 pine trees to alleviate *qi* (氣) at Puyongdae (芙蓉臺) opposite Hahoe Village. It was designated as a natural monument in 2006 (an area of 145,219 m^2) and has been managed since that time.

Sŏngbaksup (forest outside the castle in Kyŏngsan-ri, Sŏngju) is a traditional, rural and *yŏpsŭng* (厭勝) forest. It is located in Kyŏngsan-ri, Sŏngju-ŭp, Sŏngju-kun, Kyŏngsangbuk-to, and is a forest developing on a slip-off slope by Ich'ŏn stream. It is known to have been artificially created to hide the nearby male Tanggŏn (skullcap) Rock and female Chokturi (headpiece) Rock from each other (Natural Research Institute of Cultural Heritage 2007, 90) but there is no known specific data whereby it may be known whether it was artificially created or whereby its functions as a *yŏpsŭng* may be concretely confirmed. It has been administered since it was designated as a natural monument in 1999 (an area of 39,944 m^2).

Karosup (forest traversing the landscape from south to north in Sach'on-ri, Ŭisŏng-kun) is a traditional ancient, rural and windbreak forest. It is located in Sach'on-ri, Chŏmgok-myŏn, Ŭisŏng-kun, Kyŏngsangbuk-to, a developing riverside in the alluvial fan, and a branch of Mich'ŏn stream. Karosup is known to have been created to block winds from the west from Andong to Sach'on-ri by Kim Chach'ŏm (金自瞻, 1369–1454), the ancestor of the Andong Kim clan (安東金氏) in 1392, at the end of the Koryŏ Dynasty (Kim Taechong 2006; Cultural Heritage Administration of Korea 2011), but there are no basic historical materials related to it. It was designated as a natural monument in 1999 (an area of 33,862 m^2).

Sangnim (上林) in Hamyang is an ancient, traditional rural, and bank-protection (保堰, *poŏn*) forest. It is located in Taedŏk-ri, Hamyang-ŭp,

Hamyang-kun, Kyŏngsangnam-to and was previously called Taegwallim (大館林), but as the middle part of this forest was divided by a flood, it split into two parts known as Sangnim (Upper Forest) and Harim (Lower Forest). Currently, Harim has been damaged while Sangnim has been maintained mostly intact (Cultural Heritage Administration of Korea 2011). It formed along the left bank of Wich'ŏn stream, and is in the form of a straight line stretching from the northwest to the southeast. It is known that Ch'oe Ch'iwŏn (崔致遠, 857–?) created this forest in the United Silla period, when Ch'oe served as the governor-general of Ch'ŏnnyŏng-kun (formerly Hamyang-kun) (Institute for Translation of Korean Classics 1969, 196), in order to protect the farmland and village from flooding, but there is no reliable data to support this. It was designated as a natural monument in 1968 (an area of 182,665 m^2).

Kyerim (鷄林) in Kyŏngju is a mythical, historical and religious forest that has been maintained till now as it is the site related to the tale of the birth of Kim Alchi (金閼智), the ancestor of the Kim Dynasty of Silla (Kim Pusik 2009, 54). It is located in Kyo-dong, Kyŏngju-si and was designated as a historical site in 1963 (with an area of 20,023 m^2). Generally it is perceived to have been "formed," (Hwang Junghwan 1999, 443–464; Jang Dongsoo, Kim Hakbeom and Hwang Junghwan 1996, 37–49; Tokumitsu 2007, 52–60) but there is no literature that provides "the proof of the formation."

We carried out phytosociological investigations of these relic forests and ascertained the environmental conditions of each habitat and described their ecological information. To understand the tree species performance of each relic forest, Braun-Blanquet's transformation of cover-abundance value was used; namely, 9: over 76%, 8: 51–75%, 7: 26–50%, 6: 12.5–25%, 5: 5–12.5%, 4: less than 5%, 3: less than 5% with few individuals size, 2: with three or four individuals, 1: one or two individuals. Tree species diversity is described by the population size of each species and the relative proportion of each was estimated based on Mansongjŏng, Andong. For related information obtained through a survey of historical records, an eco-sociological reinterpretation of the origins of the forests was also carried out.

3. RESULTS

3.1 RELIC FORESTS BY NATURAL ORIGIN

The origins of the five relic forests studied are defined as naturally developing ones from the diversity of tree species that form each forest (Table 2). This is because the occurring tree species have the same ecological characteristics as the key species of potential natural vegetation (later PNV) in the cool-temperate southern/submontane zone and warm-temperate zone of the Korean peninsula corresponding to the site conditions of their relevant habitats. First, the major tree species of the relic forests are native species growing in response to the climatic and edaphic environments of the site conditions of the habitats, which are not alien species (introduced species or foreign species). In other words, except for *Sophora japonica and Quercus acutissima*, they are not populations planted by humans. *Quercus aliena, Carpinus tschonoskii, Cornus walteri* and *Hemiptelea davidii*, etc. are not tree species widely used in the field of landscape architecture even now.

Second, key species such as *Quercus aliena, Quercus serrata, Carpinus tschonoskii, Zelkova serrata, Cornus walteri, Hemiptelea davidii, Ulmus parvifolia, Celtis sinensis, Pinus densiflora and Salix chaenomeloides*, etc. that characterize the relic forests, are representative species through which late-successional species or pseudo-climax vegetation are diagnosed. In other words, the ecological properties of these species are not those pertaining to plant communities which are artificially maintained but to those maintained through ecological processes (See conclusions and discussions). Among them, *Pinus densiflora* and *Salix chaenomeloides* are species that form very homogeneous forests, which are uniformly reproduced with a perpetual plant community at the alluvial cone area of the fan section of rivers and at the silt estuaries of the meandering sections of rivers, respectively (Kim Jongwon 2005, 113–120; Kim Jongwon et al. 2010, 237–297). Andong's Mansongjŏng is a model of a perpetual plant community of *Pinus densiflora*, while Sŏngju's Sŏngbaksup is a model of a perpetual plant community of *Salix chaenomeloides*.

Third, it is not difficult to distinguish a natural topography from an artificial one. This is because, in general, artificial plantation accompanies the arrangement of the topography and the ground for the plantation, and as a consequence such artificial traces can be found in the shape of the habitats. If the topography is natural, the topography and ground are wild, developing through natural erosion or sedimentation mechanisms. In the relic forests in this study, the physical shape of the habitats, that is, the structures of their topography and microtopography have developed from their original shapes, which originated from natural mech-anisms. This is also proved by the fact that the key tree species that constitute the forest canopies are the constituents of the potential natural vegetation corresponding to such original topography.

Table 2. Habitats of Relic Forests and Major Tree Species Performances in the Forest Canopy

	Andong Mansongjŏng	Sŏngju Sŏngbaksup	Ŭisŏng Karosup	Hamyang Sangnim	Kyŏngju Kyerim
Altitude (m)	75	40	170	180	45
Area (m^2)	145,219	38,944	33,862	182,665	23,023
Area ratio	6.3	1.7	1.5	7.9	1.0
Topography	alluvial fan, slip-off slope	alluvial cone area, slip-off slope	alluvial cone area, fan-bank	alluvial fan, flood plain	slip-off slope, flood plain-low alluvial plain
Soil	coarse sand, sandy loam	fine sand, silt	loamy soil, gravel	coarse sand, gravel, rock	silt, clay
Tree diversity	1.0	3.73	54.32	12.99	39.95
Area (m^2) per a species	48,406	12,981	891	3,728	1,212
PNV (potential natural vegetation)	pioneer forest of slip-off slope	softwood forest of bank	deciduous broad-leaved mixed forest of mountainous stream-fan	deciduous broad-leaved mixed forest of mountainous stream	deciduous broad-leaved mixed forest of alluvion
Community type	*Pinus densiflora* community	*Salix chaenomeloides* community	*Zelkova serrate -Quercus aliena* community	*Zelkova serrate –Carpinus tschonoskii* community	*Salix chaenomeloides* community *Celtis sinensis-Zelkova* serrata community
Quercus aliena	.	.	7	4	.
Carpinus schonoskii	.	.	.	8	.
Zelkova serrata	.	.	6	5	6
Cornus walteri	.	.	6	.	.
Quercus acutissima	.	.	4	4	.
Pinus densiflora	9	.	1	.	.
Hemiptelea davidii	.	9	4	.	.
Salix chaenomeloides	.	.	2	.	7
Quercus serrata	.	.	.	6	.
Ulmus parvifolia	.	.	.	.	2
Celtis sinensis	.	.	5	2	5
Sophora japonica	.	.	6	.	4

Species with underlined cover-abundance values are the most characteristic ones in the forest canopy.

3.2. MANSONGJŎNG (COUNTERLESS PINE TREES)

Figure 1. Mansongjŏng, a red pine (Pinus densiflora) forest spontaneously occurring at a sandbar of the slip-off slope in a river channel (May 4, 2011).

Andong's Mansongjŏng (萬松亭) is commonly thought to be an artificial forest that originated from the ten thousand *Pinus densiflora* planted by the Confucian scholar Ryu Unyong (1530–1601), but this assertion has not been established both phytosociologically and ecologically. The Naktong River winding around Hahoe Village has developed a wide sandy beach on both its banks, and Mansongjŏng is located on their slip-off slope. The slip-off slopes at the mid-to-upper streams of rivers and valleys in Korea are mainly composed of sand and gravel stratum which have been deposited to form a gentle slope. The inside is relatively stable but continues to fluctuate dynamically and is affected greatly by the river at times of high water during typhoons once or twice a year or during the rainy season. Because of this, the slip-off slope maintains a kind of perpetual plant community of pioneer vegetation which coincides with the creation and extinction of forests. '*Pinus densiflora* dominant forests,' as perpetual plant communities, are the most typical natural landscapes in Korea (Kim Jongwon 2006, 9–18). Landscape paintings created with these *Pinus densiflora* forests as their background are a symbol of traditional Korean culture (Kim Yeolgyu 2006, 397–400). Mansongjŏng is one of these *Pinus densiflora* forests that have formed naturally as pioneer vegetation of a slip-off slope composed of sand and gravel stratum (Figure 1).

Thus, Mansongjŏng is not an artificial forest but a forest that has natural origins. The formation and development of Hahoe Village were possible due to the fact that such pine forests as Mansongjŏng preexisted. Mansongjŏng had its essential significance and value as a *pibo* forest that screens Hahoe Village from the seasonal northwest wind and shields it from the evil spirit of Puyongdae that overlooks the village, a function that is still valid today. The first phrase, "Mansongjŭngsusik (萬松曾手植)" of the poem "Yŏngsongjŏng (詠松亭)" in Vol. 1 of Kyŏmamjip (謙菴集) written by the Confucian scholar Ryu Unyong (1743) demonstrates the fact that the local people had long recognized the effects of Mansongjŏng forest on the village. This shows the Confucian values practiced by Ryu Unyong, whereby forests and humans coexist.

However, later scholars interpreted this phrase as meaning "I planted ten thousand *Pinus densiflora* myself," and Mansongjŏng was perceived as being an artificial forest based on a literal interpretation of the passage. As a consequence the forest has been managed as an artificial one. Because the ecological properties of its natural origins have been ignored,

Mansongjŏng pine forest has greatly declined both quantitatively and qualitatively.

If Mansongjŏng forest is considered pioneer vegetation, the passage should be understood as meaning "I managed and grew countless *Pinus densiflora* myself." In other words, the sustainability of Mansongjŏng can be achieved by an eco-logical understanding and Confucian reconsideration of it as being pioneer vegetation rather than an artificial plantation.

3.3. SŎNGBAKSUP (FOREST OUTSIDE A CASTLE)

There are no historical records for the origin of the name of Sŏngju's Sŏngbaksup except for the statement, "There had been Sŏgyosu (西郊藪), Ch'ŏnsu (泉藪) and Yulsu (栗藪) but they no longer exist" in *Kyŏngsanji* (京山誌) in 1677 and *Sŏngsanji* (星山誌) in 1832. In general, Sŏgyosu is recognized as being the same as Sŏngbaksup (Sŏngju Culture Center 2010, 27; Yea Myunghai, Lee Jaehwan and Kim Sooyeon 2006, 165–172), and as the phrase, "*ch'oninsingnimji* (村人植林地) (Sŏngju Culture Center 2010, 27)" in *Sŏngsanji* is accepted as meaning "an area where the villagers planted trees," Sŏngbaksup is also considered to be a forest with an artificial origin. From the statement in *Sŏngsanji* that Sŏgyosu is located near the rivers outside the west gate of the village, it is assumed to have existed along the bank blocks of Ich'ŏn stream, and the bank sides are areas where in phytosociology, a variety of *Salix* species can spread. The broad-leaved forest areas shown even on a topographic map with a scale of 1:50,000 in 1918 are habitats in which typical *Salix chaenomeloides*-dominant perpetual communities occurring on a slip-off slope floodplain can develop (Kim Jongwon et al. 2010, 237–297), and even now, that community still survives. The argument that people artificially created

Sŏngbaksup, based only on the record that there was no Sŏgyosu in *Kyŏngsanji* in 1677 and later the statement, *"ch'oninsingnimji"* in *Sŏngsanji* in 1832 does not stand up for the following two reasons. First, until today it has never been reported that the species *Salix chaenomeloides* has been planted to create an artificial forest. Second, *Salix chaenomeloides* has an eco-genetic property that shows a model of uniform forest (一齊林) sprouted again uniformly from a certain ecological event (flooding and felling, etc.). Thus, Sŏngbaksup due to the fact that it comprises *Salix chaenomeloides*, of which the DBH and height are uniform, should be considered a natural forest *sensu stricto* formed by natural factors. In general, from a preliminary study that *Salix chaenomeloides* grows by the volume (DBH) of 2 cm a year (Lee Changwoo 2009, 6–7), it is known that the current populations of *Salix chaenomeloides* in Sŏngbaksup are less than 300 years old. Through historical records, it is assumed that the forest was formed between 1677 and 1832, which supports the above fact.

In conclusion, Sŏgyosu in *Kyŏngsanji* and *Sŏngsanji* is now known as Sŏngbaksup, a natural forest occurring on a fine sand floodplain of a river and a typical summergreen, broad-leaved, softwood forest dominated by *Salix chaenomeloides* (Figure 2). This willow forest Sŏngbaksup is a huge natural structure that serves as a typical, traditional, rural forest that can block flooding and the northwest wind due to its location and size. It seems that it has been preserved thanks to the oral tradition of it being a *yŏpsŭng* in relation to Tanggŏn Rock and Chokturi Rock as well as due to its functions as a "forest outside a castle (sŏngbaksup)." The date of genesis and source of the view of Sŏngbaksup as a *yŏpsŭng* are unknown. But it is assumed that this view arose from a fiction created by a sage with the Confucian intention of ensuring the preservation of Sŏngbaksup at a certain time.

Figure 2. Sŏngbaksup, a relic forest characterized by king willow (Salix chaenomeloides) sprouting naturally at a slip-off slope floodplain of Ich'ŏn stream (August 1, 2006).

However, Sŏngbaksup has been greatly damaged since the 1950s as a result of urbanization and industrialization processes and has, therefore, been managed since it was designated as a natural monument—the strictest legal device to preserve natural heritage—in 1999. Nevertheless, since people have not recognized the ecological and biological processes of this natural willow forest developing on a floodplain, it has been ruined and has gradually reduced in size. Sŏngbaksup is a relic forest that demonstrates the Confucian authenticity of the ancient town of Sŏngju and the integrity of the *Salix chaenomeloides*-dominant ecosystem, which has great value as a natural heritage.

3.4. KAROSUP (CROSS-CUTTING FOREST)

Karosup is situated on a terrace by Sach'on stream, Ŭisŏng-kun. It is a huge forest with an existing size of 40 m in width and 600 m in length, and is, therefore, the largest among the relic forests studied in this article.

The actual vegetation of Karosup is phytosociologically classified as a deciduous broad-leaved mixed forest of a *Zelkova serrata-Quercus aliena* community, and its diagnostic species are *Quercus aliena, Zelkova serrata, Cornus walteri, Hemiptelea davidii* and *Celtis sinensis*, etc. These species are all major components of the PNV which appears from the integration of its natural environmental conditions at the fan area of a mountainous stream. These PNV species are ones that are spontaneously regenerated and perpetually maintained unless the habitat condition of the Sach'on-ri Karosup is transformed. As the base can be found in population research on plant groups (Lehvävirta and Rita 2002, 57–66) that will maintain the future forest, the above assertion is proven by the fact that the young populations of these species in the shrub layer in the forest are reproduced abundantly. This, ultimately, means that Karosup is a phytocoenosen that has developed naturally and spontaneously from ancient times without the help of humans.

Generally, the creation of Sŏrim (西林, West Forest) by Kim Chach'ŏm (1369–1454), known as the ancestor of Sach'on-ri village, is accepted as being the origin of Karosup (Kim Taehong 2006). However, there is no original literature proving this; it is simply assumed that a story handed down orally was eventually written down. The current Karosup is located to the west of Sach'on-ri village running north and south, from which it is known that Sŏrim, meaning "west forest" of the village, is also a karosup. Until now, '*karo*' in the Korean name 'karosup' has been interpreted as coming from the Chinese term '*karo* (街路)'meaning 'roadside', but it has been recently discovered that it actually comes from the native Korean word *karo* meaning 'width' as opposed sero meaning 'length.' The Karosup's location cutting across the alluvial plain from north to south supports the meaning that it is a windbreak and also a *yŏpsŭng* that sustains the peace of the village community situated behind it (Figure 3).

Figure 3. Karosup, cutting across a broad plain north to south along the western part of Sach'on-ri village (September 16, 2006).

Some scholars believe that Karosup was artificially created for religious reasons (Jang Dongsoo and Kim Hakbeom 1993, 19–31). However, Karosup was evaluated as a natural forest from a phytosociological analysis of the PNV. The fact that the representative species such as *Quercus aliena, Cornus walteri* and *Hemiptelea davidii* have not been used for landscape plantation until now also supports this view. Thus, Sach'on-ri Karosup is a relic forest with a natural origin rather than an artificial one.

Also, the argument that it is a religious artificial forest is not a persuasive one due to the relationship between the formation of the village and the origin of the forest. In ancient times, in mountainous inland regions, the development of indigenous villages was inevitably dependent on the local natural surroundings and environmental conditions. In other words, a scenario whereby a village was formed first, and then a forest was created to protect the village is virtually impossible in a traditional agricultural society considering the people's mode of living that was necessarily dependent on natural mechanisms. Instead, the village site would be chosen on the basis of human wisdom taking into account the environmental conditions in which a village might be built. In this context, Karosup was a natural structure that made a crucial contribution to the formation and sustainability of Sach'on-ri village. In fact, studies of the effects of the forest on the reduction of wind speed and water evaporation rate (Lee Dowon, Koh Insu and Park Chanryul 2007, 47–100) sufficiently support the assertion that Karosup existed as a natural structure even before there was the village. Therefore, the religious element behind Karosup is judged to have been caused by the hidden intention of a local scholar or the community to prevent the forest from damage at a certain point in time. Karosup is a relic forest that functions as a windbreak against the prevailing northwest wind, a *pibo* blocking evil spirits from the west and a means of buffering the flooding of Sach'on stream.

Karosup was a forest with a natural origin, therefore, and the village community clearly perceived this, but the fact that it was one that was also managed is shown in the diversity of the species in Karosup. Evidence of this is the large, old oaks (*Quercus acutissima*), a famine relief plant resource (Choe Chaha 1417)—used as a means of substantial practice of the Confucian spirit of love for the people—which are found with a high frequency in Karosup. *Quercus acutissima* is an oak species representing the *supchŏngi* (traditional forests created on a hill at the back of rural villages which function like agricultural fields). For example, the titles *solbat* (pine fields), *tot'oribat* (acorn fields) and *chukpat* (bamboo fields) are all indicative of this function. *Quercus acutissima* is characterized by relatively quick growth and a short life-span but is not a successional species of secondary vegetation but an element of substitute vegetation. In other words, the giant and old trees, *Quercus acutissima* observed in Karosup have only survived with human help. Thus, *Quercus acutissima* occurring in Hamyang Sangnim Forest and Ŭisŏng Karosup is a phytosociological foreign species among the other species in the target relic forests, which proves that Karosup is a relic forest originating from nature that was subsequently managed by the village community.

Despite this intentional management of Karosup, its plant diversity is very high. In general, it is different from afforested vegetation or park landscaped forests which are managed using uniform and simple plant species (Bae Byungho, Yoon Yonghan, and Kim Jeongho 1998, 701–710). The diversity Karosup's plant species is about fifty-four times that of Mansongjŏng—the highest diversity among the target relic forests of this study. Also, the ratio of the PNV's components indicative of the typicality of the habitat condition among the entire plant species was 78.4%—also the highest ratio. This means that Karosup is essentially different from artificial afforestation or park-forest and that it has long been managed in a way that demonstrates that the local community was in harmony with the forest's ecological properties and vitality.

Since the onset of the urban industrial era in the twentieth century, however, the original form of Karosup has been distorted by a variety of management methods that have inevitably caused its qualitative decline. A typical example is the introduction of the invasive alien species *Robinia pseudoacaccia* and the following severe spread of its population after the Japanese colonial era (Ishidoya and *Chŏng* Taehyŏn 1923, 72;

Lee Deokbong 1963, 339–364). Although it has been designated and managed as a national natural monument since 1999, the decline of the vegetation has never improved, causing the forest to lose its original form. Karosup has great academic value, however, as it has the greatest diversity of plant species among Korea's relic forests and an evidential vegetation of PNV.

3.5. SANGNIM (UPPER FOREST)

Sangnim (上林) is located in the warm-temperate evergreen broad-leaved forest zone in the southern part of the Korean peninsula and has the greatest surviving area among the target relic forests in this study. According to legend, the forest was created in the Silla Dynasty by Ch'oe Ch'iwŏn (崔致遠, 857–?) when he was the governor-general of Ch'ŏnnyŏng-kun (now Hamyang-kun) (Institute for the Translation of Korean Classics 1969, 196). It is recorded that the forest was planted by the family in 1923, based on a passage in Ch'oe Ch'iwŏn's *Sint'obi* (文昌侯崔先生神道碑), which his descendent Ch'oe Pyŏnggŭk edited in 1861; "*Kŏnhaksaru susingnimmogŏjangje* [建學士樓手植林木於長堤] (Tokumitsu 2007, 217)." There are no earlier historical records showing confirmable evidence that Sangnim is an artificially created forest. In other words, there is no reliable material supporting the content of Ch'oe Ch'iwŏn's *Sint'obi* that was edited in 1861. Since he was the governor-general of Ch'ŏnnyŏng-kun, however, it cannot be denied that Ch'oe Ch'iwŏn was at one time involved in Sangnim.

But this study reaches the conclusion that Sangnim originated from a natural forest based on a phytosociological analysis of the diversity and nativeness of the arbor species. The phrase "建學士樓手植林木於長堤" could mean that Ch'oe Ch'iwŏn built a long bank somewhere in the Sangnim area, planted some plants there and soon afterwards built Haksaru (學士樓, a pavilion).

Figure 4. The natural condition of the micro-topography on the Sangnim forest floor. The dom-inant species of the forest canopy is Carpinus tschonoskii, which is a major element of the potential natural vegetation of the Sangnim area (May 20, 2011).

Sangnim can be said to be a remnant vegetation of mixed summergreen broad-leaved forests where the typical components of PNV such as *Carpinus tschonoskii, Zelkova serrata, Chionanthus retusus* and *Celtis sinensis*, which typically occur in ground comprising coarse sand, gravels and rocks with good drainage at warm-temperate alluvial fans in southern Korea. Especially, *Carpinus tschonoskii*, the most representative phytosociological diagnostic species of the habitat conditions in which Sangnim has developed is still not known to be used even in today's landscape gardening. This tells us that the individuals of *Carpinus tschonoskii* in Sangnim have originated not from artificial plantation but from a spontaneous natural system.

An ecological proof that could support the above assertion can also be found in the structures of the surface (Figure 4) and underground of the site where Sangnim has developed. On the Korean peninsula, the natural and typical habitat of *Carpinus tschonoskii* is a site with an igneous or metamorphic lithosphere and coarse particle soil originating from these rocks. Thus, since the base topography under the surface consists of huge boulders covered by mixtures of gravels and rocks, it is not an environmental condition in which large plant species including *Carpinus tschonoskii* can be planted. Also, synchorologically, *Carpinus tschonoskii* is a key species of summergreen broad-leaved forest among the kinds of the edaphic climax forests developing in warm-temperate evergreen broad-leaved forest zone horizontally. The conclusion currently drawn from the location, topographical structure, forest size and the diversity of the plant species forming the forest is that Sangnim is definitely not an artificial forest but a natural one.

Confucian scholars Ch'oe Ch'iwŏn (崔致遠), Kim Chong-jik (金宗直) and Pak Chiwŏn (朴趾源) focused on Sangnim as originating from a natural forest *sensu stricto* as an important natural structure that has buffered the regional floods and inundation. Regarding the continental precipitation pattern of the Korean peninsula, the people's suffering from the erratic occurrence of flooding for brief periods of time is described in their historical records. The most typical example can be found in *Chŏmp'ilchae chip* (佔畢齋集) (Kim Chongjik 1996, 253–254): the following is a passage describing the panic in the rural villages around Sangnim when they were inundated by a disastrous flood in the sixth lunar month, "'the banks built with stones' collapse and 'the tall and huge trees' are swept away so that they look like mingled sand and bush." This is connected to *Changje* (長堤) in Ch'oe Ch'iwŏn's *Sindobi* through which it can be assumed that there were stone banks in Sangnim and they were built to regulate the watercourses. Also, it shows that there was an old-growth forest and that Sangnim was a forest that buffered an exceptionally severe flood.

Figure 5. Sangnim, a relic forest threatened by introduction of various facilities and exotic species (April 5, 2008).

Therefore, Sangnim was not a space of consumptive amusement or event celebration. It can be assumed that no artificial structure, whether pavilion or tower, was installed in Sangnim for almost one thousand years from the days of Ch'oe Ch'i-wŏn, the governor-general of Hamyang, Chŏmp'ilchae Kim Chongjik and Yeonam Pak Chiwŏn through the latter era of the Chosŏn Dynasty to the twentieth century. Currently all artificial structures including Hamhwaru (咸化樓), Saŭnjŏng (思雲亭), and Ch'osŏnjŏng (樵仙亭), which are the elements that deaden the originality of Sangnim, were built after the 1900s (Figure 5). Thus, Sangnim is a natural structure, that is, a natural heritage forest, and at the same time, a cultural heritage related to the practice of Confucian values. In such a context, Sangnim Forest is evaluated as one of the world's rare and precious "natural-cultural heritage forests."

3.6. KYERIM

Kyerim (鷄林) is a mythical relic forest associated with the birth legend of Kim Alchi, the founding ancestor of the Kyerim (Silla) nation. Kyerim, a summergreen broad-leaved forest consisting of various broad-leaved plant species and Najŏng, an evergreen needle-leaved forest consisting of *Pinus densiflora* only, show their ecological, sociopolitical responsiveness to the forest origin, respectively (Kim Jongwon et al. 2011, 167–214). Kyerim is generally considered to have originated from "afforestation," (Hwang Junghwan 1999, 443–464; Jang Dongsoo, Kim Hakbeom and Hwang Junghwan 1996, 37–49; Tokumitsu 2007, 217) but there is no literature or scientific grounds that confirm this.

The fragment of *Salix chaenomeloides* communities have spread around the waterway naturally flowing down in the Kyerim area that has site conditions similar to alluvial lowland, and on the plain of an alluvial highland and protruding land, a *Celtis sinensis-Zelkova serrata* community, including the diagnostic species of *Ulmus parvifolia*, is widespread. Thus, this means that Kyerim originated from natural vegetation consisting largely of two forest types of a *Salix chaenomeloides* community and a *Celtis sinensis-Zelkova serrata* community.

Among the major species comprising the actual forest of Kyerim, the PNV of the alluvial plain and lowland that ultimately forms in the environmental conditions of Kyerim is the cold-temperate southern/submontane forest or the warm-temperate summergreen broad-leaved forest consisting of *Salix chaenomeloides*, other *Salix* species, *Celtis sinensis* , *Zelkova serrata* and *Ulmus parvifolia*, etc. Thus, the existing woods in Kyerim comprise a relic forest that is a historical forest associated with the birth legend of the founding ruler Kim Alchi and a remnant forest of the PNV.

Plant species, except the elements of the PNV, are a heterogeneous species group that belongs to the ecological categories of introduced and foreign species to the habitats of Kyerim Forest. Especially, *Sophora japonica* and *Ginkgo biloba* are Chinese plant species that are classified into *Apophyten*. The year of introduction to Korea is assumed to be around the unification of the Three Kingdoms by Silla when Tang Chinese institutions were actively introduced. The period of plantation of Sophora japonica is assumed to be around the 1430s–1630s after the founding of the Confucian Chosŏn Dynasty (Kim Jongwon et al. 2011, 167–214). *Sophora japonica* in *Chosŏn no moriyabu* (Tokumitsu 2007, 52–60), and the trees are still located on the left (east) and right (west) of the Kyerim monument house (1803) respectively, which is judged to be an intentional spatial plantation around the Kyerim monument house.

Figure 6. Two elm trees barely surviving by the wall of the Kyerim monument house (left photo, September 5, 2008), and king willows (Salix chaenomeloides) occurring on low-lying ground in the Kyerim area (right photo, July 16, 2010)

The Kyerim monument house is micro-topographically located in the highest place in the Kyerim area, and is the key site from which the liveliness and ecological properties of the habitat of Kyerim forest are derived. In this way it is like the area's navel. At the rear of the Kyerim monument house are cut granite stones that resemble the Chinese character *chŏng* (井), meaning a well, which confirms the existence of a spring that symbolizes the origin of life. Later, the Silla people would hold rituals commemorating the birth of Kim Alchi there. The site environment, in which a spring wells up from the alluvial plain with everlasting water, is an environmental condition suitable as a habitat for *Ulmus parvifolia*. The flagship species representing the forest, which is the site of the birth of the founding ruler of Silla, is *Ulmus parvifolia*. This elm species, as solid as a rock neither bending nor flinching, is a quick-growing tree when young, but once grown is awesome in appearance and persistently survives a long time once rooted. *Ulmus parvifolia* is one of the plant species indicative of the natural wishes (birth-giving, life-giving and fertility-giving) of the ancient human society in the southeastern part of the Korean peninsula.

Currently, however, the *Ulmus parvifolia* of Kyerim has been severely damaged, so only two individual trees survive pressed down by the wall enclosing the Kyerim monument house (Figure 6). *Zelkova serrata* and *Celtis sinensis* fill the space instead. Since, like most elm species, *Ulmus parvifolia* has been considered to be a useful plant resource from ancient times, it has been recklessly cut down over a long period of time, and instead *Zelkova serrata* and *Celtis sinensis* have been preserved or planted on purpose to form the current forest structure of Kyerim.

The matrix of Kyerim is widely occupied by a *Zelkova serrata-Celtis sinensis* community, and the waterway in which the *Salix chaenomeloides* community has developed is a corridor in which Yongch'ŏn stream, originating between Anapchi and Hwangyongsaji, flows from left (east) to right (west) and south to Namch'ŏn stream. The Kyerim monument has settled down at the core site like a hole (穴處) in *fengshui*. Consequently, the space is structured as follows: the Kyerim monument house has settled in the remains of the well, *Sophora japonica* is arranged on the left and right (east and west) in the front yard around the monument combining with *Ulmus parvifolia* and *Zelkova serrata-Celtis sinensis* community surrounds the outside, and a *Salix chaenomeloides* community has developed in a depression where water flows like a natural moat (Figure 7).

Kyerim has been preserved as a protected forest in a historical site (Cultural Heritage Administration designated an area of 23,023 m^2 in 1963). However, the site management has included serious anti-ecological and anti-historical elements. As there was no chance for *Ulmus parvifolia* to reproduce itself due to excessive interference on the forest floor, major species (*Alangium platanifolium* var. *trilobum*, *Evodia daniellii* and

Euonymus bungeanus) of the PNV have all been removed. The forest of Kyerim does not have a multilayered structure but a single layered one that includes the introduction of foreign or introduced species (*Lagerstroemia indica, Cornus officinalis, Ginkgo biloba* and *Sophora japonica*, etc.) and off-site species (*Acer palmatum, Forsythia koreana, Chionanthus retusus, Buxus microphylla* var. *koreana and Juniperus chinensis*). Accordingly, it is no longer a natural forest but an amusement-park-like landscape. Furthermore, the hardening of the ground by excessive treading and the introduction of exogenic soil have changed the microtopography and as a result have fundamentally damaged the original habitat.

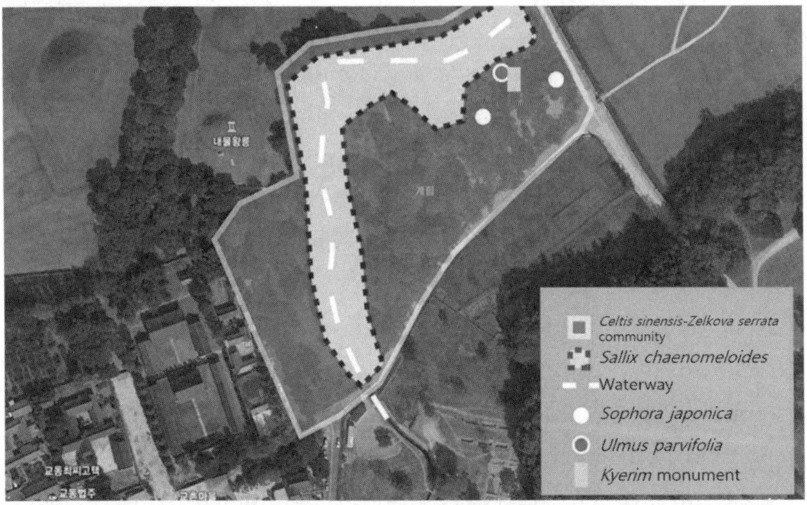

Figure 7. A map of the potential natural vegetation of Kyerim. The location of Kyerim monu-ment combining with Ulmus parvifolia shows the ecological properties and identity of Kyerim.

In conclusion, it is recognized that the identity and ecological properties of Kyerim have been thoroughly damaged due to the perception of its origin as an artificially created forest and due to excessive management caused by its objectification as a cultural heritage site. This has occurred in tandem with the decline of human and nature-friendly Confucian values caused by Korea's rapid entrance into the industrial era along with the downfall of the Confucian state, Chosŏn.

4. DISCUSSIONS AND CONCLUSIONS

4.1. CONFUCIAN VALUE, THE DRIVING FORCE OF THE PRESERVATION OF RELIC FORESTS

The driving force behind surviving relic forests originates in Confucianism, the ideological base of the modern times (historical period closest to contemporary times—Chosŏn Dynasty), and these forests have been preserved by the prophetic wisdom of the classical scholars of Confucianism. Furthermore, most relic forests remain in Yŏngnam province where Confucianism is rooted most deeply and widely.

In Confucianism, great importance is attached to customs related to community morals, which have been led by the virtuous example of Confucian scholars who have always advocated benevolent rule. Thus, scholars became the masters of community rituals and Confucian saints. As such they were the ones who best embodied the community, in other words, they were ideal men and sages (Choi Jaemok 2004, 52–67; Kaji 1999, 70–103). In this sense, the Confucian values of T'oegye (退溪) Yi Hwang (李滉, 1501–1570) or Nammyŏng (南冥) Cho Sik (曺植, 1501–1572) are connected to eco-sociology that pursues the completeness and happiness of nature, including humans, by exploring the ultimate principles of vitality and the ecological properties of nature. Here, nature would mean "good mountains and rivers," "good forests" and "good plants" with ecological completeness. The relationship between Confucian scholars and nature may be found in the name *sallim* (山林: mountains and forests), which was also used to refer to Confucian scholars in the Chosŏn period.

In the phrase "*Nagŏsallimja* (樂於山林者)" in T'oegye's *Tosan chabyŏng* (陶山雜詠) in *Tosan'gi* (陶山記) (1573), the term *sallim* would not be limited to the meaning of 'forests in mountains,' but rather, any unmanaged, natural and less artificial forests, that is, natural vegetation rather than artificial vegetation and naturally existing wild forests. Forests of more complete natural vegetation may develop near living environments and may be traditional rural forests that have been managed without any intention recently.

To Confucian scholars, these forests were places for seclusion and pursuit of study, and the more complete forests they were, the better they were as spaces for their self-cultivation in which they practiced and confirmed the contents of the scriptures of their sages (Choi Jaemok 2004, 52–67). Thus, probably in the same vein, Nammyŏng wished that he could be a scholar in the mountains and woods without taking up public office himself (Kim Chungyull 2008, 89–94/486–488). Here, *sallim* is the very forests and nature itself. T'oegye said in "Man'gosangch'ŏng (萬古常青)" in *Tosan sibigok* (陶山十二曲), that since nature is a scripture by which one gropes for the truth and living truth, one has to treat nature with respect just as one does the scriptures and saints. Forests are a part of the natural world. Moreover, if they were forests of potential natural vegetation generated from the integration of all the conditions of the place, as natural forests or nearly natural forests which were undamaged and remained close to their natural state, that is, having complete mutual relations, they would have been a space of precious opportunities in which one could "come face to face with the sages."

All the five target relic forests in this study are places where Confucian ideology and philosophy have long been practiced, and the Confucian customs remaining until the beginning of the twentieth century contributed to the survival of the relic forests. As consequential evidence, in the five relic forests of the study, there were no facilities that could prove that they functioned as spaces of play and amusement, such as pavilions or towers. This shows that relic forests protected peace (life and property) as concrete practices of love for the people, and furthermore, were perceived as "good forests" that enabled people to come face to face with the sages, showing a long tradition based on Confucian values. But the traditional culture of these relic forests was definitely spoiled during the Japanese colonial era, and ultimately, they hardly survive due to the process of industrialization and urbanization today.

4.2. CULTURAL ORIGIN AND ECOTOPE OF THE RELIC FOREST

The origin of the relic forests culture can be found in that the survival of village communities definitely depended on them. The relic forests that maintain the life, property and peace of the clan communities or village communities do not originate from artificially formed forests (Kim Hakbeom and Jang Dongsoo 1994, 30–33). In other words, a relic forest culture appeared due to a series of processes. There was initially a forest originating from a natural forest. A place where humans could settle was provided thanks to the existence of the forest, so a village was formed, and the village community came to manage the forest with an awareness of its functionalities. Thus, in the results of this research, the origin of relic forest culture has been proven to be related to the type of the source of the relic forest. The target relic forests of this study are classified into five types of cultural relic forests, namely, *pibo* forests, *yŏpsŭng* forests, windbreak forests, *poŏn* forests and religious forests (See **Table 1**). Among them, *pibo* forests and *yŏpsŭng* forests can be said to be the most typical Korean relic forests.

A *pibo* forest is one that obscures parts of the open view from a traditional Korean geomantic view of location and surrounds the space to enhance its good *qi* (氣). In addition, a *yŏpsŭng* forest is one that improves *qi* by blocking evil spirits from encroaching (Park Jaechul 2006, 223–262). A windbreak forest is one that serves to block and buffer the prevailing wind, while a bank-protection forest is one that prevents flood damage.

These various cultural types of relic forests are categorized according to two functionalities: 1) the issue of biological survival by responding to natural disasters; and 2) that of social survival centering on absolute power. Nach'ŏng called the first *ŭpsu* in Silla (Jang Dongsoo, Kim Hakbeom and Hwang Junghwan 1996, 37–49) is a typical example of the latter. Among the target relic forests in this study, Kyerim alone falls under the category of social survival while all the rest are related to biological survival. Nevertheless, both socially and biologically, the cultural origin of the relic forests results in one essential premise; namely, the struggle for the sustainability of human communities. In the long historical process, a community with an ideal form of survival transcending interests is called a '*Gemeinschaft*' while one that exists and operates with an ego-centric, calculating relationship of mutual interests is called a '*Gesellschaft* (Tönnies

2001, 17–19).' In this sense, in Braun-Blanquet's phytosociology (Braun-Blanquet 1965, 5–25), a plant community or a relic forest is not a '*Pflanzengesellschaft*' but a '*Pflanzengemeinschaft* (Braun-Blanquet 1965, 5–25).' However, relic forests and traditional villages are ecotopes that are maintained by mutual interests, which are characterized by the elements of Korea's traditional cultural landscape, which is rare in the entire world. Here, the term ecotope refers to the middle unit between ecosystem and ecoregion, meaning the integration of the natural ecosystem of the relic forests and the artificial one of the traditional villages.

Korea's relic forests' traditional village ecotope is, in fact, completely trans-itioning from the 'Gemeinschaft' of the ancient prehistoric era to the 'Gesell-schaft' of the urban industrial era (Lee Younghee and Lim Hunyeong 2010, 522–523).

4.3. RECONSIDERATIONS OF THE VALUE OF RELIC FORESTS

The disorder of species composition within the original phytocoenosen in each relic forest is not caused naturally but by humans. Although the species composition in relic forests surely derives from the properties of the integration of the relevant habitat conditions, they have been managed from a human perspective that has regarded their formation as being artificial. Foreign and exotic plant species, which never suited the ecological properties of the relic forests, have been introduced and continue to be introduced until now. Management even more violent than this has resulted in the removal of the forest itself, excluding the ecological and historical properties of the relic forests. Seven out of the eleven relic forests around the Kyŏngju area have disappeared altogether, and these are examples of the disappearance of forests due to the straightening of the river (Hwang Sookyoung 2011, 9–11).

There is a passage in *Samguksagi* (*The Chronicles of the Three Kingdoms*) that shows Ch'oe Ch'iwŏn's taste for the arts and recounts that mountains, temples and *pyŏlsŏ* (artistic spaces) (Lee Jaekeun 1996, 213–233) were his favorite places. The term *pyŏlsŏ* refers to a quiet house built separately near farmland, which might be similar to a vacation home but different in that people cultivated themselves there (The National Institute of the Korean Language 2011). Ch'oe's *pyŏlsŏ* was an aesthetic space where he explored a beautiful natural ecosystem or scenery. Thus, it is a concept fundamentally different from a Korean garden in a yard or a Western garden in which the vegetation is artificially planted, so it is appropriate to regard "*pyŏlsŏ* as another type of a pavilion or tower that accepts nature intact." Ch'oe Ch'iwŏn, who was involved in management of forests, rivers and beaches, and pavilions or towers, planting *Pinus densiflora* and bamboo trees, is said to have taken books as his pillow while appreciating nature (Kim Pusik 2009, 433/439). This has been generally accepted as a sign of realistic agonies and frustrations: (Lee Eunsun 1996, 214–215) a consumptive wandering, blaming the world, eating, drinking and playing around. However, it was both an intellectual tour defined as ecotourism and productive tourism, and most of all, responsible tourism respecting the local characteristics, natural ecosystem and natural scenery. People were greatly consoled and inspired by the respect for life of the wild natural ecosystem. For example, Ch'oe Ch'iwŏn did not take Hamyang Sangnim Forest as a space for amusement where he could build a pavilion, outlook tower or artistic space such as a *pyŏlsŏ*. We would recognize that people in the past perceived the strictly distinguished functions of relic forests according to their type. Also, there are no facilities such as pavilions, outlook towers or *pyŏlsŏ* inside Andong's Mansongjŏng, Sŏngju's Sŏngbaksup, Ŭisŏng's Karosup, or Kyŏngju's Kyerim. Therefore, the culture of relic forests such as the *pibo* forest, *yŏpsŭng* forest, windbreak forest, *poŏn* forest and religious forest are different from public spaces such as amusement parks that can be created artificially.

Relic forest culture being misunderstood as a *landscaped* space for amusement is connected to the disordered Confucian values of the late Chosŏn Dynasty and the decline of community consciousness in modern and contemporary times. As a result of the weakening of the virtues of classical Confucian scholars, anti-Confucian outcomes occurred which distorted the Confucian moral base of small communities and villages. Additionally, due to a market-based economy that underestimated or overlooked the value of the ecosystem services of the relic forests and quantified them according to their monetary value, the relic forests that have been handed down from ancient times have finally begun to disappear.

The value of the ecosystem services of relic forests are summarized as follows: (1)they are important places for feeding wildlife, providing spaces for breeding and resting shelters, for securing biological diversity and gene banks, and contributing to the ecosystem's productivity through complete mutual relations; (2)they are important for air purification and material decomposition; (3)they act as buffers against natural disasters and are useful for monitoring environmental change; (4)they are spaces for buffering the local climate and fixing greenhouse gases such as carbon dioxide; (5)they preserve aspects of the symbolism, originality and historicity of the traditional geography and culture such as *fengshui* and *yŏpsŭng*; (6)they provide opportunities for ecological education and ecological tours; and (7)they provide us with resources and stages for aesthetic and cultural activities concerned with biophilia originating from human nature.

Relic forests are a key ecosystem preserving local environmental conditions and highly valuable forests in terms of conservation biology and humanities. Therefore, relic forests are a model that will allow humans and nature to live a sustainable life in cities if they are recreated through ecological preservation and restoration.

Translated by Kim Jongwon and Kim Jeongeun

Kim Jongwon (jwkim@kmu.ac.kr) *is a professor in the Department of Biology at Keimyung University, Taegu, Korea.*

Lee Junga (momo3030@kmu.ac.kr) *is a researcher at the Korea Institute of Ecosystem Management at Keimyung University, Taegu, Korea.*

Lim Jeongcheol (gieny21@nate.com) *is a Ph.D. candidate in the Department of Biology at Keimyung University, Taegu, Korea.*

Hwang Sookyoung (1sylove@naver.com) *is a researcher at the Korea Institute of Ecosystem Management at Keimyung University, Taegu, Korea.*

References

CONFUCIANISM, KOREAN CONFUCIANISM AND ECOLOGICAL DISCOURSE

Chang Hoeik. *Sam kwa onsaengmyŏng* [Living and global life]. Sol, 1998.

Chang Sŭnggu. "T'oegye sasang ŭi saengt'ae ch'ŏrhakchŏk chomyŏng [High-lighting Yi Hwang's ecological philosophy]," *T'oegye hakpo* (The T'oegye Studies Institute) (2001).

Ch'a Sŏnghwan. "Chŏng Yagyong kyŏnghak sasang i saengt'ae hwan'gyŏng wigi ŭi sidae e chunŭn sisajŏm [The implications of Chŏng Yakyong's thought regarding the Confucian Classics in terms of the ecological crisis]," *Tamnon 201* (The Korean Association of Socio-Historical Studies) (2010).

Ch'oe Chongdŏk. *Hamkke hanŭn hwan'gyŏng ch'ŏrhak* [Environmental philosophy for all]. Dongyeon, 2003.

_______. "Yangmyŏnghak kwa hwan'gyŏng yulli [Yangming Learning and environmental ethics]," *Tongasia munhwa wa sasang* [East Asian Culture and Philosophy] (East Asian Forum on Cultural Diversity) 1 (1998).

Ch'oe Yŏngjin. "*Chuyŏk* esŏ ponŭn in'gan kwa chayŏn ŭi kwan'gye—tajagwan ŭl chungsim ŭro [The relationship between man and nature as viewed through the *Book of Changes*]," *Tongyang ch'ŏrhak* (The Society for Asian Philosophy in Korea) 13 (2000).

Confucianism and Ecology: The Interrelation of Heaven, Earth, and Humans. ed. Mary Evelyn Tucker and John Berthrong. Harvard University Press, 1998.

Han Myŏnhŭi. *Hwan'gyŏng yulli* [Environmental ethics]. Ch'ŏrhakkwa hyŏnsilsa, 1997.

_______. *Tongasia munmyŏng kwa Han'guk ŭi saengt'aejuŭi* [East Asian civilization and Korean ecologism]. Philosophy and Reality Publishing, 2009.

Hans Jonas. *Saengmyŏng ŭi wŏlli* [The phenomenon of *life*: toward a philosophical biology]. Trans. Han Chŏnsŏn. Acanet, 2001.

Han Yewŏn. "Yangmyŏnghak ŭi manmul ilch'e kwan esŏ pon saengmyŏng yulli [Life ethics as viewed through the perception of *manmul ilch'e* found in Yangming Learning]," *Yangming Study* (Korean Association of Yangming Study) 6 (2001).

Hong Won-sik and Lee Sangho. "Kyŏngbu taeunha p'ŭrojekt'ŭ wa Naktonggang kaebal e taehan 'inmun saengt'aejŏgin" chŏpkŭn [A humanistic ecological approach to the Pan-Korea *Grand* Waterway Project and Naktong River Development]," *Han'gukhak nonjip* (Academia Koreana) 36 (2008).

Hwang Kapyŏn. "21 segi yuga ch'ŏrhak ŭi paljŏn panghyang—hwan'gyŏng yulli rŭl chungsim ŭro [The developmental direction of Confucian philosophy in the twenty-first century–with a special focus on environmental ethics]," *Tongyang ch'ŏrhak* (The Society for Asian Philosophy in Korea) 12 (2000).

Joseph R. Desjardins. *Hwan'gyŏng yulli* [Environmental Ethics: An Introduction to Environmental Philosophy]. Trans. Kim Myŏngsik. Chajak namu, 1999.

Kim Kyobin. "Yangmyŏnghak kwa saengmyŏng sasang [Yangming Learning and life-ism]," *Tongyang ch'ŏrhak* (The Society for Asian Philosophy in Korea) 13 (2000).

Kim Pyŏnghwan. "21 segi yuhak ŭi kwaje wa chŏnmang—yuhak sasang kwa saeng-t'ae munje rŭl chungsim ŭro [The tasks of Confucianism in the twenty-first century and the outlook thereof—with a special focus on Confucian thought and ecological problems]," *Chungguk hakpo* 42.

Kim Myŏngsik. *Hwan'gyŏng, saengmyŏng, simŭi minjujuŭi* [Environment, life, and deliberative democracy]. Pumyangsa, 2002.

Kim Sea-jeong (Kim Sejŏng). "Wang Yangmyŏng ŭi ch'inminsŏl e taehan saengt'aeronjŏk chŏpkŭn [Ecological approach to Wang Yangming's theory of *ch'inmin* (approach the people with dignity)]," *Tongyang ch'ŏrhak* (The Society for Asian Philosophy in Korea) 11 (1999).

———. "Hwangyŏng yulli e taehan tongyang ch'ŏrhakchŏk chŏpkŭn: yuga ch'ŏrhak ŭl chungsim ŭro [Asian philosophical approach to environmental ethics: with a special focus on Confucian philosophy]," *Pŏmhan ch'ŏrhak* (Bumhan Philosophy Association) 29 (2003).

Kim T'aeo. "Hyegang sasang ŭi saengt'ae chuŭijŏk kyoyuk wŏlli [The ecological education principle contained in Hyegang's thought]," Philosophy Education (The *Philosophy Education* Society of Korea) 35 (2008).

———. "Hyegang ŭi taedongnon kwa sot'ongnon kŭrigo kyoyuk saengt'aehak [Hyegang's theories of great harmony and communication and educational ecology]," *Philosophy Education* (The Philosophy Education Society of Korea) 41 (2010).

Ku Sŭnghoe. *Ecophilosophy*. Saegil, 1995.

———. *Saengt'ae ch'ŏrhak kwa hwang'yŏng yulli* [Ecological Philosophy and Environmental Ethics]. Dongguk University Press, 2001.

Kwak Sinhwan. "Yuhak ŭi yugich'ejŏk ujuron [The Confucian theory of the organic cosmos]," *Kisul chŏngbohwa sidaeŭi in'gan munje* [Mankind in the era of technology and information] (The Society for Asian Philosophy in Korea) (1994).

———. "*Chuyŏk* esŏ ŭi chayŏn'gwan [The view of nature contained in the *Book of Changes*]," *Tongyang sasanggwa hwan'gyŏng munje* [Asian Thought and

Environmental Problems]. (Mosaek, 1996).

Lee Dong-hee (Yi Tonghŭi). "Han'guk Sŏngnihak ŭi hwan'gyŏng ch'ŏrhakchŏk sisa [Environmental philosophical implications of Korean Neo-Con-fucianism]," *Tongyang ch'ŏrhak* (The Society for Asian Philosophy in Korea) 13 (2000).

Lee Jin-Woo (Yi Chinu). *Noksaek sayu wa ek'otop'ia* [Green thought and ecotopia]. Munye Publishing, 1998.

Mun Sunhong. *Saengt'ae wigi wa noksaek ŭi taean* [Ecological crisis and green alternatives]. Nara sarang, 1992.

Murray Bookchin. *Saeho saengt'aeron ŭi ch'ŏrhak* [Toward an ecological society]. Trans. Mun Sunhong. Sol, 1999.

Pak Imun. *Munmyŏng ŭi wigi wa munhwa ŭi chŏnhwan* [The crisis of civilization and cultural transition]. Minumsa, 1996.

_______. *Munmyŏng ŭi mirae wa saengt'aehak chŏk segyegwan* [The future of civilization and the ecological view of the world]. Dangdae, 1998.

_______. *Hwan'gyŏng ch'ŏrhak* [Environmental philosophy]. Midas Books, 2002.

Peter Singer. *Tongmul haebang* [Animal Liberation]. Trans. Kim Sŏnghwan. Ingan Sarang, 1999.

Pak Imun. "Noksaek ŭi yulli [Green ethics]," *Noksaek p'yŏngnon* 15 (1994).

Pak Hŭibyŏng. "Hong taeyong sasang e isŏsŏ mul-a ŭi sangdaesŏng kwa tongil-sŏng [The relativity and similarity between nature and the self found in Hong Taeyong's thought]," *Han'guk ŭi saengt'ae sasang* [Ecological Philosophy of Korea]. Tolbegae, 1999.

Reiner Grundmann. *Marŭk'ŭsŭjuŭiwa saengt'aehak* [Marxism and Ecology]. Trans. Pak Manjun and Pak Chun'gŏn. Dongnyeok, 1995.

Ro Yŏngch'an (Young-chan Ro). "Yulgok ujuron ŭi saengt'aeronjŏk amsi tŭl [The Korean Neo-Confucianism of Yi Yulgok], *Yuhak sasang kwa saengt'aehak* [Confucianism and Ecology: The Interrelation of Heaven, Earth, and Humans] ed. Mary Evelyn Tucker and John Berthrong (Harvard University Press, 1998), trans. O Chŏngsŏn. Yemoon sowon (Yemun sŏwŏn), 2010.

Tu Weiming. "Kyemongjuŭi chŏngsin ŭl nŏmŏsŏ [Beyond the enlightenment mentality]," *Yuhak sasang kwa saengt'aehak* [Confucianism and Ecology: The Interrelation of Heaven, Earth, and Humans] ed. Mary Evelyn Tucker and John Berthrong. (Harvard Univerdity Press, 1998), trans. O Chŏngsŏn. Yemoon sowon, 2010.

Yi Chongho. "T'oegye Yi Hwang ŭi yugich'e ujuron kwa saengt'ae sasang [Yi Hwang's theory of the organic universe and ecological thought]," *Han'guk hanmunhak yŏn'gu* [Journal of Korean Literature in Hanmun] (Society of Korean Literature in Hanmun) (2004).

Yi Hyogŏl. "Hwan'gyŏng saengt'ae munje e taehan tongyang ch'ŏrhak ŭi taean [Asian philosophy as an alternative with which to resolve environmental and ecological problems]," *Chunggukhak nonch'ong* (Chinese Studies Insti-tute, Korea University) 9–1, 1996.

Yi Kiyong. "Yulgok ŭi chayŏn ihae wa ch'ŏnin kyoyŏ [Yi Yi's perception of nature and the relationship between heaven and man]," *Tongyang ch'ŏrhak* (The Society for Asian Philosophy in Korea) 13 (2000).

Yu Sŏngsŏn. "Yulgok simnon e kŭn'gŏhan hwan'gyŏng yulli ŭi mosaek [Searching for environmental ethics based on Yi Yi's theory of the mind]," *Yulgok sasang yŏn'gu* (Association of Yulgok Study) 4 (2001).

Wang Yangmyŏng ŭi saengmyŏng ch'ŏrhak [Wang Yangming's philosophy of life]. Cheonggye, 2006.

THE CONTEMPORARY CONFUCIAN HERITAGE AND THE ENVIRONMENT OF WORLDLY CONFUCIANS AND TOHAK CONFUCIANS

Book of Documents.

Brooks, David. "The New Humanism." *New York Times*. March 7, 2011. http:// www.nytimes.com/2011/03/08/opinion/08brooks.html?ref=opinion(accessed August, 28, 2011).

Herman E. Daley, *Beyond Growth: The Economics of Sustainable Development*. Boston: Beacon Press, 1996.

Nicholas Kristof. "China's Winning Schools." *New York Times*, Jan. 15, 2011.

Yi Hwang. *T'oegye sŏnsaeng ŏnhaengnok* 5.lla, B, 855.

HUMAN FULFILLMENT AND LOVE OF THE UNIVERSE: A MEDITATION ON EMOTION IN KOREAN AND CHINESE SOURCES

Chinese Classics

Tao Te Ching. Trans. Victor Mair, Bantam Books, 1990.

Tchouang-tseu, Oeuvre Complète. traduction de Liou Kia-hway, Gallimard/Unesco, Paris,

1969.

The Analects of Confucius/The Doctrine of the Mean. Trans. James Legge, New York : Dover Publications, 1971.

The I Ching or Book of Changes. Trans. Richard Wilhelm, Princeton University Press, 1976.

The Works of Mencius. Trans. James Legge, New York: Dover Publications, 1970.

Works of T'oegye and Yulgok

T'oegye

Complete Works of T'oegye. Vol.3, T'oegyehak Yŏn'guwŏn, Seoul, 1992.

T'oegye, *To Become A Sage, The Ten Diagrams on Sage Learning* [聖學十圖]. Trans. and with commentaries by Michael Kalton, Columbia University Press, 1988.

T'oegye, *Chasŏngnok* [自省錄]. Trans. into Korean by Ch'oe Chung-sŏk, Kugak charyowŏn editions, Seoul, 1998.

T'oegye Hakpo, no. 19, Transactions of the Third Annual International T'oegye Symposium, "Neo-Confucianism and Lee T'oegye," Seoul: T'oegyehak Yŏn'guwŏn, 1978.

T'oegye's Selected Works. Seoul: Minchok Munhwa Ch'ujinhwoe, 1979.

Yun Sa-Soon, *T'oegye sŏnchip*. Seoul: Hyŏnamsa, 1993.

Yulgok

Yi I, Yulgok, *Anthologie de la sagesse extrême-orientale*. Trans. into French of the *Sŏnghak chibyo* [聖學輯要] by Philippe Thiébault, Autres Temps, 2009.

Yulgok chŏnsŏ. Edition of the Academy of Korean Studies, II, 1984, Manŏn pongsa, *Ten-Thousand Characters Memorial* [萬言封事].

Yulgok chŏnsŏ. Edition of the Academy of Korean Studies, V, 1985, *Sŏnghak chibyo, Compendium of Sage Learning* [聖學輯要].

Yulgok chŏnsŏ. Edition of the Academy of Korean Studies, III, 1987, Letters.

Yulgok chŏnsŏ. Edition of the Academy of Korean Studies, IV, 1988, Yŏksuch'aek, *Book on the Changes and Numbers* [易數策].

Yulgok chŏnsŏ. 1 vol. Poetry. Seoul: Sŏnggyun'gwan University Press, 1958/1986.

Other References

Bergeron, Marie-Ina, *La Chine et Teilhard.* Jean-Pierre Delarge, Paris: éditeur, 1976.

De Bary, William T., *The Message of the Mind in Neo-Confucianism.* Columbia University Press, 1989.

Demieville, Paul, *Choix d'Etudes Bouddhiques* (1929–1970). Leiden, 1973.

Macintyre, Alasdair, *After Virtue.* a study in moral theory, Duckworth, 1981/1996.

Nylan, Michael, *The Five Confucian Classics.* Yale University Press, 2001.

Pascal, Blaise, *Pensées.* Paris: Texte établi par Louis Lafuma, 1962.

Ricoeur, Paul, *Philosophie de la Volonté.* I/II, Paris: Aubier, 1960/1988.

Ricoeur, Paul, *Du Texte à l'Action.* Essais d'Herméneutique II, Paris: Seuil, 1986.

Ro Young-chan, *The Korean Neo-Confucianism of Yi Yulgok.* SUNY Press, 1989.

Schweitzer Albert, *The Teaching of Reverence for Life.* Holt: Reinehart and Winston, 1965.

Teilhard De Chardin, Pierre, *Réflexion et Prière dans l'espace-temps.* Paris: Seuil, 1972.

Teilhard De Chardin, Pierre, *The Future of Man. Trans.* Norman Denny, Harper & Row, 1964.

Thiebault Philippe, *La Pensée Coréenne.* Autres Temps, 2006.

Tu Wei-ming, *Confucian Thought.* Selfhood as Creative Transformation, SUNY Press, 1985/1991.

Tu Wei-ming and Tucker Mary Evelyn ed., *Confucian Spirituality.* Vol. 1/2. New York : A Herder and Herder Book, 2003/2004.

Tucker Mary Evelyn and Berthrong John ed., *Confucianism and Ecology–The Interrelation of Heaven, Earth, and Humans.* Center for the Study of World Religions, 1998.

Waley, Arthur, *An Introduction to the Study of Chinese Painting.* New York: Grove Press, 1958.

THE ECOLOGICAL DIMENSION IN KOREAN LITERATI PAINTING: THEORY AND ART

Kim Sisŭp(金時習). Maewol dangjip(『梅月堂集』).

Koryŏ-sa (『高麗史』).

Sin Sukju(申叔舟), *Pohan Chaejip*(『保閑齋集』).
Sŏ Gŏjŏng(徐居正), *Tongmunson* (『東文選』).
Yi Inro(李仁老), *P'ahanjip* (『破閑集』).
Yi Kyubo(李奎報), *Tongguk Isanggukjip*(『東國李相國集』).
Yi Saek(李穡), *Mok'un Chip* (『牧隱集』).
Yi Sŭnghyu(李承休), *Tong'an Kosajip*(『動安居士集』).
Xu Jing(徐兢), *Gaoli Tujing* (『高麗圖經』).

Secondary Sources

Acker, William. 1974. *Some T'ang and Pre-T'ang Texts on Chinese Painting*, Leiden, E. J. Brill.

Ahn, Hwi-joon (安輝濬), 1987. *Han'guk Hoehwa-sa* (『韓國繪畵史』, History of Korean Painting), Seoul: Ilchi-sa.

Barnhart, Richard M., et al. 1997. *Three Thousand Years of Chinese Painting*, New Haven: Yale University Press.

Bush, Susan. and Shih, Hsio-yen. 1985. *Early Chinese Texts on Painting*, Cambridge: Harvard-Yenching Institute.

Ch'oe Yongho. 1999. "Private Academies and the State in Late Choson Korea." in Haboush and Deuchler, eds. , *Culture and the State in Late Choson Korea*, Cambridge, Mass. : Harvard University Press. pp. 15–45.

Egami, Yasushi. and Kobayashi, Hiromitsu. 1994. *Woodcuts in the Nanzenji Bizangquan*, Tokyo: Yamakawa Publishing Co.

Fuller, Michael A. 1993. "Pursuing the Complete Bamboo in the Breast: Reflections on a Classical Chinese Image for Immediacy." *Harvard Journal of Asiatic Studies* 53:1. pp. 5–23.

Guo Ruoxu(郭若許). 1967. *Duhua jianwen zhi* (『圖畵見聞誌』) (compiled after 1076). in *Songren huaxue lunzhu* (『宋人畵學論著』), Taipei: Shih chiai shuchu.

Hong, Sonp'yo(洪善杓). 1987. "Yi Kyu-bo ui hoehwakwan (李奎報의 繪畵觀 : Yi Kyu-bo's Views on Painting)." *Misul Charyo* (『美術資料』) vol. 39. pp. 28–45.

_______. 1990. "Koryo sidae ui hoehwa iron (高麗時代의 繪畵理論: Art Theory in Koryo dynasty)." *Kogo misul* (『考古美術』). 187. pp. 3–23.

_______. 1999. *Choson sidae hoehwa-sa ron* (『朝鮮時代繪畵史論』 Art Historical Theory in Choson Dynasty). Seoul: Munye ch'ulp'an-sa.

Kikutake Junichi and Chong, Woo-taek. 1998. *Koryo sidaeuiPulhwa* (『高麗時代의 佛畵』 : Koryo Buddhist Painting). Seoul: Sigong-sa.

Kim Daewon. 2011. "Koryo hwaron ui mun'kijok hoehwagwan yon'gu (高麗畵論의 文氣的 繪畵觀 研究 : A Study on the Literary Views on Painting in Koryo Art Theory)." *Soyehak yongu* (『書藝學研究』 18).

Kim, Sisup(金時習). 1973. Maewol dangjip (『梅月堂集』) in Ch'oe Chin-won(崔珍源). *Maewoldangjip haejae*(『梅月堂集解題』), Songgyunkwan University Taedong munhwa yon'guwon.

Ko, Yusop(高裕燮). 1963. "Koryo sidae hoehwa ui oegukgwa ui kyoryu (高麗時代의 繪畵의 外國과의 交流 Foreign interaction of Koryo dynasty painting)." *Hanguk misulsa kup mihak nonsu* (『韓國美術史及美學論收』), Seoul: T'ongmun-kwan. pp. 69–81.

Kukje han'guk hakhoe, 1987. *Silk Road wa Han'guk munhwa* (The Silk Road and Korean Culture), Seoul: Sonamu.

Loehr, Max, 1968. *Chinese Landscape Woodcuts-From an Imperial Commentary to the Tenth-Century Printed Edition of the Buddhist Canon*, The Belknap Press of Harvard University Press.

Paik, Insan(白仁山). 2003. "Sonjo nyon'gan muninhwa samchol (宣祖年間 文人畵 三絶 : Three Literati Masters from the Reign of Sonjo)." *Kansong Munhwa* (『澗松文化』) vol. 65. pp. 103–127.

Soper, Alexander Coburn. 1951. *Kuo Jo-hsu's Experiences in Painting*, Washington, D. C. : American Council of Learned Societies.

Suzuki, Kei(領木敬). 1981. "Rinsen kchi shu no Gaki to Kaku Ki ni tsuite (林泉高致集の <畵記>と 郭熙について, *Linchuan Gaozhi's Huaji* and Guo Xi)." Bijutsushi (『美術史』) 30. pp. 1–11.

Yi Songmi(李成美). 1986. "Koryo ch'ojo taejangkyong ui Ojebijangjon p'anhwa Koryo ch'oki sansuhwa ui ilyongu (The Woodblock prints of the Imperially-composed Explanation of the Secret Treasure A Study of Early Koryo Landscape Painting)." *Kogo misul*(『考古美術』)169–170. pp. 14–70.

Yi Tongju(李東洲). 1987. *Hanguk Hoehwasa-ron* (『韓國繪畵史論』 Discussion on Korean Painting History), Seoul: Yolhwa-dang.

Yi Un'gyong, 1999. *Ch'anggang Cho Sok ui Hoehwa* (『滄江 趙涑의 繪畵』 : Paintings by Ch'anggang Cho Sok), M. A. Thesis, Seoul: Ewha Women's University.

Yu, Jianhua(兪劍華). ed. , *Chungguo hualun leibian* (『中國畵論類編』 Chinese Painting Theory by Categories), 2 vols. , Beijing: Chungguo gudian ishu.

YI T'OEGYE ON REVERENCE (KYŎNG) FOR NATURE: A MODERN NEO-CONFUCIAN ECOLOGICAL VISION

Primary Sources

TC. Yi T'oegye 李退溪. 1986. *T'oegye chŏnsŏ* (退溪全書, Complete works of Yi T'oegye), enlarged edition, 5 vols. Seoul: Sŏnggyun'gwan University Press.

T'oegye sŏnsaeng munjip (退溪先生文集, Collected literary works by Master T'oegye).

Translations and Modern Works:

Abe Yoshio. 1965. *Nihon shushigaku to Chōsen* (Japanese Chu Hsi school in relation to Korea). Tokyo: Tokyo University Press.

Berthrong, John. 1994. *All Under Heaven: Transforming Paradigms of Confucian-Christian Dialogue*. Albany, NY: SUNY Press.

_______. 1998. "Motifs for a New Confucian Ecological Vision." In Tucker and Berthrong, eds. *Confucianism and Ecology: The Interrelation of Heaven, Earth, and Humans*. Cambridge, MA: Harvard University Press, 237–263.

Bergmann, Sigurd and Heather Eaton, eds. 2011. *Ecological Awareness: Exploring Religion, Ethics and Aesthetics*. Studies in Religion and the Environment/ Studien zur Religion und Umwelt, Bd. 3. LIT Verlag.

Chan, Wing-tsit. 1963. *A Source Book in Chinese Philosophy*. Princeton University Press.

_______. 1967. *Reflections on Things at Hand: the Neo-Confucian Anthology by Chu Hsi and Lü Tsu-Ch'ien*. New York: Columbia University Press.

_______. 1985. "How T'oegye Understood Chu Hsi." In Wm. T. de Bary and J. Kim Haboush, eds., *The Rise of Neo-Confucianism in Korea*.

Chan, Wing-tsit, ed. 1986. *Chu Hsi and Neo-Confucianism*. Honolulu: University of Hawaii Press.

Ch'oe Kŭndŭk. 1992. T'oegye sasang ŭi sijŏk chomyŏng (T'oegye's thought from a poetic perspective), *Han'guk yuhak sasang yŏn'gu* (Studies in Korean Confucian thought). Seoul.

Ching, Julia. 1977. *Confucianism and Christianity: A Comparative Study*. New York and Tokyo: Kodansha International.

_______. 1993. *Chinese Religions*. Maryknoll, NY: Orbis Books.

_______. 1997. *Mysticism and Kingship in China: The Heart of Chinese Wisdom*. Cambridge University Press.

_______. 2000. *The Religious Thought of Chu Hsi*. Toronto and Oxford: Oxford University Press.

Chung, Edward Y. J. 1994a "Confucianism and Women in Modern Korea: Continuity, Change and Conflict." In Arvind Sharma and Katherine Young (eds.), *The*

Annual Review of Women in World Religions, vol. 3, 142–188. Albany: SUNY Press.

Chung, Edward Y. J. 1994b "Confucianism: A Living Religious Tradition in Contemporary South Korea." *Korean Studies in Canada* 2:13–22.

_______. 1995. *The Korean Neo-Confucianism of Yi T'oegye and Yi Yulgok: A Reappraisal of the Four-Seven Thesis and Its Practical Implications for Self-Cultivation*. Albany: SUNY Press.

_______. 1998. "Confucian-Christian Dialogue Revisited: A Korean and Comparative Study." *Chonggyo-wa munwha* (Journal of Religion and Culture) IV: 221–249. Seoul National University.

_______. 2004. "Confucian Spirituality in Yi T'oegye: A Korean Interpretation and Its Implications for Comparative Religion." In Tu Weiming and Mary Evelyn Tucker, eds., *Confucian Spirituality*, vol. 2B, 204–225.

_______. 2006. "Confucian Li (Ritual) and Family Spirituality: Reflections on the Contemporary Korean Tradition of Ancestral Rites." A paper presented at the 2006 Annual Meeting of American Academy of Religion, Washington, DC, November. 17–21.

_______. 2009. "Sagehood and Religious Practice in Yi T'oegye's Neo-Confucianism." In *Literature and Thought of Yi T'oegye: Program for the 22nd International Conference on T'oegye Studies* (Aug. 27–30, 2009), The International T'oegyehak Society, 263–291.

_______. 2010. "T'oegye's Religious Thought: A Neo-Confucian and Comparative Perspective." In *East Asian Confucianisms: Interactions and Innovations*. New Brunswick, NJ: Confucius Institute and Rutgers University Press, 193–210.

_______. 2011. "Self Transcendence as the Ultimate Reality in Interreligious Dialogue: A Neo-Confucian Perspective." *Studies in Religion / Sciences Religieuses* vol. 40, no. 2 (June 2011): 152–178.

de Bary, William. T. 1981. *Neo-Confucian Orthodoxy and the Learning of the Mind-and-Heart*. New York: Columbia University Press.

de Bary William T. and JaHyun Kim Haboush, eds. 1985. *The Rise of Neo-Confucianism in Korea*. New York: Columbia University Press.

Gardner, Daniel K, trans. 1990. *Chu Hsi: Learning To Be a Sage: Selections from the Conversations of Master Chu*. Berkeley and LA: University of California Press.

_______. 2009. *The Four Books: The Basic Teachings of the Later Confucian Tradition*. Indianapolis/Cambridge: Hackett Publishing Company.

Girardot, N. J., James Miller, and Xiaogan Liu, eds. 2001. *Daoism and Ecology: Ways within a Cosmic Landscape*. Religions of the World and Ecology series. Cambridge, MA: Center for the Study of World Religions and Harvard University Press.

Kalton, Michael C., trans. 1988. *To Become A Sage: The Ten Diagrams on Sage Learning by Yi T'oegye*. New York: Columbia University Press.

Kearns, Laurel and Catherine Keller, eds. 2007. *Eco-Spirit: Religions and Philosophies for the Earth*. The Forum on Religion and Ecology. Fordham University Press.

Keum, Jang-tae. 1998a. *Confucianism and Korean Thought*. 2 vols (translated from the original Korean edition) Seoul: Jimoondang Publishing Co.

_______. 1998b. *T'oegye-ŭi sam kwa ch'ŏrhak* (T'oegye's life and thought). Seoul; Seoul National University Press.

Kim, Yŏng-suk. 2009. "T'oegye si e natanan tohak chŏk sŏnggyŏk kwa hyŏng-sang" (The Neo-Confucian nature and formation of T'oegye's poetry), *Literature and Thought of Yi T'oegye: Program for the 22nd International Conference on T'oegye Studies* (Aug. 27–30, 2009), The International T'oegyehak Society, 145–164.

Kwŏn, O-bong. 1992. *T'oegye si taejŏn* (T'oegye's poetry: a compendium). Pohang: Yŏgang Press.

Lau, D. C., trans. 1979. *Confucius: The Analects*. New York: Penguin Classics.

_______. 1970. *Mencius*. New York: Penguin Classics.

Lee, Dong-hee (Yi Tonghŭi). 2011. "Nonpyŏng: Saengt'aehak kwa Han'guk ŭi yugyo sasang—chuje II" (Discussant's Commentary: Ecology and Korean Confucianism—panel theme II), Program of the Fifth Keimyung Inter-national Conference on Korean Studies: Ecology and Korean Confucianism), Keimyung University, Daegu, Korea (June 2–4), pp. 119–124. Note: this paper was presented in Korean as a commentary on three conference papers in panel II including mine.

Lee, Peter K. H., ed. 1992. *Confucian-Christian Encounters in Historical and Contemporary Perspectives*. Lewiston/ Queenstown: The Edwin Mellen Press.

Liu, Ning. 2009. "T'oegye ŭi sip'ung kwa kŭ chŏngsin chŏk kich'o" (The nature of T'oegye's poetry and its spiritual foundation), *Literature and Thought of Yi T'oegye: Program for the 22nd International Conference on T'oegye Studies*, The International T'oegyehak Society, 329–337.

Nasr, Seyyed Hossein. 1996. *Religion and the Order of Nature*. New York and Oxford: Oxford University Press.

Neville, Robert C. 2000. *Boston Confucianism: Portable Tradition in the Late-Modern World*. Albany: SUNY Press.

Ro, Young-chan. 1989. *The Neo-Confucianism of Yi Yulgok*. Albany: SUNY Press.

Taylor, Paul W. 1986. *Respect for Nature: A Theory of Environmental Ethics*. Princeton, N.J.: Princeton University Press.

Taylor, Rodney. 1991. *Religious Dimensions of Neo-Confucianism*. Albany: SUNY Press.

Taylor, Rodney. 1998. "Companionship with the World: Roots and Branches of a Confucian Ecology." In Tucker and Berthrong, eds., *Confucian Ecology*, 40–57.

Tu, Wei-ming. 1985a. *Confucian Thought: Selfhood as Creative Self-Transformation*. Albany: SUNY Press.

______. 1985b. "T'oegye's Perception of Human Nature: A Preliminary Inquiry into the Four-Seven Debate in Korean Neo-Confucianism." In de Bary and Kim Haboush, eds., *The Rise of Neo-Confucianism in Korea*.

. 1989. *Centrality and Commonality: An Essay on Confucian Religiousness*. Albany: SUNY Press.

______. 1998. "The Continuity of Being: Chinese Visions of Nature." Tucker and Berthrong, eds. *Confucianism and Ecology*, 105–121 (this article was originally published in Tu 1985a).

______. 2004. "The Ecological Turn in New Confucian Humanism: Implications for China and the World," epilogue in Tu and Tucker, eds., *Confucian Spirituality*, vol. 11b, 480–508.

______. 2011. "Keynote Speech." Program of the 5th Keimyung International Conference on Korean Studies: Ecology and Korean Confucianism, Keimyung University, Daegu, Korea (June 2–4, 2011), 15–22.

Tu, Weiming and Mary Evelyn Tucker, eds. 2004. *Confucian Spirituality*, vol. 11b. New York: The Crossroad Publishing Company.

Tucker, Mary Evelyn. 1991. "The Relevance of Chinese Neo-Confucianism for the Reverence of Nature," *Environmental History Review* 15, no. 2 (summer 1991): 55–67.

______. 1998. "The Philosophy of Ch'i as an Ecological Cosmology." In Tucker and Berthrong, eds., *Confucianism and Ecology*, 187–207.

______. 2007. "Ethics and Ecology: A Primary Challenge of the Dialogue of Civilizations." In Kearns and Keller, eds., *Eco-Spirit: Religions and Philosophies for the Earth*, 495–503.

Tucker, Mary Evelyn, and John Berthrong, eds. 1998. *Confucianism and Ecology: The Interrelation of Heaven, Earth, and Humans*. Cambridge, MA: Center for the Study of World Religions and Harvard University Press.

______. 1998. "Introduction: Setting the Context." In Tucker and Berthrong, eds. *Confucianism and Ecology*, pp. xxxv-xlv.

Tucker, Mary Evelyn, and John Grim. 1998. "Series Foreword." Tucker and Berthrong, eds. *Confucianism and Ecology*, pp. xv-xxxiii.

______. 2007. "The Greening of the World's Religions" *The Chronicle Review* 53:23 (Feb. 9, 2007), page B9.

Tucker, Mary Evelyn and Duncan Ryuken Williams, eds. 1998. *Buddhism and Ecology: The Interconnection of Dharma and Deeds*. Religions of the World and Ecology series. Cambridge, MA: Center for the Study of World Religions and Harvard University Press.

Yi, Chang-wu and Se-hu Chang. 2007. *T'oegyesi p'uli* (T'oegye's poetry explained). Daegu: Yŏngnam University Press.

Yun, Sa-soon. 1991. *Critical Issues in Neo-Confucian Thought: The Philosophy of Yi T'oegye*. Honolulu: University of Hawaii Press (translated from the original Korean edition).

Note on the Citation and Transliteration Style:

Korean names and titles are Romanized according to the standard McCune-Reischauer system, and Chinese terms according to the Wade-Giles system (my preference over the Pinyin system for a pronunciation and writing reason). For T'oegye's writings cited, only the Korean titles are given, as this is the standard style. To avoid confusion, the titles of the primary Chinese sources are given in Chinese only. Since this is a topic on a leading Korean thinker, most of the romanized philosophical terms are given for the Korean pronunciation and then for the Chinese with a slash between them; e.g., *kyŏng / ching* (reverence).

Furthermore, all references to T'oegye's *Complete Works (T'oegye chŏnsŏ*; hereafter abbreviated as *TC*) are cited in the notes. For the reader's convenience as well, most of the relevant modern or Western sources are directly cited in the text, except those lengthy ones included in the notes for further discussion and supplementary information.

ECOLOGY AND COSMOLOGY: A KOREAN NEO-CONFUCIAN APPROACH

Chan, Wing-tsit. (trans.) *A Source Book in Chinese Philosophy*. Princeton: Princeton University, 1963.

Panikkar, Raimon. *The Rhythm of Being: The Gifford Lectures*. Maryknoll: Orbis, 2010.

Ro, Young-chan. "Ecological Implication of Yi Yulgok's Cosmology," *Confucianism and Ecology*. Mary Evelyn Tucker and John Berthrong ed., Cam-bridge: Harvard University, 1998.

Tu Wei-ming. *Centrality and Commonality: An Essay on Confucian Religiousness*. Albany: State University of New York Press, 1989.

Tucker, Mary Evelyn, and Grim, John ed. *Worldviews and Ecology: Religion, Philosophy, and the Environment*. Maryknoll: Orbis 1994.

White, Lynn, Jr. "The Historical Roots of Our Ecological Crisis," in *Western Man and Environmental Ethics: Attitudes toward Nature and Technology*. Ian G. Barbour (ed.), Reading, Mss.: Addison-Wesley, 1973.

Yulgok chŏnsŏ [栗谷全書, *Complete Works of Yi Yulgok*]. Vol. 1, Seoul: Sungkyunkwan University, 1971.

THE TRANSFORMATION OF CONFUCIANISM IN CONTEMPORARY KOREA: HOW IT HAS LOST MOST OF ITS METAPHYSICAL UNDERPINNINGS AND SURVIVES TODAY PRIMARILY AS ETHICAL RHETORIC AND HERITAGE RITUALS

Clark Sorensen and Sung-Chul Kim. 2004. "Filial Piety in Contemporary Urban Southeast Korea: Practices and Discourses." *Practice and Discourse in Contemporary East Asia*. Charlotte Ikels·Filial Piety(ed). Stanford, California: Stanford University Press. p. 173.

Ch'oe Yŏngsŏng. 1997. "The history of Korean Confucian thought: the modern and contemporary period". *Han'guk yuhak sasangsa*. vol. V: Kŭn . hyŏndae p'yŏn. Seoul: Asea munhwasa.

Don Baker. 2009. "Shamans, Catholics, and Chŏng Yagyong: Tasan's defense of the ritual hegemony of the Confucian state." *Tasanhak 15*. pp. 139–79.

Eun Ki-soo. 2008. "Family values changing —but still conservative." *Social Change in Korea*. Kim Kyong-dong(ed). Seoul: Jimoondang. p. 149.

Gallup Korea. 2004. "The religion and religious attitudes of Koreans: a study of religion based on a comparison of survey results from 1984, 1989, 1997, and 2004". *Han'gugin ŭi chonggyo wa chonggyo ŭisik: '84nyŏn, '89nyŏn, '97nyŏn, '04nyŏn chosa kyŏlgwa rŭl pigyohan chonggyo yŏn'gusŏ* . Seoul: Gallup Korea. 101.

Gallup Korea. 2004. *Han'gugin ŭi chonggyo wa chonggyo ŭisik*. p. 84.

Hahm Chaibong. 2004. "Constitutionalism, Confucian Civic Virtue, and Ritual Propriety." *Confucianism for the Modern World*. Daniel A. Bell and Hahm Chaibong(ed). Cambridge, UK: Cambridge University Press.

Han'guk chonggyo sahoe yŏ'guso(ed). 1993. *Han'guk chonggyo yŏn'gam* [Yearbook of Religion in Korea]. Seoul: Korea Halimwŏn. pp. 212–251.

Kim Hoil. 2000. *Han'guk ŭi hyanggyo* [The Confucians shrines of Korea]. Seoul: Taewŏnsa.

Km Changt'ae. 1999. "Hyŏndae Han'guk yugyo ŭi pyŏndong kwa hyŏnhwang chosa"

[An investigation of the current situation of Confucianism in Korea and how it has changed], *Han'guk hyŏndae ŭi yugyo munhwa [Confucian culture in contemporary Korea]*. Seoul: Seoul National University Press.

Kwang Yeong Shin and Chulhee Chung. 2001. "Confucian Tradition and democracy in South Korea." Paper presented at the second Biennial Conference of Korean Studies Association in Australasia. (Available at http://arts.monash.edu.au/korean/ ksaa/conference/04chulheechungkwangyeongshin.pdf)

Lauren Pfister. 1995. "The Different Faces of Contemporary Religious Confucianism: An Account of the Diverse Approaches of Some Major Twentieth Century Chinese Confucian Scholars". *Journal of Chinese Philosophy 22*. pp. 5–80.

Minja Kim Choe. 2006. "Modernization, gender roles, and marriage behavior in South Korea". *Transformations in Twentieth Century Korea*. Chang Yun-Shik and Steven Hugh Lee. New York: Routledge. pp. 291–309.

Moon Ok-pyo. 1998. "Ancestors Becoming Children of God: Ritual Clashes between Confucian Tradition and Christianity in Contemporary Korea," *Korea Journal* 38:3. p. 152.

Namhee Kim·Hea Jun Yoon·Gary N. McLean, 2010. "Policy Efforts to increase women faculty in Korea: reactions and changes at universities." *Asia Pacific Education Review* 11. pp. 285–299.

National Statistical Office. 2005. *Census*. p. 32.

National Statistical Office. 2006. *Census in'gu chut'aek ch'ongchosa: chŏpsu chipgye kyŏlgwa* [in'gu pumun] [The broad results from the 2005 census of the population and housing: The results of the compilation of the overall totals, population section]. Seoul: T'onggyech'ŏng. p. 32.

National Folk Museum(ed). *Han'guk ŭi chesa* [Korea's Sacrificial Rites]. Seoul: National Folklore Museum.

Park, Keun Hae. 1979. *The New Spirit Movement*. Seoul: Naeway Business Journal and Korea Herald. p.15, p. 22, p. 28, p. 26.

Robert E. Buswell, Jr(ed). 2007. *Religions of Korea in Practice*. Princeton, New Jersey: Princeton University Press. pp. 383–82, 434–445.

James Grayson. 2009. "Ch'udo yebae: A Case Study in the Early Emplantation of Protestant Christianity in Korea". *Journal of Asian Studies*. vol. 68 no. 2. pp. 413–434.

Robert Neville. 2000. *Boston Confucianism: Portable Tradition in the Late-Modern World*. Albany: State University of New York Press.

Shin, Doh C. 1999. *Mass Politics and Culture in Democratizing Korea*. Cambridge: Cambridge University Press. p. 75.

Yang Jonghae. 2009. "Globalization and value change in Korea, with a special emphasis on the impact of the recent economic crisis and neoliberal reform on the Confucian value system" *Korea Confronts Globalization*. Chang Yun-Shik, Hyun-Ho Seok, and Donald L. Baker(ed). New York: Routledge. p. 201.

Yoon, Hong-Key. 2006. *The Culture of Fengshui in Korea: An Exploration of East Asian Geomancy*. Lanham, MD: Lexington Books. pp. 201–213.

Yun Sŏngbŏm. 1970. "Han'gukchŏk sinhak: ilmyŏng sŏng ŭi sinhak". *Kidokkyo* sasang no.150. pp. 134–151.

ECOLOGISM AND CONFUCIAN PRO-LIFE-ISM

Kim Chonguk. *Pulgyo saengt'ae chŏlhak* [Buddhist Ecological Philosophy]. Tongguk University Press, 2004.

Kim Uktong. *Han'guk ŭi noksaek munhwa* [The green culture of Korea]. Munye Publishing, 2000.

Hwang T'aeyŏn. "Kŭndae hamnisŏng inyŏm kwa hwan'gyŏng wigi ŭi hamnijŏk ihae [The ideology of modern rationality and the rational understanding of the environmental crisis]." *Konggan kwa sahoe* [Space and Society] (Korean Association of Space and Environment Research) 9 (1997).

Pak Hyŏnjŏng. "Hans Magnus Enzensberge ŭi saengt'aejuŭi pip'an [Hans Magnus Enzensberge's criticism of ecologism]." *Togil munhak* [German Literature] (Koreanische Gesellschaft fűr Germanistik) 116 (2010).

Kim Wŏnjung. "Taeji yulli ŭi an'gwa pak: in'gan chungsimjuŭi esŏ saengt'ae chungsimjuŭi ro ŭi chŏnhwan [Inside and outside land ethics: moving from anthropocentrism to eco-centrism]." *Hyŏndae yŏngŏ yŏngmunhak* [Modern English Literature] (The Modern English Society of Korea) 54–1 (2010).

Mary Evelyn Tucker and John Berthrong ed. *Confucianism and Ecology: The Interrelation of Heaven, Earth, and Humans*. Harvard University Center for the Study of World Religions Publications, 1998.

Michael C. Kalton. "Extending the Neo-Confucian Tradition: Questions and Reconceptualization for the Twenty-First Century." Mary Evelyn Tucker and John Berthrong ed. *Confucianism and Ecology: The Interrelation of Heaven, Earth, and Humans*. Harvard University Center for the Study of World Religions Publications, 1998.

Tu Weiming, "Beyond the Enlightenment Mentality." Mary Evelyn Tucker and John Berthrong ed. *Confucianism and Ecology: The Interrelation of Heaven, Earth, and Humans*. Harvard University Center for the Study of World Religions

Publications, 1998.

Kaji Nobuyuki. Trans. Kim T'aejun. *Yugyo ran muŏsin'ga* [What is Confucianism]. Chiyoungsa, 1996.

Yang Haerim. "Saengt'ae minjujuŭiwa saengt'ae kongdongch'ejŏk sayu [Eco-democracy and the concept of Eco-community]." *Hwan'gyŏng ch'ŏrak* (Han'guk hwan' gyŏng ch'ŏrakhoe) 10 (2010).

Cho Chŏngok. "Isangjŏk saengt'aejuŭijŏk chayŏn'gwan e taehan ch'ŏlhakchŏk in'ganhakchŏk hwan'gyŏng yullijŏk koch'al: togil sangt'ae kongdongch'e ŭi ye [A philosophical, human, and environmental ethical consideration of the ideal ecological view of nature]." *Ch'ŏrhak kwa hyŏnsanghak yon'gu* (Han'guk hyŏnsanghakhoe) 25 (2005).

Mun Sunhong. "Pullip wi ŭi sasang: kŭnbon saengt'aehak ŭi ch'angsija Arne Naess [The philosophy of the blade of grass: Arne Naess, the creator of deep ecology]." http://newhamgil.cafe24.com/xe/? document_srl=1677

(accessed May 29, 2011).

Gregory Bateson. Trans. Pak Chidong. *Chŏngsin kwa chayŏn* [Mind and nature: a necessary unity]. Kkach'i, 1990.

Hitoshi Imamura and Shinsuke Imamura. 儀禮のオントロギ-人間社會を再生産 するもの [Rites and ceremonies used to reproduce the ontology of human society]. Tokyo: Kodansha, 2007.

The Book of Changes [周易].

The Doctrine of the Mean [中庸].

The Book of Rites [禮記].

Xun Zi [荀子].

THE CURRENT STATE OF THE ECOLOGICAL DISCOURSE WITHIN KOREAN CONFUCIANISM AND ITS FUTURE OUTLOOK

Berry, Thomas. *The DREAM of the EARTH*. San Francisco: Sierra Club Books, 1988.

Ch'oe Han'gi. *Injŏng* [人政], *Ch'uch'ungnok* [推測錄], *kihak* [氣學], *Sin'git'ong* [神氣通].

Han Myŏnhŭi. *Hwan'gyŏng yulli* (Environmental ethics). Philosophy and Reality Publishing, 1997.

_______. *Tongasia munmyŏng kwa Han'guk ŭi saengt'aejuŭi* (East Asian civilization and Korean ecologism). Philosophy and Reality Publishing, 2009.

Kato Hisatake. *Hwan'gyŏng yulli* (Environmental ethics). Trans. Han Kwihyŏn.

Dongnam Planning, 2001.

Kim Chaehŭi. *Sin'gwahak sanch'aek* (Promenade through new science). Kamyŏngsa, 1995.

Kim Kukt'ae. "Kwahak kisul munmyŏng ŭi panhwan'gyŏngsŏng (The anti-environmental nature of scientific and technological civilization)." *Kwahak sasang* 17 (1996).

Kim Sea-jeong. "Hwangyŏng yulli e taehan tongyang ch'ŏrhakchŏk chŏpkŭn: yuga ch'ŏrhak ŭl chungsim ŭro (The Asian philosophical approach to environmental ethics: with a special focus on Confucian philosophy)." *Pŏmhan ch'ŏlhak* (Bumhan Philosophy Association) 29 (2003).

______. "Saengt'aegye wigi wa yuga saengt'ae ch'ŏrhak ŭi paljŏn panghyang (The crisis of ecosystems and the direction of the development of ecological philosophy within Confucianism)." *Ch'ŏlhak yŏn'gu* (Korean Philosophical Society) 85 (2003).

______. "Yuga saengt'ae tamnon ŭl t'onghae pon yuga saengt'ae yulli (The ecological ethics of Confucianism as viewed through ecological discourses in Confucianism)." *Tongsŏ ch'ŏlhak yŏn'gu* (Korean Society For Philosophy East-West) 50 (December 2008).

Kim Uktong. *Han'guk ŭi noksaek munhwa* (The green culture of Korea). Munye Publishing, 2000.

Kukyŏk Yŏyudang chŏnsŏ. Vol. 1, Trans. Institute of Honam Studies, Jŏnju University. Yeogang Publishing, 1999.

Merchant, Carolyn. *Chayŏn ŭi chugŭm* (The Death of Nature). Trans. Chŏn Kyuch'an et al. Mito, 2005.

No Hŭijŏng. "Hwan'gyŏng yullihak esŏ ŭi kaech'eron kwa ch'ongch'eron ŭi t'onghap (The integration of individualism and synopticism in environmental ethics)." Ph.D. diss., Korea National University of Education, 2002.

Naess, Arne. "The Shallow and Deep, Long-Range Ecology Movement: A Summary." *Inquiry* 16 (1973).

Pak Hŭibyŏng. *Han'guk ŭi saengt'ae sasang* (Ecological philosophy of Korea). Tolbegae, 1999.

Pak Imun. *Munmyŏng ŭi wigi wa munhwa ŭi chŏnhwan* (The crisis of civilization and cultural transition). Minŭmsa, 1996.

T'oegye chŏnsŏ [退溪全書].

Tamhŏnjip [湛軒集].

Tucker, Mary Evelyn and John Berthrong eds. *Confucianism and Ecology*. Harvard University Press, 1998.

Tucker, Mary Evelyn and John Berthrong. Trans. Oh Chŏngsŏn, *Yuhak sasang kwa saengt'aehak* (Confucian thought and ecology). Yemun sŏwon, 2010.

Yulgok chŏnsŏ [栗谷全書].

Zimmerman, Michael E. 2 eds. *Environmental Philosophy—From Animal Rights to Radical Ecology*. New Jersey: Prentice Hall, 1998.

THE ORIGIN AND PRESERVATION OF RELIC FORESTS AND CONFUCIANISM IN KOREA

Books

In English

Braun-Blanquet, J. 1965. *Plant Sociology*. Trans. and ed. G. D. Fuller and E. S. Conard. New York and London: Hafner.

Tönnies, F. 2001. *Community and Civil Society*. Trans. and ed. J. Harris and M. Hollis. Cambridge: Cambridge University Press.

In Classical Chinese

Ch'oe Chaha. 1417. *Hyangyak kugŭppang* [鄉藥救急方, Emergency Remedies for Folk Medicine].

In Japanese

Ishidoya, T. and *Chŏng* Taehyŏn. 1923. *Chosŏn samnim sumok kamyo* [朝鮮森林 樹木鑑要, Illustrated Forestry Trees of Chosŏn]. Seoul: the Japanese Government-General of Korea, Forestry Experiment Station.

In Korean

Choi Jaemok (Ch'oe Chaemok). 2004. *Swipke ingnŭn T'oegye ŭi* Sŏnghaksipto (Easy to Read *Ten Diagrams on Sage Learning* [退溪聖學十圖] by T'oegye). Seoul: Yemoon sowon (Yemun sŏwŏn).

Institute for the Translation of Korean Classics, Trans. and ed. 1969. *Kukyŏk sinjŭng Tongguk yŏjisŭngnam* [國譯 新增 東國輿地勝覽, Augmented Survey of the Geography of Korea]. Paju: Korean Studies Information.

Kaji Nobuyuki. 1999. *Yugyo ran muŏsin'ga?* (What is Confucianism?). Trans. Kim T'aejun. Seoul: Chiyŏngsa.

Kim Chongjik. 1996. *Kukgyŏk* Chŏmp'iljae chip [國譯 佔畢齋集, Collected Works of Chŏmp'iljae Kim Chongjik]. Trans. Im Chŏnggi. Seoul: Institute for the

Translation of Korean Classics.

Kim Chungyull (Kim Ch'ungyŏl). 2008. *Nammyŏng Cho Sik ŭi sŏnbi hangmun kwa sŏnbi chŏngsin* (Nammymyŏng Cho Sik's Scholarship and Sŏnbi Spirit). Vol. 25, *Han'guk chŏrhak ch'ongsŏ*. Seoul: Yemoon sowon.

Kim Hakbeom (Kim Hakpŏm), and Jang Dongsoo (Chang Tongsu). 1994. *Maŭlsup Han'guk chŏnt'ong purak ŭi tangsup kwa sugumagi* (The Korean Village Grove). Seoul: Youlhwadang.

Kim Jongwon (Kim Chongwŏn). 2006. *Nokchi saengt'aehak* (Vegetation Ecology). 2 ed. Seoul: World Science.

Kim Jongwon, and Lim Jeongcheol (Im Chŏngch'ŏl). 2007. *Chŏnt'ong maŭlsup e taehan singmul sahoehak chŏk koch'al* (A Phytosociological Review of Traditional Rural Forests). In *Maŭlsup kwa ch'amsari* (Rural Forests and True-life). Taegu: Keimyung University Press.

Kim Jongwon, et al. 2010. *Hach'ŏn saengt'aehak kŭrigo Naktonggang* (Stream Ecology and the Nakdong River). Taegu: Keimyung University Press.

Kim Pusik. 2009. *Samguksagi* [三國史記, *The Chronicles of the Three States*]. Trans. and ed. Lee Byeongdo (Yi Pyŏngdo). Seoul: Eulyoo.

Kim Yeolgyu (Kim Yŏlgyu). 2006. *Han'guk munhwa sangjing sajŏn 1* (Dictionary of Korean Myths and Symbols 1). Seoul: Doosan Dong-A.

Korea Forest Service (Sallimch'ŏng). 2006. *Sallim yujŏn chawŏn pohorim ŭi pojŏn kwalli pangan surip ŭl wihan yŏn'gu* (A Study on the Establishment of Conservation and Management of Forest Gene Resources). Seoul: KFS.

Lee Dowon (Yi Towŏn), Koh Insu (Ko Insu), and Park Chanryul (Park Ch'annyŏl). 2007. *Chŏnt'ong maŭlsup ŭi saengt'aegye sŏbisŭ* (Ecosystem Services of Traditional Village Groves in Korea). Seoul: Seoul National University Press.

Lee Eunsun (Yi Ŭnsun). 1996. "*Ryŏmal-lach'o ŭi sahoe pyŏndong kwa sasang* (Thought and Social Change of the Late Koryŏ Dynasty and Early Silla Dynasty)." in *Han'guk sahoe sasangsa*. Paju: Jisik-Sanup.

Lee Jaekeun (Yi Chaegŭn). 1996. "Pyŏlsŏ chŏngwŏn," *Chogyŏnghak taegye*, vol. V, *Tongyang chogyŏngsa* [東洋造景史]. Seoul: Munwoodang (Munudang).

Lee Younghee (Yi Yŏnghŭi), and Lim Hunyoung (Im Hŏnyŏng). 2010. *Taehwa: han chisikin ŭi sam kwa sasang* (Conversation: Life and Thought of an Intellectual). Paju: Han'gilsa.

Kungnip munhwajae yŏn'guso ch'ŏnyŏn kinyŏmmul sent'ŏ (National Research Institute of Cultural Heritage). 2007. *Ch'ŏnyŏn kinyŏmmul (surimji) monit'ŏring mit silsa kiban kuch'uk pogosŏ* (An Actual Investigation and Monitoring of a Natural Monument (silva)). Taejŏn.

Sŏngju munhwawŏn, trans. and ed. 2010. *Kukgyŏk sŏngsanji* [國譯星山誌]. Sŏngju: Sŏngju Culture Center.

Tokumitsu, Nabuyuki. 2007. *Chōsen no moriyabu* [朝鮮の林藪, Chosŏn's Forests]. Trans. *Saengmyŏng ŭi sup* (Forest of Life). Seoul: Geobook (Kŏbuk).

Journal Articles

In English

Lehvävirta, S., and H., Rita. 2002. Natural Regeneration of Trees in Urban Woodlands. *Journal of Vegetation Science* 13, no. 1: 57–66.

In Korean*

Bae Byungho, Yoon Yonghan, and Kim Jeongho. 1998. Vegetation Structure and Ecological Restoration of Disturbed Forest Due to Artificial Plant. *Environmental Sciences* 2, no. 2: 701–710.

Choi Jaiung, and Kim Dongyeob. 2000. A Study on the Structure and Conservation Condition of Rural Community Forests as Culture in Korea. *Journal of Korean Institute of Traditional Landscape Architecture* 18, no. 351–65.

Hwang Junghwan. 1999. A Study on the Locational and Landscape Characteristics and Its Meaning of the Old Forests in Kyongju. *The Journal of Gyeongju University* 12, no. 2: 443–464.

Hwang Sookyoung. 2011. The Analysis of Vegetation Structure of Historical Forests in Gyeongju. M.D. diss., Keimyung University, Taegu.

Jang Dongsoo, and Kim Hakbeom. 1993. A Study on the Origin of Korean Village Grove Mentioned in Ancient Documents. *Journal of Korean Institute of Traditional Landscape Architecture* 11, no.1: 19–31.

Jang Dongsoo, Kim Hakbeom, and Hwang Junghwan. 1996. A Study on the Transition of Kyungju City Forests. *Korea Planners Association* 31, no. 3: 37–49.

Jang Dongsoo, Lee Kyumok, and Kim Hakbeom. 1993. A Study on the Tendency and Characteristics of Planted Forests in Kyung-Sang-Do Province. *Journal of Korean Institute of Traditional Landscape Architecture* 11, no. 2: 77–89.

Kang Hyunkyoung, et al. 2004. Management Guidelines of Village Groves through an

---

* Editor's note: In this section of the references the preferred romanization of the authors' names and the original English translations of the titles of their articles have been used at the request of the authors of this article.

Analysis of Growth Environments--Focusing on Village Groves in Gyungsang and Gangwon Provinces--. *Journal of Korean Institute of Traditional Landscape Architecture* 22, no. 2: 63–74.

Kim Hakbeom. 1992. A Study on the Cultural Background of Village Grove. *Yonam Jr. Coll. Livestock @ Horticulture. J.* 11: 239–257.

Kim Hakbeom, Jang Dongsoo, and Lee Seungje. 2003. A Study about Improved Plans of Management of Korean Village Groves. *Journal of Korean Institute of Traditional Landscape Architecture* 21. no. 4: 90–93.

Kim Jongwon. 1993. A Review of the Current Status of Green Environment in the Republic of Korea. Seoul: KETRI.

_______. 2005. What is Problem on the *Pinus densiflora* Forests in Korea in Relation to Erratic Fires and Pine Wilt Disease. *Journal of Ecology and Field Biology* 28, no. 2: 113–120.

Kim Jongwon, and Lim Jeongcheol. 2006. A Phytosociological Review of the Traditional Rural Forests (Maeul-soop). *Academia Koreana of Keimyung Univesity*. 33: 81–114.

Kim Jongwon, et al. 2011. An Eco-sociological Review on the Origin of Relic Forests in Korea: Case-studies on the Mansongjŏng of Andong, Karosup of Ŭisŏng, Sŏngpaksup of Sŏngju, Sangnim of Hamyang and Kyerim of Kyŏngju. *The Fifth Keimyung International Conference on Korean Studies*: 167–214.

Lee Changwoo. 2009. Spatial Distribution Patterns of Major Willow Species (Salicaceae) in Upo Wetland. M.D. diss., Keimyung University, Taegu.

Lee Deokbong. 1963. A Study of Pangjunghyangyangmok (方中鄕藥目) of Hyangyakkugŭppang (鄕藥救急方). *The Journal of Asiatic Studies* (Korea University) 6, no. 2: 339–364.

Park Jaechul. 2006 Concept and Case of Village Grove. *Academia Koreana of Keimyung Univesity* 33: 223–262.

Park Jaechul, et al. 2004. Research Paper: A Study on the Restoration of Neunggil Village Forests in Jinan. *Journal of Korean Society of Rural Planning* 10, no. 3: 27–32.

Yea Myunghai, Lee Jaehwan, and Kim Sooyeon. 2006. A Study on Special Structure of Regional Cities in Seongju the Chosun Dynasty. *Architectural Institute of Korea* 22, no. 3: 165–172.

Web-sites

Cultural Heritage Administration of Korea. *Information about Culture Heritage*. http://www.cha.go.kr (accessed September 27, 2011).

Kim Taehong. 2006. *Retrace the Course of Sach'on Village*. The Head Family of the Kims of Andong, Top'yŏng Ŭikong Family (安東金氏 大宗會 都評議公派). http://www.andongkimc.kr (accessed April 25, 2011).

The National Institute of the Korean Language. *Pyŏlsŏ*.

http://www.korean.go.kr/eng/index.jsp (accessed May 10, 2011).